LANDSCAPE AND HISTORY

GLOBALITIES

Series editor: Jeremy Black

GLOBALITIES is a series which reinterprets world history in a
concise yet thoughtful way, looking at major issues over large
time-spans and political spaces; such issues can be political,
ecological, scientific, technological or intellectual. Rather than
adopting a narrow chronological or geographical approach,
books in the series are conceptual in focus yet present an array of
historical data to justify their arguments. They often involve a
multi-disciplinary approach, juxtaposing different subject-areas
such as economics and religion or literature and politics.

In the same series

Why Wars Happen
Jeremy Black

A History of Language
Steven Roger Fischer

The Nemesis of Power
Harald Kleinschmidt

*Geopolitics and Globalization
in the Twentieth Century*
Brian W. Blouet

Monarchies 1000–2000
W. M. Spellman

A History of Writing
Steven Roger Fischer

*The Global Financial System
1750 to 2000*
Larry Allen

Mining in World History
Martin Lynch

*China to Chinatown: Chinese Food
in the West*
J. A. G. Roberts

Landscape and History since 1500

IAN D. WHYTE

REAKTION BOOKS

For Kathy, Rebecca and Ruth

Published by Reaktion Books Ltd
79 Farringdon Road, London EC1M 3JU, UK

www.reaktionbooks.co.uk

First published 2002

Printed and bound in Great Britain by
Biddles Ltd, Guildford and King's Lynn

British Library Cataloguing in Publication Data
Whyte, I. D. (Ian D.)
   Landscape and History since 1500. - (Globalities)
   1.Human ecology - History 2.Landscape ecology - History
   I. Title
   304.2

ISBN 1 86189 138 5

Contents

1   Landscape and History   7
2   Early Modern Landscapes   27
3   Enlightenment, Picturesque and Romantic Landscapes   70
4   Industrial and Imperial Landscapes   122
5   Modern and Post-Modern Landscapes   164

REFERENCES   219
BIBLIOGRAPHY   238
PHOTOGRAPHIC ACKNOWLEDGEMENTS   251
INDEX   252

ONE

Landscape and History

Landscapes are important because they are the product of one of the most enduring sets of linkages: the relationships between the physical environment and human society.[1] They are created by people through their engagement with the world around them. They are, then, social constructions, whether intentionally or unintentionally, but they need to be viewed within the context of their own natural and cultural histories in order to be properly understood. Landscapes are the result of attitudes as well as actions, so that ideologies are important in appreciating them. The history of landscape is inevitably grounded in the analysis of its visible features, but such structures are created and destroyed within ideological contexts that need to be appreciated for a full understanding of landscape.[2] For individuals, landscapes may be real, lived-in places, or distant, half-fantasized ones. Landscapes can be familiar and comfortable, exotic or unattractive, valued or inspiring. They are the product of changes through time, often over thousands of years. Sometimes such changes occur slowly and subtly, at other times rapidly and dramatically. Landscapes are all around us, something we interact with daily, both physically and in our imaginations, forming backdrops to the whole stage of human activity.[3] Landscapes are never unchanging, although the pace at which they change has varied through time and over space in the half millennium considered by this book. Because of their time-depth, landscapes involve interactions between the present and the past, and give a sense of identity at individual, local, regional and national scales. Landscapes are multi-layered, and constitute a form of memory in which is stored the history of successive periods of human activity on the surface of the earth. They are palimpsests that hark back to earlier engagements with the environment by different societies, emphasizing change, both ancient and recent.

Because people have markedly different views about landscapes, their nature is contested,[4] which makes landscape 'a concept of high tension'.[5] Attitudes to landscape have changed markedly over time, as people's perceptions and interpretations have altered in the light of their own changing experience. Landscapes that today are valued for aesthetic or environmental reasons, and which now may be carefully managed, were not created intentionally, in the main, but have developed as a by-product of historical processes. Social structures, cultural traditions, economic activities and political patterns have all played crucial roles in the shaping of landscapes. The values placed on different types of landscape are not fixed, but have changed over time and may represent different things to different people at any one period.

The ways in which people interact with their environments to produce landscapes depend on time, place and historical context, but also on age, gender, socio-economic status, ethnicity, race and other variables. Views of landscape can be contested by different groups within a society. The anti-enclosure sentiments in the poems of John Clare (1793–1864) indicate an opposition between elite views of landscape and more down-to-earth peasant viewpoints. At a personal level, they also highlighted internal tensions within Clare as a poet: he despised his uneducated fellow labourers, who in turn despised him for his education; he wrote about the injustices created by the imposition of enclosure by the landed elite, yet was forced to do so using the literary forms and conventions of this very group.[6] Landscapes can be contested by different social, cultural and ethnic groups – the perspectives of North American Indians or Australian Aborigines versus European settlers, for example. A good modern instance of a contested landscape is Stonehenge and its environs, where archaeologists, tourists, Druids, New Age travellers, English Heritage and the National Trust all have their own images, symbolism and views regarding the ways in which the area should be preserved and its landscapes managed and consumed.[7]

But landscape is more than just a particular assemblage of natural and man-made features; any landscape is composed not only of what lies before our eyes but what lies within our heads.[8] Perception specialists argue that landscapes cannot be defined simply by itemizing their parts. The landscape perceived by one person is not the same as that perceived by another, even within the same culture. Every individual has his or her own personality and cultural viewpoint, which filter and distort information, giving a selective impression of what a landscape is like; such views may be close to reality or may contain major misconceptions.[9] D. W. Meinig has suggested that ten people might view a landscape in ten different ways, in terms of representing nature (the insignificance of human activity), habitat (people's adjustment to nature), artefact (human impact on nature), system (the scientific view of the processes of interaction between society and environment), problems (which can be solved through social action), wealth (property), ideology (cultural values or social philosophy), history (chronology), place (the identity that locations have) and aesthetics (the artistic qualities of place).[10]

So the interpretation of landscapes can depend upon the values and attitudes of individuals: a capitalist might interpret landscape in monetary terms, an artist in aesthetic terms and a scientist in ecological terms. Impressions of landscape can also vary between people who are detached observers, or 'outsiders', and those who are 'insiders', living and working within particular landscapes and interacting with them on a daily basis. The outsiders see landscapes afresh, while to the insiders they are subservient to everyday life, work and social interactions. Understanding people's perceptions of places is important in that what people do with their environment arises from how they see it. Considerations of landscape perception are not purely academic then; they are also important in practical terms.[11] Decision makers operating in response to a particular landscape will base their decisions on the environment as they perceive it, rather than how it really is.[12] Cultural factors condition landscape perceptions to a considerable degree.

Individuals have personalized attitudes to landscape, but there are also wider consensuses. Some influential perceptions of spatial differences that have landscape dimensions are ancient and deep-rooted. For instance, the modern north–south divide in England has been traced back to the early thirteenth-century split between King John and his barons.[13] In terms of a contrast in landscape as well as in society, this divide gained a peculiar slant in the nineteenth century with the rise of industrialization, when, as in Mrs Gaskell's novel *North and South* of 1855, it referred to contrasting states of minds as well as contrasting landscapes and societies.[14]

Although some perceptions of landscapes can be enduring, popular tastes regarding which types of landscape are favoured change over time, as do the standards by which landscape is judged. In the modern world, it is hard to experience landscape without preconceived images. In the nineteenth and early twentieth centuries, expectations raised by black and white photographs were likely to be exceeded by reality, but today coloured photographs, films, television documentaries and travel brochures present much higher-quality images, which may be more 'real' than the places they depict. Landscape tastes also reflect nationality. American landscape tastes, it is claimed, involve strong preferences for wilderness over culturally modified scenery. By contrast, English tastes incline towards neat, tamed countryside, with clear references to the past. Such generalizations, however, must be treated with caution. David Lowenthal and Hugh Prince considered that it was unsafe to generalize about national attitudes to landscape in England because of the pronounced class differences.[15]

Modern landscape tastes have been moulded by perceptions and preferences that have developed over many centuries. Landscape tastes have varied in the past, and they also differ today, between different countries and social groups, and are likely to continue to change in the future. There are, nevertheless, continuities in our perceptions of landscapes. Most of the views from the 'stations' or viewpoints described by Thomas West in his *Guide to the Lake District*, first published in 1778, are still considered attractive today. On the other hand, Peter Howard's study of the changing popularity of different British landscapes, measured by the subjects of pictures exhibited at the Royal Academy from 1768 onwards, shows some rapid and quite marked shifts.[16] The attraction of moorland, for instance, in areas such as the Pennines and Dartmoor, began to be apparent only at the end of the nineteenth century, just in time to exert a powerful influence on the choice of locations for future national parks.[17]

Modern concerns about environmental changes at a global scale, such as climatic change, tropical deforestation, desertification and sea-level rise, are all bound up with landscape. Change, rather than stability, may be the normal state for landscapes, at many different spatial scales and speeds.[18] Rates of landscape change have accelerated over time with the advances in technology, the growing complexity of society and increases in population. The extent and rate of landscape change can be measured in some circumstances – for example, seventeenth-century Dutch reclamation or Parliamentary enclosure in late eighteenth- and early nineteenth-century England – but it is much harder to measure small-scale, frequent changes operating over long timescales than the occasional 'revolutions'.[19]

In recent decades, European planners and academics have shown a growing interest in the classification and evaluation of historic landscapes in relation to their scenic, ecological, heritage and recreational value as part of the development of policies for conservation and management. This is manifest not only in the designation of particularly valued areas and places with enhanced protection against unsuitable development, such as World Heritage Sites and national parks, but in the country-side more generally in relation to debates about, for example, the siting of wind farms or the spread of new housing, retail and industrial developments. There is also concern for the impact on landscape of trends in agriculture. Within the European Union, price support systems and grants have encouraged the destruction of landscape features such as hedges, wetlands and ancient woodlands in lowland areas, while in the British uplands, habitats such as heather moorland have been lost, and a spread of erosion has occurred. In Britain, the virtual collapse of the markets for the products of hill farming, and the impact of the foot-and-mouth outbreak of 2001, has widened the debate on the extent to which agriculture in such areas needs to be maintained for purposes relating to landscape management and the viability of rural communities, rather than for economic reasons.

In the near future, changes in EU agricultural policies, which now show a greater concern for the protection and sustainable management of rural landscapes, are likely to be of major importance in relation to the themes of continuity and change in the landscapes of Britain and Europe.

APPROACHES TO LANDSCAPE

A range of theoretical approaches has deepened our understanding of many aspects of the character and spatial variation of landscape in the past and at the present. Much of our sensitivity towards landscape is a relatively modern development, which emerged among European elites during the Renaissance. Hence the Eurocentric approach of this book, which explores the complex relationships between landscape and history over the past five centuries, focusing on Britain but ranging more widely to embrace Europe, the Americas, colonial and imperial contexts. The geographical focus of the book, starting with the British Isles and then working outwards, also reflects the author's own background, experience and research interests. It must be emphasized that the European view of landscapes, the Western landscape aesthetic, is far from being the only one, but historically it has been very important and powerful.[20] The approach of this book is interdisciplinary, and draws on material from social, economic and cultural history, environmental history, the history of art, historical geography, archaeology and planning; but it is grounded in landscape history and historical/cultural geography. The focus is specifically on rural landscapes. The growing influence of towns, cities and urban systems on rural landscapes cannot be ignored, but the evolution of townscapes, the most complex cultural landscapes of all, deserves a volume to itself and is not considered here. The approach taken is a broadly chronological one. Each chapter reviews a range of themes, highlighting both objective and subjective aspects of landscape. These include landscape change in British, European and wider contexts, and the inter-relationships between historical trends and landscapes, particularly the effects of cultural, demographic, economic, environmental and political changes, as well as changing perceptions and portrayals of landscape through art, cartography and literature.

In medieval times, the word 'landscape' referred to an area owned by a lord or inhabited by a particular group of people. The modern use of the term goes back to the sixteenth century, when Italian and Dutch painters began to use it to indicate a representation of scenery. The term 'landscape' embraces a bewildering diversity of definitions.[21] It is often used imprecisely and ambiguously, with multiple layers of meaning. Landscape has been seen as a useful concept, because it is free from fixed positions, elusive in meaning yet all-embracing in scope.[22] It is frequently seen as an integration of natural and human phenomena, which can be studied objectively and empirically, classified, analyzed and mapped. While scenery is considered to be something to which everyone can react aesthetically, landscape is something to be examined with a trained eye. We also need to penetrate below superficial levels of meaning and interpretation, however, to understand deeper meanings, through studying the iconography of landscape, a term derived from art history.[23]

The study of past landscapes, how they have changed through time and how people have related to them, bridges the gulf between the arts and the sciences. As a result, it has spread over a number of disciplines, involving archaeologists, historians, anthropologists, sociologists, geographers and art specialists, among others, and incorporates a range of approaches. In recent years, landscape change and the nature of human impact on the environment have also been central concerns of the emerging discipline of environmental history. Approaches to landscapes have included the study of their history and development (via landscape archaeology, landscape history and historical geography), consideration of the changing perceptions of landscape, and research into the links between past landscapes and political ideologies, economic change and social structures, via cultural and historical geography. The adoption of post-modernist approaches within geography has led to major reassessments of the portrayal of landscape in the past through media such as cartography, art and literature.[24]

Relationships between landscape and history have usually been considered in terms of the latter influencing the former.

Landscape history and archaeology have been concerned with the ways in which societies have modified landscape at a variety of scales, which range from individual decision-making to national and imperial policies. In this approach, landscape has been treated in an objective, empirical manner as an object of study. It has also been considered as a surface phenomenon, the expression of underlying economic, social, cultural and political influences, which were themselves controlled by deeper structures, such as feudal or capitalist modes of production. The interaction between landscape and history is, however, a two-way one. Landscapes can also influence history, particularly through the ways in which people have perceived, described, depicted and reacted to them.

Within Europe, the study of the rural landscape developed out of work on settlement geography in the 1890s and 1900s.[25] Within history, the study of landscape evolved as a separate branch of study, heavily influenced by both geography and archaeology.[26] Early studies of the agrarian landscapes of western Europe favoured a static approach, neglecting the processes of change. The work of early writers such as August Meitzen focused on the importance of ethnicity during the Great Migrations of early medieval times in producing the settlement patterns and agrarian structures that were still discernible in the nineteenth century. More recently, within archaeology, the growing awareness of the limitations of site-oriented studies has generated a wider interest in field survey to provide information about human activities in wider contexts, and this has given rise to the sub-discipline of landscape archaeology. In this approach, archaeological landscapes exist as past surfaces within a defined timespan, which are influenced by antecedent features and later modifications. A past landscape surface can be buried, eroded or changed by human and environmental processes. Landscape surfaces produced by the cultural and physical processes of one period influence the activities of later inhabitants, so that landscapes are not simply passive creations of human activities, but dynamic, interactive elements in the development of societies. This requires us to consider what the antecedent and subsequent character of a landscape has been in order to understand it at any particular period.[27]

Objective approaches to the study of landscape have focused on the examination of changes over time caused by natural and especially human forces. The impact of the physical environment on cultural landscapes is evident in the character of traditional construction materials used for building houses and making field boundaries, an area of study that has been called the 'structure and scenery approach',[28] and which was well exemplified by A. E. Trueman.[29] William Mead has highlighted the close relationship between field boundaries and geology at a very local scale for a small area of the Yorkshire Dales.[30] In Britain, a highly empirical school of landscape history and archaeology has developed that sometimes seems to forget that the landscapes under consideration are the products of human activity.[31] The creation of landscapes has often been visualized indirectly and abstractly through the impact of population levels, the layouts of field systems and the organization of settlement patterns, rather than as the product of real people.[32] In an 'old' country such as Britain and in most countries of Western Europe, there are few single-phase landscapes; almost all are multi-period and multi-functional. Even landscapes such as an eighteenth-century park and an area of Parliamentary enclosure, which might seem to have been deliberately planned and created within a short timespan, have been influenced by antecedent elements in the cultural landscape, and have also been subject to subsequent modifications.[33]

In Britain, this approach to landscape has been particularly associated with the historian W. G. Hoskins. Hoskins made statements about the landscape that were based on evidence derived from fieldwork, maps and documentary sources. Such statements could be tested, but, at the same time, his work was not fully objective and contained marked preferences and biases. Hoskins's English landscape reflected his own interests and prejudices – he was in favour of early modern times and against the impact of the Industrial Revolution. Post-modernist explanations of landscape have emphasized that landscapes are texts with multiple meanings. Hoskins's most famous book, *The Making of the English Landscape* (1955),[34] was in some respects

W. G. Hoskins's English Landscape, one man's particular, sometimes idiosyncratic view; another layer on an already deeply layered text rather than a palimpsest with a single 'real' or 'authentic' meaning.[35] Hoskins's view of the English landscape was evocative and richly observed, but it was also conservative and strongly anti-modernist.[36] His comment that 'Since the last years of the nineteenth century ... and especially since the year 1914, every single change in the English landscape has either uglified it or destroyed its meaning, or both', and that over 'Poor devastated Lincolnshire and Suffolk ... drones day after day the obscene shape of the atom-bomber, laying a trail like a filthy slug upon Constable's and Gainsborough's sky' hardly seems likely to guarantee objectivity.[37] Nevertheless, Hoskins's approach to the study of landscape has continued to be influential, notably in America.[38]

Within British historical geography, the traditional objective approach to the study of landscape, heavily influenced by geographers such as H. C. Darby, involved looking at static cross-sections of landscape at particular periods – most notably in Darby's studies of the English landscape at the time of Domesday Book – and the examination of landscape change over time.[39] These approaches focused on the mapping of data extracted from historical sources, and the careful scholarly criticism of such source material. The quantitative revolution in geography in the 1960s and early '70s, which also influenced landscape approaches in archaeology, added the use of spatial models to explain patterns in past landscapes and of statistical techniques for the analysis of data.[40]

In America, the study of landscape by geographers has been strongly influenced by the work of the Berkeley School, and in particular by Carl Sauer, who introduced ideas derived from German geography. Sauer's style of cultural geography concentrated on the visible forms of landscape, such as farms and field patterns. Cultural landscape forms were seen in simple materialist terms as the results of the activities of people who were trying to satisfy their basic needs. Culture was considered simply as a set of shared practices common to a particular human group, practices that were learned and passed on to later generations. Critics have viewed this interpretation as cultural determinism, because it ignores the ideologies of the people who created the visible landscape features, which were not just the result of a struggle for existence within a specific set of environmental and technological frameworks. More recent writing in this vein, while continuing to stress the importance of making a living in terms of creating landscapes, also stresses the significance of culture – the beliefs, values, patterns of behaviour and technical skills that are learned and transmitted by groups of people.[41]

Landscape history has often been studied at a relatively small scale, at local or regional levels, with a focus on the purely agrarian, on field systems or settlements, rather than on the broader contexts of rural landscape. Much work of this kind has been highly specific in time and place, and has shown a lack of concern for broader temporal and spatial trends, issues and problems.[42] Relatively few studies have tried to follow landscape change across a range of environments within particular regions throughout long time periods, which span prehistoric and historic phases.[43] A good deal of environmental history has also been very place-specific, because of the nature of the evidence used. Historical geography also possesses the ability to see the 'big picture', however, and looks at trends at continental and global scales, as in Michael Williams's study of the forests of North America.[44]

SUBJECTIVE APPROACHES

In recent years, landscape has been seen in less concrete, visible terms and more subjectively.[45] An alternative set of approaches to landscape emphasizes its symbolic qualities, rather than focusing on the physical and structural aspects of landscapes as artefacts.[46] Landscape, in this view, is the external world mediated through subjective human experience. Landscape is not merely the world we see; it is a construction of that world. Landscape is thus a social and cultural product, a way of seeing projected on to the land, with its own techniques and compositional forms, a restrictive gaze that diminishes other modes of experiencing our relations with nature. Landscapes are not merely 'there' on the ground, but are socially constructed within a complex set of linkages among variables, such as race, class and gender. Landscapes are culturally determined, not just because they are the products of human decisions, but because they are understood through sets of perceptions that are themselves culturally and historically conditioned.[47] Such approaches are concerned with how landscapes are perceived, interpreted and represented. Reading the landscape is contingent on the eye of the beholder, involving the personal view and the cultural background of the observer.[48] Early humanistic work on the representation of place by regional novelists such as Thomas Hardy and Walter Scott falls into this category.[49] It is suggested that landscapes cannot be seen in unmediated ways. All landscape representations are culturally situated and are viewed according to particular aesthetic conventions. This view of landscape has been especially characteristic of recent cultural geography.

Hoskins suggested that we consider landscape as a text, but recent interpretations of landscapes as texts see them as having multiple layers of meaning, capable of being read in different ways, with a wide range of simultaneously valid interpretations.[50] If landscapes are texts that are interpreted and read according to an ingrained cultural framework of interpretations, they may be inculcating their readers with a set of notions about how society is organized without the readers' being aware of this. Landscapes, as Simon Schama suggests, can be considered as culture before they are nature, constructs of the imagination projected on to wood, water and rock.[51] While a landscape historian might study a forest in terms of its species composition and past systems of management, focusing on the evidence of past human activity, a cultural geographer might be concerned with the different social meanings associated with human reactions to and relations with the forest. Forests might be seen as paradisal, spiritual or mythological landscapes, as ecologically friendly through their absorption of atmospheric carbon dioxide, or as strongly gendered in terms of being areas of women's fear and masculine activities.[52] Landscapes may thus be used to pass on messages and rules from one generation to another, and not merely within pre-literate societies.

Subjective approaches to the study of landscape went through various shifts during the twentieth century. One, associated with modernism, tried to read the history of landscape mainly through the history of landscape painting. Another was linked with postmodernism. It removed the role of painting from centre-stage towards a semiotic and hermeneutic approach. Semiotics concerns the way in which signs are produced and given meaning, while hermeneutics includes the study of interpretation and meaning, and treats landscapes as allegories of psychological or ideological themes.

How do culturally induced reactions to landscape develop: by cultural conditioning or in response to more basic needs? Jay Appleton has argued that our responses to landscape unconsciously reflect ways of evaluating territory in early hunter-gatherer societies.[53] The importance of being able to see without being seen confers a sense of security. A landscape that offers both a prospect and a refuge is something that appeals to ancient survival needs buried deep in the human psyche. Such views, Appleton argues, would translate naturally into an aesthetic appreciation of landscape once the importance of evaluations for basic survival had vanished. Research on modern people's ideal landscapes has demonstrated a distinct preference for savannah/parkland views with scattered trees, groups of trees and open grassy areas. These are the kinds of landscape that were depicted by Claude Lorrain and created by Capability Brown. This could be interpreted as indicating that such artists and landscape gardeners were successful because, accidentally or otherwise, they hit upon the type of landscape that subconsciously appealed to people. On the other hand, it could be argued that unconscious cultural conditioning is at work, so that modern respondents automatically selected such landscapes as ideal. G. H. Orians has suggested that, since humans originated in savannah environments, landscapes of mixed grassland with groups of trees should stir strong positive emotions, which helps to explain the popularity of garden landscapes.[54] Denis Cosgrove disagrees, believing that any such links that might once have existed have been transformed, overlain and mediated by social, cultural, economic and personal meanings.[55]

Modern cultural landscape studies have focused on human agency, and on the social and economic processes underlying it, sometimes to the neglect of the physical environment, the role of which is often simplified and misunderstood. Many landscape changes caused by human activity are actually accomplished by physical processes operating at a speed or on a scale that is greater than normal.[56] Equally, models of human agency in landscape change can also be simplistic.

W. J. T. Mitchell has argued that landscapes are instruments of cultural power, of imperialism or nationalism.[57] They have been seen as an ideological class view, as a discourse in which various political positions can be situated. Indeed, Mitchell has hypothesized that there is a link between the flourishing of landscape art and imperialism, as seen in ancient Rome, China, seventeenth-century Holland and France, and eighteenth- and nineteenth-century Britain, although the exact nature of the connections is unclear.

Attempts to decode the symbolic meanings and messages contained in landscapes are relatively recent.[58] Landscapes may be seen as assertions of power: of man over nature, or of one social group or political ideology over another. Examples include landscape parks (Chapter 3), Victorian grouse moors (Chapter 4) and modern capitalist farming landscapes (Chapter 5). Our cognition of landscapes is, however, both selective and distorted. Current ideas about symbolism and landscape have been heavily influenced by post-modernist writers, especially Roland Barthes and Michel Foucault. There is, nevertheless, the problem that symbolism in landscapes may be the fabrication of the outsider, and may say more about them than the landscapes they study.[59]

In the 1980s, cultural geographers redefined landscape as a concept with subjective and artistic resonances, and focused on the creative and experiential aspects of human relations with the environment. Geographers have been increasingly interested in using a range of landscape representations, including art and literature, as sources for answering geographical questions.[60] One of the most challenging interpretations of landscape has been that of Cosgrove, who considers that landscape is not an object but 'a way of seeing' rooted in ideology.[61] It represents a way in which certain classes of people have signified themselves and their world through their imagined relationship with nature, and through which they have underlined and communicated their own social role and that of others with respect to external nature. It is an artist's, an elite, way of seeing the world. So the landscape idea is a way in which some Europeans have represented to themselves and to others the world around them and their relationships with it, and through which they have commented on social relations. This way of seeing has a specific history in the West, in the transition of Western social formations from feudal-use values in land to the capitalist production of land as a commodity for the increase of exchange value. Cosgrove's interpretation of landscape is linked to ideas regarding space that first developed in Renaissance Italy, and connected with the appropriation of land by an urban merchant class that was buying rural estates (Chapter 2).

The development of a new relationship between humans and the environment at the time of the Renaissance was associated with the establishment of linear perspective, sophisticated map projections, landscape painting and the construction of rational human landscapes. Landscape is thus intimately linked with a new way of seeing the world as a rationally ordered, designed and harmonious creation, the structure and mechanism of which are accessible to the human mind and eye. The idea of landscape developed in a context of new ways of representation, such as linear perspective and improved techniques of surveying and cartography. This landscape idea has then a definite history stretching from the Renaissance to modern times. This history can be understood only as part of a wider history of economy and society. Cosgrove's landscape idea originated with early modern capitalism and the decline of feudal systems of land tenure. Landscape developed as land acquired capital value and became itself a form of capital.

In Cosgrove's view of landscape, there is a close link between landscape and art. Wealthy landowners had landscape architects remodel their estates and then had them painted. Cosgrove has examined the idea of landscape in a rather restricted sense of its artistic conceptions within the European humanist tradition. For Cosgrove, landscape is not the world that we see, but a particular construction of it that is historically specific. Cosgrove sees landscape as a form of representation, not an empirical object, a cultural image, a pictorial way of representing, that structures or symbolizes our surroundings. Landscape can be represented on the ground, but also on canvas or paper. A landscape's meanings draw on the cultural codes of the society for which it was made. Such codes are embedded in the power structures of society. Cosgrove and other cultural geographers have borrowed the concept of iconography from art history to make sense of the symbolism of built, visual and verbal landscapes. They look for the ideas contained in the imagery, seeing landscapes as encoded texts whose meanings can be deciphered by those knowing the key, and look not just for more obvious, superficial symbolic meanings but deeper-seated layers of meaning.[62]

As a view of landscape, however, Cosgrove's approach has been challenged. First, his Eurocentric focus has been criticized because it cannot be translated into other cultures. His 'idea of landscape' may date from the Renaissance, but both landscapes and ideas about landscapes existed centuries earlier.[63] The appreciation and representation of landscape can be identified, for instance, in medieval and Classical literature, while the richness, complexity and antiquity of the Chinese tradition of landscape painting, which itself strongly influenced European landscape aesthetics in the eighteenth century, emphasize that the Western landscape tradition is not the only one. Cosgrove's essentially Marxist approach has also been criticized for its focus on class as the major influence in the production of landscape representation, and for reading landscapes only through the perspective of class structure and focusing on the views of the ruling classes regarding what qualifies as landscape.

Gillian Rose believes that the landscape way of seeing was a masculine gaze, and that Cosgrove does not take into account gender differences in relation to landscape.[64] To what extent is landscape, and its study, gendered? In eighteenth-century Britain the capacity to read landscape as a whole was seen as one of the qualifications of a man of taste, but not an accomplishment for an educated woman.[65] Enlightenment thinkers considered that only educated European men were able to think in rational and abstract terms, objectively and disinterestedly. Women were held to lack the intellectual breadth of mind to be able to read landscape. In the nineteenth century, for that reason, landscape was not considered as a suitable subject for women painters. Women were also outside the framework of science and scientific organizations, such as the Royal Geographical Society. Women travellers often had difficulty in accommodating their different viewpoints and perspectives with the masculine, imperialist tradition of exploration and conquest.[66]

Landscape and politics have a long association. For much of its history, landscape has been closely bound up with the practical appropriation of space. There are close connections between landscape and cartography, with the survey and mapping of newly-acquired and then improved commercial estates in the hands of an urban bourgeoisie, and with military survey and fortification design. In painting and garden design, landscape achieved visually and ideologically what surveying and map-making achieved practically: the control and domination of space and its transformation into the property of the individual or the state. More recent work on landscapes has been concerned with their role in creating national identity, and on landscapes in the context of colonialism and post-colonialism. In creating overseas colonial empires, European nations, especially Britain and France, interpreted the landscapes that they found in terms of European landscape aesthetics. Representations of exotic colonial landscapes were mediated through European conventions such as the Picturesque (Chapter 3).

Landscape aesthetics can be appreciated through many forms, including poetry, fiction, travel literature, landscape gardening, architecture and art. One approach has focused on attempts to read the history of landscape through the history of landscape painting. Representations of landscapes in paintings, on maps and in other media reflect not merely changes in the skills of depiction, whether literary or graphic, but changes in tastes and attitudes to the works of the human race and how they relate to nature. Landscape art from whatever period contains visual prejudices, conscious or unconscious, which affect how we respond to landscape and pictures of landscape.[67] Art in the Western world since the Renaissance has been dominated by the urge to depict the world as realistically as possible, but in terms of particular points of view that have been racially and culturally defined. Artistic representations of landscape do not present 'natural' or unbiased views of the world, even when, as in early seventeenth-century Dutch landscape and townscape painting, they seem superficially to record the everyday and mundane accurately and faithfully.

For early writers such as Kenneth Clark, 'landscape' merely meant a good view of an area of countryside. 'Art' was what happened to that landscape when it was translated into a painted image.[68] Landscape was the raw material waiting to be processed by the artist. Paintings are now, however, considered to contain complex ideological messages, both superficially and at greater depth. The interpretation of landscape art has moved away from Clark's emphasis on its philosophical context to considerations of its social and economic background. One of the key watersheds was John Berger's comment that Mr and Mrs Andrews, in Gainsborough's famous painting of 1749, looked smug and self-satisfied not because they were fitting into the Augustan and Rousseauesque tradition, but because they owned the land behind them.[69] In this interpretation, a landscape has already been changed by our perception of it. Landscape is land that has already been aesthetically processed. In deciding what makes an attractive view, we are judging and selecting. Landscape is what a viewer has selected from the land, edited and modified on the basis of conventions about what makes a 'good view'. Our response to it may be recreational, aesthetic or spiritual, or involve all three approaches at the same time.

As graphic, pictorialized sources of information about human and physical environments, maps are closely linked to landscape, and the two have often developed together – in sixteenth-century Italy or the late sixteenth- and early seventeenth-century Netherlands, for example. Maps and landscape art shade into each other through high vantage points and bird's-eye views to a truly vertical perspective. Maps, like any other document, are socially constructed forms of knowledge, which reflect the societies that produced them and their values, as much as the landscapes that they portray. Their codes are historically specific; they are not in themselves either true or false. In the selectivity of their content, they are social products that highlight the concerns of their cartographers and the patrons who commissioned them.

Maps have provided ways in which power could be gained, administered and legitimized. Map-making has usually been associated with elites; with internal administration linked to the growth of nation states, with defence or with territorial expansion. Maps have supported the exercise of power at a range of scales from the individual estate to global empires. Like cannon and warships, they were weapons of imperialism, sometimes anticipating expansion and empire building by making advance claims to territory. Equally, once lands had been accessed, they helped to create the myths that held nations and empires together. At one scale, the history of the map was closely linked to that of the nation state, since the state was a major patron of cartographic activity. At another scale, cadastral or estate maps were linked to the rise of agrarian capitalism, providing control and organization through information on ownership, tenancy and rents.[70] Maps, then, are purposive interpretations of, and commentaries on, the human and physical world and the landscapes resulting from their interaction.[71] What is distinctive about them is not their distance from reality, but the fact that they are systematic. They are descriptive, not only of the world they seek to portray, but also of the system that produced them. Maps also represent technology, and technology has often been used as a rationale for conquest and dominance. Contrasts in cartographic approaches over time can be demonstrated at a macro scale by the difference in world views between the medieval *Mappa Mundi* in Hereford Cathedral and the nineteenth-century Mercator projection of the world, which highlighted the British Empire in red, one reflecting the place of the world in divine creation, the other the place of Britain in world domination.[72]

It is one of the standard tenets of landscape history, as it has developed in Britain and Europe, that everything is older than we think. W. G. Hoskins believed that the English landscape was mainly the creation of the last 1,500 years.[73] Since then, this timescale has been extended back to cover most of the 10,000 years since the last Ice Age; the environmental and landscape impacts of even Mesolithic cultures are seen today as having been far from negligible.[74] Even in an 'old country' such as England, it has been estimated that about 60 per cent of the hedged and walled landscape dates from after 1450, and 30 per cent from after 1750.[75] The rural landscape, the pattern of fields, roads, buildings and many earthworks were created largely within the last 500 years, the period on which this book is focused.

TWO

Early Modern Landscapes

LANDSCAPES AND FEUDALISM

The landscapes of early-sixteenth-century Europe mostly developed under the impact of feudalism, underlain by the legacies of prehistoric, early-historic and Roman times. A good deal of landscape change occurred under feudalism in medieval and post-medieval times, rather than during the period of the Great Migrations at the end of the Roman Empire. Feudalism was a form of social organization that was based on land as the primary means of production. Land was held and worked communally by peasants, who rendered labour and produce to their feudal lords in return for protection. Feudal lords maintained themselves through the institution of the manor, the means by which feudalism was articulated in the landscape. Within feudalism, land was held principally for its use rather than its exchange value. People were closely linked with, and dependent upon, their local environment, because of the difficulty of transporting bulk foodstuffs from areas of surplus to those of deficit. The medieval manor, and the feudal system that underpinned it, has been seen as a stable, sustainable system, in which many of the resources, representing different components of the landscape, were held and worked in common by communities in a balanced, equitable form of resource management, which helped to reduce the risk of shortages and starvation.[1] Holdings within open fields were worked by individuals in scattered strips, which minimized the danger of complete crop failure by giving cultivators a range of soil and drainage conditions. Apart from the arable and meadow land, the waste provided a range of resources including fuel, timber and construction materials, as well as common grazing. Difficult environments, such as wetlands, were exploited surprisingly intensively, again frequently on a communal basis, as sources of fish, fowl, timber, turf, reeds and peat.[2]

The classic model of the feudal mode of production emphasizes the manor as the unit of organization, with village-scale farming systems and collectively-regulated resources, such as open fields and common waste. Open field systems, which occurred, in different forms, from Ireland to eastern Europe and Scandinavia, were not the only distinctive element of the feudal landscape. Equally characteristic of feudalism was the castle, which emphasized the system's military basis, and the church, which represented an organization that was a great feudal land-holder in its own right, as well as a powerful source of social control. There was, however, no single 'feudal landscape', just as there was no single, monolithic feudal system: feudalism and its landscapes varied nationally and regionally, as well as changing over time. The build-up of population throughout Europe in the twelfth and thirteenth centuries demonstrated that the feudal system could become strained. Population growth led to the creation of new settlements, and the taking into cultivation of increasingly marginal land, the clearance of woodland and the drainage of wetlands. Between the eleventh and the thirteenth century, the landscape impact of woodland clearance in Europe, first in internal frontiers and then in external ones as the population increased, was one of the most dramatic landscape changes made anywhere in the world up to that time.[3]

EUROPEAN LANDSCAPES IN 1500

In 1500 European landscapes were still essentially feudal, and the pace of landscape change was slow. Early modern Europe, from the Mediterranean to the fringes of the Arctic, was characterized by a great variety of cultural landscapes, the patterns of which reflected geology, climate, vegetation, soils and topography, as well as political, economic and social influences.

In the nineteenth and early twentieth centuries, French geographers, notably Vidal de la Blache, identified a complex mosaic of landscape units, or *pays*, within France. Within each *pays*, the physical environment, the farming systems, settlement patterns, vernacular building traditions and cultural traits were closely inter-related to form landscape units that were clearly distinguishable by local inhabitants, as well as by academics. Within a single province, such as Champagne, there might be more than 30 individual *pays*, some recognized only locally, some defunct by modern times, but all once recognizable visually.[4] The distinctive identities of such *pays* often went back many centuries, and, if more blurred than formerly, are often still evident today. While such regions have been studied in more detail in France, they existed widely throughout pre-industrial Europe. In England, where patterns of *pays* have been obscured by early industrialization and urbanization, patterns of 'farming regions', similar in many respects to *pays*, have been identified by economic historians. While these evolved over time and sometimes changed their character quite markedly as a result of agrarian improvement, they were probably at their most distinctive in the sixteenth and seventeenth centuries.[5]

Away from areas of Mediterranean farming, and outside the mountains and the northern taiga, a major contrast in improved landscapes existed between enclosed and more open areas, in France *bocage* and *champagne*, in England wood pasture and *fielden* or *champion*.[6] The boundary between the two types did not necessarily reflect differences in topography, climate or soil fertility. In France, there was some correspondence between areas of nucleated settlement with extensive open fields and well-drained loessic soils, but the fit was not a close one. In the Limagne, east of the Massif Central, classic Mediterranean landscapes were found (though without olive trees), 300 km north of the Mediterranean.[7]

In England, Oliver Rackham has made a distinction between 'ancient' and 'planned' countryside, the former characterized by enclosed fields that evolved gradually, in many areas from prehistoric times, the latter the result of a major replanning exercise in late Anglo-Saxon and Norman times, the context of which is still poorly understood, but which is part of a pattern found more widely in western Europe during the same period.[8] In the areas of planned countryside, prehistoric and Roman landscapes were swept away and replaced by open field systems and nucleated settlements. In England, this zone of planned countryside was then replanned in an even more systematic way during the era of Parliamentary enclosure in the later eighteenth and early nineteenth centuries.[9] The origins of non-planned landscape zones could be complex, and have been disputed. Tom Williamson has claimed that the automatic identification of wood pasture areas with late settlement is misleading, and that some of the woodland areas were as densely populated at the time of Domesday Book as open field areas.[10] Neither were champion areas necessarily distinguished by unity of lordship. Williamson traces the origins of the contrast between champion and wood pasture to differences in settlement created between areas of initial Anglo-Saxon occupation in south-east England and later settled areas in the Midlands, which affected the landscape in later times through differences in structures of kinship.

In areas of old enclosures or bocage, such as west Cornwall and Brittany, the field boundaries often consisted of massive stone and earth banks topped by hedges, which in some cases originated in prehistoric times. The boundaries between open field and enclosed regions, however, were not fixed. In western France, the area of bocage expanded from the sixteenth century onwards with the clearance of waste, and also by the replacement of open fields.[11] Much of the bocage in the Vendée was created as late as the seventeenth century. Different again were the Mediterranean landscapes, where, within a wide range of environments from the mountains down through the hills to the coastal plains, a greater variety of crops was grown than in transalpine Europe. They included tree and shrub crops such as olives, vines, figs, citrus fruits, almonds and chestnuts, as well as field crops such as rice, using a patchwork pattern of squarish fields, terraces and irrigation systems.

As regards rural settlement patterns, Brian Roberts has identified a core area from the Seine to the Elbe, extending northwards into Denmark, with a band across central England, which was characterized by irregularly laid-out villages and hamlets, a pattern that in many areas had evolved in early medieval times from one of dispersed farmsteads and small hamlets.[12] A peripheral zone, comprising Scandinavia, the Atlantic fringes of Europe and the Alpine foreland, was characterized by settlement dispersed in single farmsteads and hamlets. In much of eastern Europe, and some parts of eastern France and northern England, villages with regular plans along streets or around greens were common. These had been laid out during the medieval expansion of Christian Germanic peoples against the Slavs, the Magyars and the Baltic tribes, or, as in northern England, during phases of internal colonization. In the Mediterranean, villages sited on hilltops for defence against pirates were common in many areas, although here, too, some districts were dominated by dispersed settlement. In the southern Apennines, villages with populations of 3,000 or more were found. The dangers of malaria in the marshy lowlands of the Mediterranean reduced population and settlement there, and made the hills and mountains more attractive, despite their difficult topography.[13] At a local scale, settlement patterns might mirror environmental contrasts, with large villages on the best soils, hamlets on more marginal land and isolated farms at the fringes of colonization, but such simple determinism broke down at a larger scale – some highly fertile areas, such as parts of south-east England, had dispersed settlement.

Landscape units were rarely as uniform or as simple in origin as they appear on small-scale maps. In west Brittany, the bocage was a patchwork that had developed gradually. It was intermixed with quite extensive areas of open fields in an almost uninterrupted belt along the coast, with smaller blocks of open field strips further inland.[14] There were also marked landscape contrasts within the open field areas, the field systems of which exhibited numerous and complex variations.[15] The principal differences were between areas such as Midland England, where open fields were extensive and dominated the landscape, with comparatively limited areas of grazing, and those like Ireland, Scotland and southern Norway, where open fields formed small islands of improvement in a sea of rough pasture and waste. In such areas, the infield–outfield systems were often used: most of the manure and a range of other fertilizers, such as seaweed and turf pared from the pasture, were used to keep the small areas of infield under continuous cultivation, while the surrounding outfields, only lightly manured, were cropped much less intensively.[16] In mountain and upland areas, where there was plenty of rough pasture, systems of transhumance were widespread, where the high summer grazings were exploited using temporary settlements – saeters in Norway,

The remnants of a nineteenth-century *shieling* hut in central Lewis in the Outer Hebrides; the last phase of a long tradition.

shielings in Scotland, booleys in Ireland. Transhumance declined only with the penetration of more commercialized systems of livestock farming at various dates from the sixteenth to the twentieth centuries.[17]

At a smaller scale, the complex relationships between environment and socio-economic and social structures produced a wide range of traditional building styles, which formed an integral part of the landscape. Because of the difficulty and expense involved in transporting building materials any distance other than for prestige, high-status projects, most houses below those of the gentry were built using local materials, in styles and with layouts that reflected the nature of the local environment and the needs of the local economy. The contrast between the vernacular buildings of the ordinary people and the polite architecture of the more well-to-do could sometimes be relatively muted, since similar materials and layouts might be used, as in the timber-frame tradition of southern England and the North European Plain, or it could be very marked, as on a map of Carrickfergus drawn around 1560, on which the round, windowless turf cabins of the native Irish stand out sharply from the stone houses of merchants and craftsmen in the more prosperous town centre.[18]

Contrasts also existed between the log construction used in areas with plentiful timber, such as eastern Europe and Muscovy, and those with less timber but little good building stone, as in the timber-frame housing tradition of the North European Plain. In clay lowlands with no timber, walls of solid-clay construction were common, while areas with stone but little timber, such as upland Britain, used both mortared and dry-stone walling. There were differences between the layouts of farmsteads in arable and pastoral areas; in the former, there was a greater need for outbuildings that provided storage for grain, tools, plough teams and carts. Layouts of farm buildings around courtyards were characteristic of larger farms in some arable areas, such as the Paris Basin.[19] Long houses, with people and cattle accommodated under the same roof, were once thought to have been characteristic mainly of the poorer pastoral areas of northern and western Europe,[20] but the excavation of deserted villages in lowland England has shown that they were replaced with better-quality accommodation in late medieval times.[21] This emphazises how increasing prosperity could alter housing traditions. The Great Rebuilding of southern and central England in Tudor times led to the conversion or replacement of traditional houses over a wide area within certain social classes, as did a similar trend in northern England a century or so later.[22] Earlier traditions of building lingered on in outbuildings and minor structures when they had been abandoned for domestic accommodation – in the corbelled stone shieling huts of parts of Ireland and the Scottish Highlands and similar field shelters in upland France and the Balkans, which echo a tradition going back to Bronze Age or even Neolithic times.

THE TRANSITION FROM FEUDALISM TO CAPITALISM

The transition from feudalism to capitalism involved many complex, inter-connected elements, but all were related to a major shift in the ways in which European societies used their environments and how this was reflected in the landscape. The self-contained world of the manor became integrated into the space-economy of the region and then the nation state, becoming commercially oriented and specialized in the process. By the thirteenth century, the revival of trade and the growth of towns were encouraging the increasing commercialization of agriculture close to the larger urban centres in areas such as Flanders. The massive mortality of the fourteenth century caused by famines, notably in 1315–17, the Black Death in 1348–9 and later outbreaks of bubonic plague, reduced population by a third or more in Europe, cutting back to approximately the levels of around 1200. This drastically altered the balance between population and resources, and helped to weaken feudalism. In England, the population fell from around 6 million in 1300 to about 1.5 million in 1450.[23]

Population decline on this scale inevitably affected the landscape. The actual processes at work are not very clear, because documentation is limited. Abandonment of settlement and regeneration of woodlands did occur,[24] although in many parts of France, for example, temporary abandonment was much more common than permanent desertion, even during periods of instability such as the Hundred Years War (1337–1453) and the Thirty Years War (1614–48). In the Sierra Nevada of southern Spain, the Reconquista led to major depopulation after the converted Moorish population rebelled in 1568. Three-quarters of the villages were deserted, and only limited numbers of Christian settlers moved in to balance the large number of inhabitants who had been expelled.[25] Many more marginal communities declined because of labour shortages, due to the availability of better quality land in lowland areas. Settlement changes often operated within the context of individual estates, as particular landowners reorganized and concentrated their reduced labour force. A shift from intensive arable farming with ample peasant labour to less intensive crop production or extensive livestock farming occurred in areas such as the English Midlands and the Paris Basin. In Alsace, many smaller settlements were deserted as the population became concentrated into larger villages.[26] In the landscape this was shown by the extensive abandonment of cultivation in favour of pasture, and the retreat of rural settlement from marginal areas, as in the Cheviots and Dartmoor in England. Substantial reversion of improved land to forest occurred in central and eastern Europe. After the Black Death, in order to attract and retain tenants, landlords had to rent out demesnes and reduce feudal restrictions. The renting of land in itself promoted a cash economy, which further encouraged social change with the emergence of rentier landlords, groups of wealthier peasants and increasing numbers of landless labourers.

The transition from feudalism to capitalism varied in timing between different regions and countries, and is most easily (though not perfectly) measured in the decline of labour services. It had a characteristic geographical pattern at a range of scales from that of the feudal kingdom, through regions to individual estates. Feudalism disappeared most slowly in core areas rather than peripheral ones, in areas of large-scale grain production rather than in livestock areas, in old-settled areas rather than recently-cleared districts, and in areas where feudal control was strongest. Remnants of feudalism often survived when the dominant mode of production had shifted decisively towards capitalism, such as the continuation of thirlage to estate mills in late eighteenth-century Scotland. On the other hand, the reverse occurred in eastern Europe, east of the Elbe, in a huge territory that had been won from the Slavs and colonized in medieval times. In this zone, which had been characterized by freer tenures than in western areas, a 'second feudalism' was later imposed, as lords built up estates and extended their powers over their peasantry. A focus on demesne cultivation and the production of large grain surpluses for western European markets provided the context in which, through a manorial structure in some areas and a system resembling plantations in others, a once-free peasantry became enslaved. The process was under way by 1300 and was nearly complete by the later sixteenth century, by which time demesne cultivation had largely disappeared from western Europe, with the commutation of labour services into money payments. In the process of expanding demesnes in countries such as Poland, peasants were often dispossessed and relocated in new, planned street villages.[27]

ENVIRONMENTAL CHANGE AND LANDSCAPE: THE LITTLE ICE AGE

For much of this book the focus is on landscape change under the impact of human activity, but on the 500-year timescale considered here cultural landscapes were also subject to the impacts of environmental changes, although it is dangerously easy to be simplistic and deterministic about the nature of the relationships involved. In reality, changes in environmental constraints interacted with demographic, economic, social and political variables to affect landscapes in complex ways, which makes it difficult to generalize from individual case studies. By the early fourteenth century, with the encouragement of a warm phase of climate, settlement had expanded under pressure of population into many marginal areas, such as the upland zones of Britain, parts of Scandinavia and the Alps.[28] The drastic cut in population during the fourteenth century, possibly assisted by a shift to wetter, cooler climatic conditions, led to the desertion of many marginal settlements. On Dartmoor, the high-lying settlement of Hound Tor was one of many to be abandoned. In Scandinavia, around 40 per cent of farms were deserted in parts of Norway and even Denmark, and 25 to 40 per cent in some areas of Sweden. The valley of Jostedalen in Norway was deserted after the Black Death, and recolonized only with population growth in the sixteenth century. Shortly afterwards, cooler conditions and advancing glaciers made conditions in the valley increasingly difficult – there were avalanches, rockfalls, floods, cold summers and poor harvests.[29] Many of the farms deserted in Scandinavia and elsewhere in Europe at this time were marginal climatically and/or possessed small areas of cultivation, although it should be noted that studies of farm and settlement desertion have often been focused at a fairly broad regional level, and that the reasons behind desertion have more often been inferred than demonstrated.[30] The southward spread of the limits of summer sea ice in the Atlantic helped to isolate the Norse colony in Greenland and, together with colder, wetter conditions, formed the background to its complete demise by the early sixteenth century. In Iceland, cooler conditions and the spread southwards of the summer sea ice limits led to the abandonment of cereal cultivation in the fifteenth or sixteenth century.[31]

By the mid-sixteenth century, with population on the increase, limits of settlement and cultivation were expanding once more, often into areas that had been cleared and colonized in medieval times but that were subsequently abandoned. In some areas, however, renewed settlement growth was halted and even reversed in the seventeenth century by the continued climatic deterioration of the Little Ice Age. Its chronology is imprecise and regionally varied, but it seems to have involved a trend towards cooler and wetter conditions in the later sixteenth and especially the later seventeenth centuries. Increasing storminess around the North Sea had already brought a higher incidence of coastal flooding in late medieval times.[32] These trends continued with accelerated coastal erosion in parts of eastern England, and on the German and Danish North Sea coasts. Blown sand blocked river mouths and buried settlements in north-east Scotland and parts of Denmark.[33] Cooler conditions from Britain and Norway through the Vosges to the mountains of eastern Europe drove tree lines and cultivation limits downhill. In the coldest spell, at the end of the seventeenth century and into the early years of the eighteenth, Alpine, Scandinavian and Icelandic glaciers advanced substantially. Around Mont Blanc, they overran fields and even settlements, while the cold summers meant that crops failed to ripen.[34] Around the fringes of the Jostedalsbreen ice cap in Norway, farms were affected by avalanches, rockfalls and floods as an indirect result of the advancing ice.[35] New glaciers formed on the Hardanger plateau, and permanent snow returned to the highest British mountains, implying average annual temperatures at least 2 °C below those of the mid-twentieth century.[36] At the end of the seventeenth century, a run of wet, cool summers and long, cold winters brought disaster to livestock farmers in the southern uplands of Scotland, and this probably encouraged the abandonment of some smaller, more marginal farms.[37] At the same time, the limits of summer sea ice pushed south of Iceland. The associated cooler conditions caused Icelandic farming and fishing to suffer as a result. Even in lowland areas, the length of the growing season in north-west Europe in the seventeenth century was five weeks shorter than during the medieval optimum. Climatically marginal land was not necessarily all high-lying, though. Wetter conditions on some of the English claylands, due to heavier rainfall and reduced evaporation, may have been a factor behind the desertion of villages such as Goltho in Lincolnshire.[38]

CHANGING AGRICULTURAL LANDSCAPES

By the mid-sixteenth century, the population was starting to expand again, until, in the early to mid-seventeenth century, many areas had exceeded their early-fourteenth-century demographic peak. The population of France, Germany and England had stood at *c.* 22 million in 1200 and *c.* 40 million in 1340, but had dropped to *c.* 27 million by 1470 only to rise to *c.* 42 million by 1620.[39] Population growth and increasing commercialization, associated with the stimulus of urban markets, began to affect the European landscape, although agricultural progress and its associated landscape changes were mainly a feature of only a few areas: northern Italy, southern France, the Low Countries and parts of eastern England. In these regions, agricultural output was increased by more sophisticated rotations, the introduction of new crops, improved techniques of cultivation, and also by the reclamation of new land. In the Low Countries, the elimination of fallowing and the incorporation into rotations of fodder crops such as turnips, lucerne and sown grasses, and the growing of industrial crops such as flax, hemp, madder and woad, were also features. The wide range of fertilizers used also encouraged the intensification of animal husbandry.[40]

In particular, the changing relationship between society and environment in post-medieval times was reflected in the landscape by enclosure, the reclamation of land from marshes and the sea, and the clearance of woodland and heath. In some districts, much enclosure and intake of new land in the sixteenth and seventeenth centuries was undertaken on a piecemeal, small-scale basis by individual peasants or small groups of farmers, from lowland common pastures, wood-pasture and heath or upland waste. In England, in the southern Pennines and parts of Cumbria, the improvement of small areas of waste by land-hungry squatters produced a system of smallholding agriculture that was combined with domestic textile manufacture. This created a densely-settled, busy landscape that is still distinctive today. Enclosure of this sort was often allowed by manorial lords in situations where pasture was plentiful, the squatters eventually being formally entered in the manorial court rolls.[41] In Scotland, population growth was accommodated by the splitting of existing townships and an associated enlargement of the cultivated area, and by the creation of new marginal crofts, often with names incorporating elements such as hill, muir, moss and bog. These indicated the environments from which they had been reclaimed.[42]

Such activities were relatively unobtrusive, but some large-scale enclosure in late fifteenth- and sixteenth-century England attracted wider attention, because perceived associated threats of depopulation and reductions in grain supplies came to the notice of the government. In addition, it was the subject of polemics by writers such as Sir Thomas More. Enclosure was thus relatively well documented. It was encouraged by economic conditions, especially the shift of prices in favour of wool and against cereals. In parts of the Midlands and eastern England, communities of mixed-farming smallholders were evicted, and their farms were amalgamated and enlarged into big commercial sheep runs. Many of the communities involved had already suffered population decline, but the density of deserted villages from this period in some areas helps to explain the concern of Tudor governments.[43] In fact, the scale of the problem was exaggerated, for recent research suggests that enclosure in England between 1450 and 1599 accounted for only about 3 per cent of the total enclosed land, compared with nearly 25 per cent between 1600 and 1699. The seventeenth century was a period of more widespread, but less obtrusive, enclosure from both open fields and waste, often by private agreement between small groups of landowners, in which a substantially greater area was probably enclosed than in either the eighteenth or the nineteenth centuries.[44]

Reclamation was especially active around the North Sea, at the core of the emerging 'world system'.[45] It was spurred, especially in the Netherlands, by population increase and urban growth, which generated demand for food surpluses from commercial agriculture, and was encouraged by urban investment in land improvement. In the Netherlands, which were never heavily feudalized, reclamation from the sea made steady progress between 1100 and 1500, but it experienced a major increase between 1500 and 1650. This was encouraged by a number of severe sea floods in the sixteenth century, and aided by technical innovations such as the bucket dredger and more powerful windmills. Between 1615 and 1640, around 1,800 ha (4,500 a) were being reclaimed each year. Coastal reclamation by dykes represented 80 per cent of this. Between 1540 and 1715 in Zeeland alone about 70,000 ha (175,000 a) were reclaimed. By 1640, the cultivated area in the Noorderkwartier, north of Amsterdam, had increased by more than 40 per cent as a result of reclamation. Coastal reclamation accelerated earlier, because the marine clays were very fertile and the land was not subject to shrinkage. The drainage of inland lakes and wetlands presented greater difficulties, requiring investment in chains of windmills to pump water up into the canals.

During the seventeenth century, reclamation from inland waters by pumping increased dramatically. Some drainage of shallow lakes had been achieved in the sixteenth century, but from the early seventeenth century the development of improved windmills, able to lift water more than 3 m (9 ft), encouraged a considerable expansion of this type of reclamation. The first major project was the drainage of the Beemster lake, covering some 6,912 ha (27 sq miles) and about 4 m (12 ft) deep. Amsterdam merchants provided the capital, the Dutch engineer, Jan Leeghwater, the expertise. Within five years, with the use of more than 40 windmills, some 7,000 ha (17,500 a) of land had been reclaimed and 207 new farms established. The technique involved surrounding a lake by a dyke and pumping water out into a drainage canal, which was connected, via sluices, to a river or the sea. Progress continued until the late seventeenth century, when the amounts of both types of reclamation fell abruptly.[46] The peak of Dutch drainage activity between 1600 and 1625 coincided with the 'golden age' of the Dutch economy and landscape art.

Reclamation was also a feature of the English Fens, where the Dissolution of the Monasteries had led to the neglect of medieval drainage systems. In the early seventeenth century, the Fens were still largely undrained medieval landscapes, whose people were as distinctive as their surroundings, as the antiquarian William Camden (1551–1623) observed:

> the inhabitants of this and the rest of the fenny Country [are] fen men; a sort of people (much like the place) of brutish uncivilized temper envious of all others whom they term Upland men, and usually walking aloft upon a sort of stilts; they all keep to the business of grazing, fishing and fowling. All this country in the winter time, and sometimes for the greatest part of the year, laid under water.[47]

Villages were on dry sites, slightly elevated above the Fens with areas of open field on better-drained soils.

Severe floods in 1570 led to a Dutchman, Humphrey Bradley, being commissioned in 1589 to drain marshes in the English Fens, but little was achieved until James I, concerned by major floods in 1607, 1613 and 1614, brought in Cornelius Vermuyden, who worked at first in Yorkshire and around the Humber. In 1630–31 the Fourth Earl of Bedford and a group of thirteen landowning partners or 'adventurers' undertook to drain the peat of the southern Fens. They employed Vermuyden, who planned a series of new waterways, including the Old and New Bedford Rivers. By 1637, much of the work had been carried out, with further activity during the 1650s. Vermuyden used technology that had already been tried and tested in the Netherlands and Italy. He appears not to have appreciated the danger of peat shrinkage, however, and by 1700 the new drains were already above the level of the peat, increasing the risk of flooding. The use of windmills in the eighteenth century and steam engines in the nineteenth was necessary to keep water levels down.

In the seventeenth century, reclamation was undertaken widely elsewhere in Europe, from the Somerset Levels to the Vistula, often with the aid of Dutch engineers and colonists. Religious intolerance in Roman Catholic countries such as

France, and concern by local people over the loss of traditional rights in marshland areas, caused problems that delayed some reclamation schemes and prevented others from being started at all. In other cases, hard-won land was eventually lost through failure to maintain the drainage systems during war or political shifts, which sometimes led to the expulsion of the Dutch colonists, as in France after the revocation of the Edict of Nantes in 1598. One of the most impressive schemes, the reclamation of the Moeres depression in Flanders – the remains of extensive medieval peat workings like the Norfolk Broads, on which 140 new farms had been established – was lost during the Thirty Years War when the land was deliberately flooded to protect the city of Dunkirk. The island of Amager, on which part of Copenhagen was built, was drained as early as 1515 by Dutch settlers. Other Dutchmen settled in Sweden and drained the Göteborg marshes from 1618. Much inland drainage from peat bogs and riverside marshes was also undertaken by Dutchmen in Brandenburg, east Prussia and Poland. Groups of Dutch settlers on the Vistula, encouraged by Danzig merchants, drained marshland as far inland as the area around Warsaw. Other colonists were active round the shores of the Baltic, in Muscovy and in the Ukraine. Their work was also seen on the western and northern coasts of France, in the Po valley and the Rhône delta, in the Pontine marshes near Rome and in northern Germany, and in many of the valleys of eastern Europe. Humphrey Bradley worked on the Channel, Atlantic and Mediterranean coasts of France, achieving considerable success in some areas, but failing in others because of local opposition.[48]

Forests, outside Scandinavia and eastern Europe, were mostly deciduous, although conifers were being introduced into some parts of Germany by 1500. There had been some recovery and expansion of the forest area in the fourteenth and fifteenth centuries as a result of depopulation, which led to settlement abandonment and a fall in the demand for timber. From the sixteenth century onwards, however, the attack on woodland was renewed. Only 6–7 per cent of England was wooded by the seventeenth century, barely 2 per cent of Ireland.[49] In central and eastern Europe, however, extensive forests still survived. Prussia was still about 40 per cent forested in the eighteenth century, and further east reserves of timber were even greater.

The forests of the Mediterranean were by this time increasingly confined to mountain areas, but even there they were under pressure from the demand for timber for fuel, ship-building and construction. Simply keeping warm in winter required up to 10 cubic metres of fuel wood per family per year, the growth of 4 ha (10 a) of mature forest. A village of 100 families relying on wood for fuel would have needed access to up to 400 ha (1,000 a) of forest.[50] An awareness of the undesirable environmental impacts of deforestation and erosion is evident in mid-fifteenth-century Venice, where the high rate of wood-land clearance in the Veneto increased the volume of silt brought down by the rivers into the lagoon surrounding the city. From the mid-sixteenth century, local shortages forced Venice to draw timber supplies from the other side of the Adriatic.[51] Everywhere timber was in demand for making char-coal for iron smelting. Charcoal was a much more efficient source of heat than wood, but 5–10 kg (11–22 lb) of wood were required to make 1 kg (2.2 lb) of charcoal.[52] Although the iron industry was becoming increasingly concentrated in areas such as the Basque Country and the Milan district, which had high-quality iron ores, reserves of nearby timber for charcoal and access to markets by river and coastal transport, low-grade iron was produced much more widely. It has been established since the 1970s that the old idea of England's woodlands being depleted by the charcoal iron industry, forcing it to retreat from southern areas of production like the Weald ever north-wards and westwards in search of new fuel supplies, is a misunderstanding. Techniques of coppice management allowed deciduous woodlands to be maintained as renewable resources and cropped regularly. Coppice gave three or four times as much fuel wood as natural forest. In Furness, in the southern Lake District, the area of woodland actually expanded under the demand for charcoal for iron smelting and other uses, as land was converted from pasture to coppice.[53] It is not clear, however, how widely coppice management was practised among the deciduous woodlands of continental Europe, and to what degree it helped to maintain fuel supplies. Around the

Mediterranean it seems only to have been widespread in the southern Apennines.[54]

The iron industry is too simple a scapegoat for the destruction of woodlands. Given that charcoal was too fragile to transport far, it was important for ironworks to be established in areas with a sustainable fuel supply, especially with the development of larger, more expensive blast furnaces from the early seventeenth century. The effects of grazing animals and clearance for agriculture – the burning of forest for shifting cultivation continued in Finland into the twentieth century – were also major causes of deforestation. In eastern Europe and Scandinavia, large-scale commercial logging was confined mainly to areas adjoining rivers and coasts. Timber was floated down the Seine from Burgundy and down the Rhine from the Black Forest.

In bocage areas with little continuous woodland, hedgerow trees were a major source of timber. In some areas woodland seems to have been poorly managed; Lowland Scotland had probably been largely deforested by 1500. The Scots do not appear to have had a medieval tradition of coppicing.[55] When Samuel Johnson visited Scotland in 1773 he remarked on the absence of trees between the Anglo-Scottish Border and the north-eastern Lowlands. Keeping a tight hold of his walking stick, he commented on the value of such a piece of timber in Scotland! Doubtless he was exaggerating, for he was writing at a time when many landowners were starting to establish blocks of woodland around their country seats, which made the landscape less treeless than it had been in earlier times.[56]

The needs of both rural and urban populations for fuel had other impacts on the landscape in areas where woodland was not available, or was too valuable, because alternative fuel sources had to be found. Atlantic Europe and some coastal and interior lowlands elsewhere had the benefit of peat. Sometimes the extraction of peat for fuel led to landscape transformation on a grand scale. It is only relatively recently that the true origins of the Norfolk Broads have been established, as medieval peat workings supplying a densely populated area in the thirteenth century. It has been estimated that some 25.5 million cubic m (900 million cubic ft) of peat were removed over three centuries before flooding caused by higher sea levels and increasing storminess during the fourteenth century led to the abandonment of the workings.[57] By the seventeenth century, local people had forgotten that the Broads were artificial. Dutch and Flemish cities too were largely fuelled by peat and the workings, pumped out and drained, were frequently reclaimed.[58] While deforestation has been studied in some detail, the scale of peat removal by small-scale cutting or larger-scale extraction, and the impact of this on the landscape, on drainage regimes and on vegetation patterns, has been greatly underestimated. In upland areas such as the south Pennines, a far greater quantity of peat may have been removed than from the Norfolk Broads. By the seventeenth century, in parts of north-east Scotland, surviving peat mosses had to be carefully managed to conserve the remaining resources for as long as possible, although the subsoils of worked-out peat bogs could sometimes be drained and reclaimed, if they did not flood, as was the case with Kilconquhar Loch in Fife.[59] In areas where charcoal was not readily available, peat could be used for smelting lead or iron. Some Scottish island communities, without peat or timber, were forced to burn animal dung for fuel, despite its value as a fertilizer.[60]

At this period, industries were generally widely scattered and small in scale, their impact on the landscape often, as yet, fairly localized. Iron was smelted at small bloomery sites, whose remains today may often amount to only small piles of slag. Ores of lead and copper were mined by shallow workings on veins exposed at the surface. In areas where stone was readily available, quarrying was done in a limited way by every community. In most areas, coal mining involved simple outcrop workings or the sinking of shallow shafts, or bell pits. The textile industries affected the density of settlement but were undertaken mainly at a domestic scale. Even those processes that needed water power, such as the fulling of woollen cloth, were still limited in scale and impact.

The growing power of the Tudor state brought an end to private warfare in England and the need for castles and strongholds. The growing prosperity of Tudor England, particularly the profits from more commercialized agriculture, encouraged a burst of country-house construction, which was further facilitated by the profits from newly-acquired former monastic lands. In 1577 William Harrison wrote of England that:

> Every man almost is a builder and he that hath bought any small parcel of ground, be it never so little, will not be quiet until he have pulled down the old house ... and set up a new after his own devise.[61]

Houses no longer had to be sited with defence, or their function as demesne centres, in mind. Without the need to maintain large bands of retainers, the sizes of landowning households declined. New or remodelled landowners' houses, freed from their medieval defensive needs, reflected comfort, privacy, light and better sanitation, seen particularly well at Hardwick Hall, 'more glass than wall', in Derbyshire. The great houses of Elizabethan courtiers have been called 'prodigy houses' because of their strangeness and distinctiveness, unlike country houses from any other period – daringly experimental, extravagant in their proliferation of detail, incorporating Classical detail without full use or understanding of the rules of Classical style. Classical motifs were often adopted as decorative features, but not the full logic of Italian Renaissance Classicism. In both England and Scotland, the monarchy set the trend directly through the construction of new palaces, and also indirectly as courtiers vied with each other to build houses that would impress their rulers, accommodating them and their retinues on royal progresses. Occasionally, notably in the case of Cardinal Wolsey at Hampton Court, they overdid the magnificence, with disastrous results.[62]

In many parts of Britain, however, the impetus to rebuild came as much from the gentry and yeomen as the great proprietors, with the accent on the use of new materials, such as brick, as well as new styles. The Great Rebuilding of Tudor England saw the widespread replacement of medieval-style yeoman and gentry hall-houses of timber-frame construction by more modern structures.[63] In Scotland and Ireland, with more unruly societies, the use of castles and fortified houses died out more slowly. Although internal feuding declined in Scotland in the

'Hardwick Hall, more glass than wall': a classic Tudor 'prodigy house' built between 1590 and 1597.

Changing tastes. Leamaneh Castle, Co. Clare, Ireland. The more spacious and airy 17th-century block offers far greater comfort than the cramped medieval tower house on the right.

early seventeenth century and the Anglo-Scottish border was rapidly pacified after the Union of the Crowns in 1603, the Highlands remained turbulent, and new tower houses continued to be built on their fringes throughout the first half of the seventeenth century. Nevertheless, early-seventeenth-century tower houses, epitomized by Craigievar and a group of neighbouring castles in north-east Scoland, successfully integrated design features adapted from French châteaux with the spartan medieval tower-house layout. Only after 1660 did more peaceful conditions in the Scottish Lowlands encourage the construction of the first undefended mansions in neo-Classical styles, such as Kinross House and Hopetoun House, while existing fortified houses, such as Traquair House, were converted or extended by the addition of non-defensive wings.[64]

LANDSCAPE PERCEPTIONS

Landscape perceptions in Europe at the start of our period are not easy to assess directly. One point of entry to this topic is to consider to what degree wilderness still existed in Europe and to what extent it had been reduced by the medieval expansion of population, settlement and cultivation. According to a traditional view of the English landscape, there was still a good deal of woodland to clear in medieval times, and many areas of real wilderness survived well after the eleventh century.[65] More modern research has emphasized the scale of prehistoric landscape change, the density of late prehistoric settlement, and elements of continuity in post-Roman times between Britons and Saxons. On this basis, there may not have been much wilderness left in England by the sixteenth century, although the perceptions of someone living in southern England would doubtless have differed from those of the inhabitants of northern areas, where there were extensive tracts of fell and moorland. Surviving areas of woodland such as the New Forest were seen as being occupied by people on the margins of society, potential troublemakers on a small scale, such as poachers – although at least not by bands of outlaws. Robin Hood and his 'merrie men' lived on in legend, but they have no real counterparts in England from early modern times. Eighteenth-century highwayman such as Dick Turpin were more likely to be encountered lurking on the heaths around London than infesting remote moorland districts.

In northern and western Britain things were different. In Scotland, J. R. Short has argued, wilderness vanished only with the Jacobite defeat at Culloden in 1746.[66] This seems a curious yardstick. Certainly for the Lowlands it seems too late a date, despite the amount of reclamation of peat bogs and drainage of lochs that remained for improving landowners of the late eighteenth and early nineteenth century to accomplish. The establishment of extensive sheep farms in the Southern Uplands by medieval monastic orders had already brought these hills within the orbit of semi-commercialized agriculture. More meaningful perhaps was the date of the killing of the last recorded wolf. A report of the killing of a creature near Tomatin in the Findhorn Valley in 1743 is of dubious authenticity.[67] The last records of bounties paid for the killing of wolves, in Sutherland, date from the 1620s. In Ireland, the last wolves seem to have been killed in County Cork around 1709–10.[68] Irish woodlands were supposedly burnt to prevent their being used as refuges by rebels.

On the Continent, however, wilderness areas were still extensive. In France, bands of brigands and outlaws continued to flourish into the nineteenth century.[69] Wolves had been extinct in England from about 1300, perhaps even earlier in Wales, but in France they continued to pose a threat to travellers, even between the Channel coast and Paris, in the early eighteenth century.[70] Forest areas such as the Ardennes and Lorraine sheltered the human equivalents of wolves: bandits, highwaymen and army deserters, as well as refugees in times of war.[71] England was already lightly wooded compared with Scandinavia and eastern Europe, where, outside mountain zones and some coastal marshes, the largest areas of true wilderness in Europe probably survived. Fear of wilderness remained – in the attitudes of lowland dwellers travelling in upland areas like the Pennines or the Alps, in fen country or in forests. Their fear of forests, with their wild beasts and wild people, has come down to us, transferred from central Europe, in tales such as *Hansel and Gretel, Little Red*

Riding Hood and *Snow White*. The history of forests in Europe has tended to remain on the margins of landscape research, as areas into which cultivation and improvement expanded rather than as landscapes in their own right.

MAP MAKERS AND LANDSCAPE

Sixteenth-century Europe saw a revolution in the production, understanding and consumption of maps, which was both a cause and an effect of changing perceptions of landscape. This was associated with greater interest in navigation and astronomical theory, progress in military science and engineering, and agricultural changes that involved the surveying of estates, or of areas of newly-reclaimed land. In many parts of Europe, maps were little understood in 1500, while by 1600 they were familiar everyday objects to a wide range of the literate elite. Artistic developments, especially in Italy and the Low Countries, were also influential. By 1600, every literate person was a potential customer for the rapidly-expanding map-publishing industry. The crucial developments in surveying techniques occurred on the Continent in the late fifteenth and early sixteenth centuries: the magnetic compass had been applied to land surveying by the start of the sixteenth century, and the principles of triangulation using the theodolite were developed soon after.

The Italian Renaissance was as much a cartographic as an artistic achievement, united by similar ideas. Map makers such as Cristoforo Sorte (*c.* 1506–94) produced treatises on landscape art, while artists like Leonardo da Vinci (1452–1519) undertook surveys and drew maps. Bird's-eye views of cities, popular in the early sixteenth century, stood somewhere between art and cartography. Surveyors and cartographers like Sorte were also artists. He wrote a treatise on landscape painting that discussed in detail the theory of linear perspective.

A crucial element in this cartographic revolution was the development of the scale map, although its origins are far from clear. Erhard Etzlaub of Nuremberg was producing scale maps of the area around the city in the late fifteenth century, but the first examples from England date from the 1540s. The earlier traditions of perspective bird's-eye views and pictorial maps continued and even flourished, but increasingly pictorial features were superimposed on properly-surveyed scale maps. Maps were produced at different scales for a range of purposes, but from the standpoint of landscape the three most important categories were the regional map, the estate plan and maps produced for military purposes. In different parts of Europe the nature and chronology of topographic mapping varied. Italy, southern Germany, the Low Countries and England were more advanced than other parts of Europe, although within Italy progress was earlier and faster in Venice than elsewhere.[72] The development of more accurate large-scale maps was often linked with the increasing commercialization of agriculture.[73] In the late sixteenth-century Veneto, many maps were produced in conjunction with water-management schemes. In Spain and France, with less advanced agriculture, the widespread use of estate plans did not develop until the late seventeenth or even the eighteenth century. The use of maps for any purpose developed much more slowly in northern and eastern Europe. In England, there was a long tradition of producing written surveys of areas of land, such as the layout of strips within open field systems. Gradually such surveys came to be accompanied, and then replaced, by scale maps. Changes in land ownership following the Dissolution of the Monasteries may have provided a spur to the production of estate maps, which from an early date were carefully decorated and coloured, emphasizing proprietors' pride in the possession of land as well as more utilitarian functions. Changes in land ownership increased litigation over property rights, which generated another context in which maps became useful.[74] In the Netherlands in the late sixteenth and early seventeenth centuries, the demand for detailed and accurate maps was related to military operations as well as water control.[75]

Improved surveying techniques encouraged the production of more accurate maps using the plane table, the theodolite and triangulation, the last described in a book by Gemma Frisius, published in Louvain in 1533, and first noted in England by William Cuningham in *The Cosmographical Glasse* of 1559. Triangulation was certainly used for a map of Bavaria by Philipp

Apianus in the late 1550s. An important element of the revolution in cartography was military use. The new geometric styles of fortification, which were designed to counter the increasing use of artillery, developed in late fifteenth-century Italy, soon spread throughout Europe. The mathematical and engineering skills required to plan such systems lent themselves to accurate ground survey. In the early sixteenth century, there was no strict division between artist, military engineer and cartographer. Men such as Leonardo da Vinci and Albrecht Dürer (1471–1528) were active in all these fields. Italian military engineers may have introduced the idea of the scale map into England in the 1540s, although the Netherlands and published treatises such as those of Dürer are other possible sources. The pictorial maps of fortifications in Tudor England provide us with the first glimpses of the English landscape as it appeared to contemporaries.

Maps were a valuable form of political knowledge, and this knowledge represented power, a fact well appreciated by William Cecil, Lord Burghley, Secretary of State and Lord High Treasurer to Elizabeth I, the most cartographically-minded statesman of his day, who had a large collection of maps, many of them annotated in his own hand.[76] Burghley, and indirectly Elizabeth, were backers of Christopher Saxton (*b.* 1542), who undertook the first complete county-by-county survey of England and Wales in a series of 34 maps produced between 1574 and 1579. Saxton was not the only English regional cartographer of his day, but he was the first to survey the entire country. The link between mapping and royal power was emphasized when Saxton's maps were first published in atlas form in 1579, with the royal insignia on every map and a title page showing Queen Elizabeth flanked by figures representing astronomy and geography.[77] The extent to which Saxton used triangulation or merely sketched in his detail from suitable vantage points has been widely debated. He seems to have travelled alone, using locally recruited assistants. Since he completed several county surveys each season, he must have worked rapidly. He may have used a crude form of triangulation based on compass bearings, but without the use of accurately measured baselines. William Ravenhill has suggested that he

Landscapes of power: part of Saxton's 1570s map of Lancashire, emphasising the visual dominance of the parks and mansions of the gentry and aristocracy.

used the chain of warning beacons as observation points, and the local knowledge of the men who maintained them.[78] The result was an impressively accurate and detailed set of maps for their day. Saxton initiated the tradition of county cartography in Britain and, in terms of the quality of detail, his maps were not significantly improved upon for nearly 200 years. Although, curiously, not showing roads, and not always marking the boundaries of the hundreds into which counties were subdivided, his maps provide a detailed picture of the English landscape. Particular emphasis was given to the parks and mansions of major landowners, who were potential customers for his work. Saxton's maps were used at every level of government from county to national, but, perhaps more importantly, they introduced maps to a much wider public, including many landowners who may have been encouraged to commission their own private estate surveys. As perceptions of landscape at a range of scales, Saxton's maps were very influential to a rapidly expanding market.

In France, François I (1515–47) was the counterpart of Henry VIII as the first monarch with a strong sense of the political value of maps. During the 1560s and 1570s, roughly contemporary with Saxton, the French cartographer Nicolas de Nicolay completed a number of surveys of French provinces, but the outbreak of civil war prevented him from undertaking a fully national survey. Despite a lag in cartographic development at the end of the sixteenth century caused by internal unrest, by the mid-seventeenth century France was on the brink of the major cartographic developments of Louis XIV's reign (1643–1715).[79]

Sixteenth-century maps were more than just representations of landscape, they articulated symbolic values too: they emphasized the growing control of territory, and the landscapes within it, by developing nation states. The way in which Saxton's maps, bound in atlas form, continuously repeated the symbols of royal authority emphasized the link between the survey and the state. The title page, showing Elizabeth I standing on a map of England, emphasized how rapidly map-making had become harnessed as a tool of government. Maps also emphasized the mythology of the origins of states and dynasties. They should not be judged too simplistically, though. The failure of Saxton and his contemporaries to cope with the problem of showing relief other than as 'sugar-loaf' hills can easily be attributed to a lack of technique. But it also emphasized the perceptions of contemporaries, who saw upland areas as being of little value and interest – so why bother showing them in detail? Nor were estate maps simple workaday surveys. They emphasized pride of ownership and seigneurial power as much as later paintings of country houses and their surrounding parks.

In Ireland, mapping was associated with the extension of English rule with Tudor military campaigns, and represents the dynasty's greatest cartographic achievement. In 1550, the English government had little knowledge of the geography of Ireland beyond the Pale. By 1610, the whole country had been mapped, parts of it in considerable detail. The work of cartographers such as Robert Lythe, who surveyed Munster and Leinster between 1568 and 1571, Richard Bartlett, who mapped Ulster between 1597 and 1603, and John Browne, uncle and nephew, who covered Connacht in the 1580s, were particularly notable. Their maps captured some curious contrasts between ancient and modern in the Irish landscape, such as one showing a group of Irish rebels defending a crannog – a lake dwelling with prehistoric origins as a settlement form – with modern handguns. Cartography made less progress in Scotland, apart from maps drawn by engineers employed by the invading English armies of the 1540s, but the late sixteenth-century surveys of Timothy Pont, inspired by Saxton's work and possibly backed by James VI, represented a brave attempt to survey a much wilder country. They were eventually published by the Dutch house of Blaeu in the mid-seventeenth century.[80]

Late sixteenth-century cartographers, such as John Norden and William Smith, produced groups of county surveys that improved upon Saxton in that they showed roads and consistently marked county subdivisions. Nevertheless, English county cartography in the seventeenth century also represented a decline from Saxton's work, in that maps, from those of John Speed at the start of the seventeenth century to ones by John Morden at its end, relied largely on copying from Saxton and other sources rather than undertaking new surveys. Maps became more attractively embellished, but not significantly more accurate. To some extent this represents the development of a centralized map-publishing industry based in London. New surveys were time-consuming and expensive compared with compiling new maps from existing sources. But it may also have reflected a sense that the pace of change in the seventeenth-century English landscape, at the scale covered by county maps, was relatively slow. The continuity in the ways that landscapes were perceived, and the lack of appreciation of significant landscape change, is seen in England by the way in which Camden's *Britannia*, first published in 1586, was continually republished until 1806.[81]

THE EMERGENCE OF LANDSCAPE ART AND THE IDEA OF LANDSCAPE

The origins of 'landscape' as a term were in late fifteenth-century Renaissance humanism. For much of its history, landscape has been closely related with the practical appropriation of space through survey and cartography, the sciences of ballistics and fortification, and the construction of map projections. In art and garden design, landscape achieved visually and ideologically what survey and map-making did in practical terms – the control and domination of space, using the same techniques, the application of Euclidian geometry, in this case by means of theories of linear perspective. There were close links between the landscape idea and the development of linear perspective as a way of controlling space; both were linked to the growing domination of the natural environment associated with the development of capitalism. Ideas about linear perspective developed in Tuscany during the fifteenth century, and revolutionized spatial perceptions in the West.[82] Linear perspective was first discussed by Leon Battista Alberti in *Della Pittura* in 1435–6. At a more esoteric level, Euclidian geometry was also important in uniting the arts and sciences in their approach to landscape. The new genre was related to concepts of authority and control. The illusion of control provided by the new ways of structuring the world through landscape art was often matched by real power and control over farms and estates by artistic patrons.[83]

Landscape painting first emerged in the two most economically advanced, densely populated and highly urbanized areas of Europe, northern Italy and Flanders. In the early fifteenth century, artists such as Jan van Eyck began painting detailed and accurate landscape backgrounds in paintings, the main subjects of which were religious and historical. Similarly, in fifteenth-century Italy, growing emphasis on the design and brushwork of the artist, rather than on the use of expensive materials, gave artists more freedom to display their skills. Landscape backgrounds began to be used to demonstrate artists' technical and imaginative skills on pictures that were still religious in their main subjects. In the late fifteenth and early sixteenth centuries, landscape began to assume a more independent role in paintings. Landscape was peripheral, the background setting for main subjects, particularly religious ones. Landscape without a human subject was rare in finished, formal paintings and can hardly be said to have existed as a separate genre. The existence of watercolour sketches and drawings by Dürer and Lucas Cranach (1472–1553), as scenes that were later used as backgrounds for religious subjects, shows the potential of landscape art. With growing urbanization, it has been suggested that the desire for freedom and solitude in rural settings grew, and subjects such as St Jerome in the Wilderness became pretexts for elaborate landscape paintings in which the religious subject was diminished. In the northern European Renaissance, landscape gradually acquired greater licence to dominate paintings. The first independent, finished landscapes in European art were by Albrecht Altdorfer (*c.* 1480-1538) and Joachim Patinir (*c.* 1485–1524), religious subjects subordinated to huge, sweeping landscapes. But the landscapes in such paintings often contained allegorical and narrative elements from the lives of the religious figures, a disguised symbolism. Despite this, there is a feeling that such artists were nevertheless celebrating the beauty of the natural world. Patinir was recognized by Dürer and other contemporaries as a master of landscape, although it is not clear to what extent he was being proactive or whether he was responding to a new demand for such works, possibly from the Italian market.[84]

By the fifteenth century, Lombardy was the most advanced agricultural region in Europe; hydrological science and surveying were also well developed there. During the later sixteenth century, the Venetian state was involved in large-scale drainage, reclamation and irrigation work within its land empire, the 'Terraferma', in north-east Italy. At the same time, and not coincidentally, there was considerable interest in the artistic representation of landscape. As Venetian maritime trade waned during the sixteenth century, so the Terraferma assumed growing importance, particularly as a source of food, because the expanding Ottoman Empire was threatening existing overseas areas of grain supply. Venetian nobles began to buy estates outside the city and to have villas built on them. This importance was reflected in the scale of land improvement and its careful organization, with the establishment in 1556 of a ministry to supervise and regulate land drainage and irrigation. Each new scheme considered by the Provveditori ai Beni Inculti had to be accompanied by a detailed survey. As a result, technical advances in survey and cartography went hand in hand with the creation of planned, geometric landscapes aimed at commercial agricultural production, with new crops such as rice and maize as well as cereals. Between 1560 and 1600 more than 150,000 ha (262,500 a) were reclaimed by drainage operations and an equally significant area improved by irrigation. At the same time, Venice was making important contributions to the arts dealing with landscape, notably in the design of villas by Andrea Palladio (1508–80), where architecture and landscape were planned together.[85]

The growth in popularity of landscape painting in Italy during the sixteenth century was linked to the contemporary flowering of villa life, which in turn related to the idealization of the countryside, intensified by rapid urban growth. Estates were seen as refuges from the pressures of urban life, and from dangers such as outbreaks of plague. Villas on the Venetian *terraferma* were summer retreats for urban patricians who patronized scholars, writers and poets. The mood of literary Arcadia was captured by Venetian artists such as Giovanni Bellini, Titian and Paolo Veronese. Villas were sited in locations with panoramas of the surrounding countryside. Their main reception rooms were often on the first floor to take advantage of the views. The villas, however, were also, in the main, functioning estate centres. Palladio integrated landscape and architecture in his designs. The Villa Rotonda near Vicenza, the least functional of his villas, has been the most widely admired and copied. Built in the early 1550s, it had no connection with farming and was constructed simply for the pleasure of a retired official of the papal court. Villa gardens overlooked the surrounding country, too. There was a resurgence of interest in pastoral and Georgic modes of poetry. Villas and their gardens, often parts of unified designs, provided a context in which the appreciation of landscape emerged as a cultural activity. In Renaissance Italy, where there were such close links between literature, landscape art, gardening and architecture, villa design became a central element in thinking about nature.

In the seventeenth century, with the decline of Venice, only Rome among Italian cities remained a great cultural centre. New and influential landscape images were being produced in Rome and its surrounding countryside, especially by resident French painters such as Claude Lorrain (1600–82), who settled in Rome in 1627, and Nicolas Poussin (1594–1665). Claude's landscapes were based on the detailed study of nature, but his approach was very different from that of contemporary Dutch

Claude Gellée, called 'Le Lorrain', *Landscape with Hagar and the Angel*, 1646–7, National Gallery, London.

painters. Claudian landscapes incorporated views towards a light source with a foreground framed by dark side screens, often trees and sometimes Classical ruins. The central view was crossed by bands of light and shade leading the eye into the depth of the picture. Claude's landscapes were generalized, idealized pastoral ones with sheep and cattle grazing without fences or hedges, set in a golden age of harmony between man and nature, a dream of Classical innocence.

Flemish landscape art was more empirical than Italian art, which in turn was more characterized by intellectual theory.

Flemish art involved realistic, empirical representations of rural life based on careful observation. There was a focus on seasonal changes in the landscape and in the patterns of work associated with them. As in northern Italy, the countryside was permeated by urban capital. A new, commercialized agriculture was developing, with urban finance enabling reclamation and drainage behind the coastal dunes and along the Scheldt estuary. In the late sixteenth century, Flanders was devastated by war and many painters moved north to the United Provinces, which had declared independence from Spain in 1579, and settled in Amsterdam and other towns. There, a Calvinist religious culture and a middle class of merchants and shipowners provided a ready market for secular art. Seventeenth-century Dutch art emphasized a 'landscape of fact', the experiential world of the rising middle classes of Amsterdam and Haarlem.[86] It is no coincidence that the Dutch golden age of maritime expansion was also the age of flourishing art. Patrons required paintings of an unadorned, realistic rural world, flat landscapes with large areas of sky. Paintings of this era are often recognizable topographically as real, or only slightly altered, landscapes.

The traditional view of art history maintains that naturalistic landscape painting first emerged in the Netherlands in the early seventeenth century. At a general level, the popularity of rural landscapes was linked with rapid urban growth. More specifically, however, it has been suggested that something dramatic happened in Haarlem around 1620, as if the scales had suddenly and collectively fallen from Dutch artists' eyes, so that they could see and faithfully transcribe the landscapes around them. But these artists were seldom transcribing the landscapes in which they lived uncritically and mechanically: they relocated monuments, dramatized their locations and painted imaginary 'composite' landscapes. The choice of landscape subjects, their dramatization, manipulation and naturalization, were related to a unique conjunction of political, economic and religious circumstances in a country convulsed by rapid social and economic change.

As in sixteenth-century Venice, there was a link between landscape art, surveying and cartography. By the seventeenth century, Amsterdam had overtaken Venice as Europe's main centre for map production. Commercial activity and farming tended to be excluded from landscape paintings, as were the ships of the Dutch East India Company, in favour of archaic representations of ferryboats on rivers, rather than barges on new canals. Such images gave urban dwellers passports to the countryside, and encouraged nostalgia and perhaps a sense of guilt for a past landscape that was being rapidly changed by contemporary commercial enterprise. Such pictures were a visual appropriation of the dominance of the countryside, in which, in reality, there was always danger of flooding, by an increasingly prosperous urban bourgeoisie, whose roots in the land were often close and who were actively investing capital in rural landscape change. The naturalization of the land played an important part in creating changed communal identities within a nation that had a high proportion of immigrants. Immigrants were attracted by the prosperity of Amsterdam and the northern Netherlands, by an open market economy with capital being amassed for investment, and by Protestantism. A. J. Adams has suggested that paintings could either act to influence people to identify with each other or, alternatively, to widen social divisions.[87] Paintings of Dutch landscape subjects were very well received and avidly collected in the Netherlands, and were the most popular genre of painting at this time. A large proportion of the land around the great Dutch cities was owned by those who worked it, not by feudal lords. Since there was no monarch to symbolize national identity, the Dutch turned to their land in the creation of a communal identity.

EUROPE AND A WIDER WORLD: THE COLONIZATION OF NORTH AMERICA

By the beginning of our period, the passage to the Indies via the Cape of Good Hope had been opened, Madeira, the Canary Islands and the Azores had been settled, and the New World discovered. Expanding European nation states still had some internal frontiers, however. In the early seventeenth century, Ireland provided a land of opportunity for English and Scots settlers that rivalled, and complemented, North America. Late-sixteenth-century English colonies in Ireland were mostly small and localized in their impact, but the settlement of Munster from south-west England from the 1580s was on a much larger scale, transporting traditions such as fruit growing from Devon and Somerset to a broadly similar environment.[88] The plantation of Ulster in the early seventeenth century was undertaken substantially by settlers from south-west Scotland, who also brought their farming systems and settlement patterns to the new country.[89]

The most dramatic aspect of landscape change at this period, however, was the discovery and colonization of the Americas, which drastically altered the balance between population and resources within Europe by providing huge reserves of new land and a range of alternative opportunities. It also marked the start of what Donald Worster has called 'global havoc', a major phase of capitalist expansion, environmental upheaval and landscape change of unparalleled scale and impact.[90] Studies of the colonization of new places show how the images of their landscapes are modified, becoming more realistic, as new information becomes available. Early portrayals of New England as a kind of Garden of Eden were altered by experience, and were transferred to Europe by emigrant letters and return migrants. But some stereotypes were so deep-rooted and persistent that information that undermined them was excluded and discounted for a long time, until the whole image had to be comprehensively revised. In all colonization processes there was a gap between landscapes of the imagination and geographical reality. Where the gap was wide, settlers arrived poorly prepared and adjusted to environmental conditions with difficulty – they had to modify their approaches, retreat or die.

In a new-found environment it is not what people actually see as much as what they want to see or think they see that influences their reaction to the landscape.[91] The British who went to America saw it in terms of what they were running away from, as well as what they actually found. Some features, however, could not be masked by illusion: early settlers in North America were surprised by the emptiness of the interior, the violence of the landscape and the harsh extremes of climate.[92] They expected monotony from the Atlantic, but not from the land. As a result, analogies with the sea occur frequently in accounts of early travellers in the American prairies.

The image of America in 1492 as a pristine wilderness was largely an invention of nineteenth-century romantic and primitivist writers such as W. H. Hudson, James Fenimore Cooper and Henry Thoreau, as well as poets like Longfellow, and of artists like George Catlin. Ideas about the pre-Columban human impact on the American landscape have been revised in recent years, since pre-Columban population estimates for the Americas have been raised dramatically. Even seemingly unfavourable environments like the forests of the Amazon Basin are now thought to have carried substantial populations, and it is believed that the rain forest environment had been substantially affected by human activity before the arrival of Europeans. This is not a purely academic issue, but has considerable implications for modern development strategies.[93] It is now believed that in 1492 the population of the Americas may have been somewhere between 43 and 65 million – perhaps around 54 million – relatively lightly scattered over much of North America but denser in parts of central America and the Andes. Even in eastern North America, some of the best favoured areas may have supported population densities similar to those of contemporary western Europe. In fact, by 1492 Indians had modified the extent and composition of forests, created and expanded grasslands, and rearranged micro-relief with earthworks. Extensive field systems were found in many areas; sometimes the area under cultivation exceeded that of recent times. Many thousands of major earthworks, as well as villages and even towns, existed. The Mississippian site of Cahokia, with a population of around 30,000, was surpassed only by New York as the largest town north of the Rio Grande in about 1775. The amount of landscape modification by indigenous inhabitants probably exceeded that caused by the first 250 years of European settlement.[94] The fate of the Mayan empire, among others, emphasizes that landscape modification through over-expansion and resource depletion, followed by catastrophic population collapse and recolonization by tropical forests, occurred in pre-Columban America, the inhabitants of which did not necessarily live in harmony with their environment, as has often been suggested.

Environmental catastrophe and associated landscape change was not a monopoly of colonizing Europeans.

Early descriptions of New England saw the land as 'a faire virgin longing to be sped and meet her lover in a Nuptiall bed'.[95] Nevertheless, North America was hardly a virgin land when first discovered by Europeans. The wildwoods had been widely modified by human agency. Indeed, it is difficult to reconstruct the original character of the eastern forests because, though still extensive, they have been changed markedly, and their modern character may well be very different from their original species composition.[96] The scale of forest regrowth since the initial settlement can be appreciated when it is realized that in New England by about 1850, some 70 per cent of the land was cleared farmland and the rest comprised woods. Today, with massive depopulation of interior areas, these proportions have been reversed.[97] The first European settlers found stable agricultural communities with substantial settlements in many areas, ranging from the palisaded villages of the Huron and Iroquois to the pueblos of the south. In most areas the Indians had pushed agriculture close to its environmental limits. The legacy of the indigenous inhabitants in the landscape was largely dismissed by Europeans, who conveniently chose to ignore their dependence on indigenous crops, such as corn and squash, and the fact that signs of Indian cultivation were a good guide to better-quality soils. The rapid reduction of the native population caused by the introduction of diseases against which they had no immunity aided the settlers' derision of the 'savages', as they saw them.

So the 'pristine myth' developed between about 1750 and 1850, after the native population had been drastically reduced, principally by European diseases. In parts of the Caribbean, the indigenous population was cut by 99 per cent between 1492 and 1550, in Peru by 92 per cent between 1520 and 1620, and in North America by about 75 per cent between 1492 and 1800, so that settlers were penetrating an almost empty interior. This drastic population reduction caused major changes in many American ecosystems during the sixteenth and seventeenth centuries, when European populations were still small and highly concentrated, so that a major environmental recovery was possible. Tropical rain forests recolonized areas of grassland in parts of southern and central America, while the woodland cover in eastern North America also began to change. Between the decline of the Indian population on the Mid-Western prairies due to disease, and the advent of European farming in the nineteenth century, forest recolonized large areas of the eastern margins of the prairies.[98] In eastern North America, there was often continuity from indigenous Americans to European settlers in the choice of settlement sites and areas for cultivation. The greatest single landscape change produced by European colonization, however, was the clearance of forest. Before their arrival, about 45 per cent of the USA was forested, some four-fifths of it east of the Great Plains. To European settlers, wilderness and forest were almost synonymous; forests stood in the way of progress and were good only when felled, an 'enemy' that needed to be 'conquered'.[99]

Of the nations that settled North America, the Spaniards, after their original treasure-grabbing expeditions, were more inclined to treat the natives on relatively equal terms and to absorb them. This was partly because of the thinness of Spanish colonists in the areas of North America they occupied, and their need for native inhabitants not just as a labour force but as a defensive shield against the expansion of the French and British. This was reflected in the landscape by the association of the mission, the presidio or fort, and the pueblo.[100] In Texas the Spanish granted much of the land in large blocks of one square league (c. 1,792 ha/4,428 a), but along the upper Rio Grande, colonization was based on farming villages or pueblos laid out on a grid pattern with central churches and squares, associated with long, narrow strip holdings and common meadows.[101] After being converted to Christianity through the missions and being taught the rudiments of Spanish citizenship, the natives were concentrated in large villages so that they could provide food surpluses to help maintain the military garrisons.[102] Unlike the British, the Spanish did not disdain native styles of architecture; instead they fused them with Spanish forms. The extent and significance of the Spanish legacy in the American landscape has been underrated by Anglocentric historians: some twenty states of the later USA had some contact with Spain, and six American states bear Spanish names.

In place names, building styles, surviving missions and fortresses, the Spanish landscape tradition in North America is an important one.

The French, like the Spaniards, settled their North American possessions fairly lightly and had to come to an accommodation with the natives as a result. Their communities along the St Lawrence to the Great Lakes transposed farming systems characteristic of northern France – with wheat, oats, barley, cattle, sheep and pigs – into a forest environment. They also used land divisions based on strips, which may preserve echoes of field systems in Normandy.[103] Their settlement also involved the recreation of a form of feudalism, with seigneurs having certain feudal rights over their tenants, such as labour services and the compulsion to use their grain mills.[104] The use of strip holdings running from the river into the forest gave a variety of soils and encouraged houses to be located along the frontage in relatively close proximity, to give better protection. In parts of Wisconsin and along the lower Mississippi, the pattern of long lots still survives and contrasts markedly with the later American township and range grid. The Dutch, like the Spanish, favoured large land grants, such as the patroonships on either side of the Hudson Valley with frontages of 12.9 or 25.7 km (8 or 16 miles), held on condition that colonies of at least 50 adults were to be established within four years of the grant being made. Complex patterns of land division occur in some areas, such as parts of Missouri, where the original Spanish land grants in the form of huge rectangles have been subdivided by the French system of long lots, and then surrounded by the grid of the American township and range system.[105] Even in New England, land grants were large, but in the seventeenth century they were made to groups rather than individuals. Further south, Charles II granted huge areas to individual proprietors in Virginia, Maryland, Delaware and the Carolinas.

The landscape impact of early colonial settlement was particularly marked in the islands of the Atlantic and the Caribbean. As each island became incorporated into the empires of one of the European states, their landscapes were subject to rapid transformation. Their tropical landscapes were perceived as idealized Gardens of Eden, as in Shakespeare's *The*

Tempest. Adverse environmental impacts were soon evident in the Canary Islands and Madeira, where, with steep slopes and a highly seasonal rainfall, soil erosion following deforestation was rapid. On Madeira, the increasingly aridity of the environment caused most perennial streams to dry up, so that a lot of effort had to be expended in the construction of irrigation canals, the levadas that are still such a striking feature of the island today.[106] Increasing aridity in the Atlantic islands encouraged a shift of sugar production to Brazil and the Caribbean, where the cycle of environmental degradation was repeated. In drier, more semi-arid areas such as the highlands of Mexico, the introduction of European livestock, especially goats and cattle, also led to rapid landscape change and soil deterioration. The scale of change, however, was probably greater on many smaller Caribbean islands than on the mainland, where more land was available for colonization. An early feature of the exploitation of the land-scape of the New World was the development of plantation systems in many tropical and sub-tropical areas in the sixteenth and seventeenth centuries. Early crops were mainly sugar cane, indigo and tobacco. The Spanish and Portuguese may have developed plantation systems first in the Canary Islands and Madeira in the early fifteenth century, but the system spread rapidly in east Brazil in the sixteenth century and in the Caribbean, from where it reached the south-eastern parts of North America. Plantations involved centralized entrepreneur-ial production, with an efficient division of labour that used native populations and then indentured servants and negro slaves.

The labour-intensive nature of sugar-cane cultivation in particular encouraged the development of large plantations worked by slaves. The slash-and-burn system that sugar cane involved led to rapid forest clearance and soil deterioration. By about 1700, some 900 sugar-cane plantations had been estab-lished in Barbados, covering 80 per cent of the island's arable land. The islands of St Kitts, Nevis, Antigua and Montserrat followed. By 1660, Barbados had become one of the world's most densely populated agricultural areas. Terracing was intro-duced in an attempt to counter soil erosion, and slaves were used to carry soil to them from the gullies into which it had been washed. Jamaica had far more arable land than all the other English Caribbean islands put together. From 1665, small and large landowners began to establish cotton, indigo and sugar plantations in the valleys and coastal plains.

From 1612, tobacco, as a commercial crop, proved to be the saviour of the Jamestown colony, founded by the Virginia Company in 1607. Between 1617 and 1621, exports of tobacco to England rose from about 9,072 to 158,760 kg (20,000 to 350,000 lb). By the mid-1680s this had risen to 12.7 million kg (28 million lb). Given that fields could be cropped only for a few years, the scale of increase of forest clearance must have been comparable.[107] Tobacco was also tried in the Caribbean, but the realization that it exhausted soils even faster than sugar cane encouraged the removal of its cultivation from the islands to mainland America.

There were interesting national differences in attitudes to landscape change in the Caribbean. In Britain, where extensive forests had long been removed, the clearance of land was linked to ideas of improvement. By the mid-seventeenth century, it was widely believed that the expansion of cultivation beautified the landscape as well as bringing profit. This attitude was transferred to the Caribbean, where tropical forests were cleared for aesthetic as well as economic objectives in attempts to reconstruct European-style parkland landscapes. A marked acceleration in the pace of clearance was evident on Montserrat after French rule gave way to British in 1665. Rapid clearance of tropical forests was also promoted by the belief that they were unhealthy and caused disease. In 1671, when Antigua was still heavily forested, the governor of the Leeward Islands asked for 4,000 slaves to clear the island in order to improve the health of the English settlers.[108] One result of the clearance of tropical forests, as in Madeira, was a drier climate. By the end of the seventeenth century, forests had been almost eliminated on many Caribbean islands. Deforestation and over-exploitation led to rapid landscape change. The erosion that had occurred with the clearing of forests in the Canary Islands and Madeira was repeated in the Caribbean, where it was becoming evident by the mid-sixteenth century.

Montserrat was first settled by British colonists in the

1630s. Sugar production had started by 1650 and dominated the island by 1680, with other cash crops such as tobacco, indigo and cotton. European, and especially British, preferences for landscapes with extensive views over neat fields was frustrated by the dense tropical forests that came down to the beaches. Clearance with axe and fire was followed by the pasturing of livestock to prevent regeneration. In little more than 40 years, by 1673, about a third of the island had been cleared for cultivation. Deforestation in the headwaters of the island's streams increased the speed of runoff, causing devastating flash floods and gullying. Within a landscape that had been drastically modified to resemble England as much as possible, techniques of house building, especially the use of cruck construction, may have been introduced from Ireland rather than England.[109]

Although elements of feudalism persisted in the landscape, economy and society of many parts of Europe until well into the eighteenth century, by the end of the seventeenth century an increasingly rational approach was being applied to landscape in Europe, as the ideas and philosophical approaches that came to be known as the Enlightenment were starting to develop. These ideas were to transform the landscapes not only of Europe but also of many other parts of the world. Equally importantly, they were to transform how educated people perceived and portrayed landscape. It is to these ideas, and their expression and impact on the landscape, that we will turn in the next chapter.

THREE

Enlightenment, Picturesque and Romantic Landscapes

For much of the eighteenth century – the Augustan age of English literature and landscape – the pastoral tradition, which celebrated an idealized version of shepherding drawn from Virgil and other Classical authors, provided an escape, mentally and sometimes physically, from the pressures of urban and court life, not only in Britain but throughout Europe. In its most extreme form this was epitomized later in the eighteenth century by Queen Marie Antoinette playing at shepherdesses in the grounds of Versailles. To this pastoral tradition was added another, which celebrated the rural labour of cultivation, based on the Georgics of Virgil. There were, however, practical difficulties involved in translating the Classical pastoral theme and the Roman landscape to northern climes. Horace Walpole described how 'Our poets … talk of shady groves, purling streams and cooling breezes, and we get sore throats and agues in attempting to realize these visions'.[1] Increasingly, though, English poetry, such as James Thomson's *The Seasons* (1730) and Thomas Gray's *Elegy in a Country Churchyard* (1750), began to awaken interest in British landscape and nature. Gradually, inherited Classical models gave way to more nationalistic ones. The distinctive character of English society and the failure of absolutism also influenced the development of the landscape idea in the late seventeenth and early eighteenth centuries.

The landscapes that most people considered attractive were those created by civilized society. It has become almost a tradition to summarize attitudes to landscape in early-eighteenth-century England by quoting Daniel Defoe's comments on his tours of Britain. His crossing of the Pennines by Blackstone Edge, between Leeds and Manchester, during an August snowstorm reads more like the traverse of a high Alpine pass in winter:

It is not easy to express the consternation we were in when we came up near the top of the mountain; the wind blew exceeding hard, and blew the snow directly in our faces, and that so thick, that it was impossible to keep our eyes open to see our way. The ground also was so covered with snow that we could see no track ... except when we were showed it by a frightful precipice on one hand, and uneven ground on the other; even our horses discovered their uneasiness at it; and a poor spaniel dog that was my fellow traveller, and usually diverted us with giving us a mark for our gun, turned tail to it and cried.[2]

His relief was palpable when, descending below the cloud base, he saw before him a civilized landscape of fields and cottages: 'We thought now we were come into a Christian country.' Productive, prosperous agricultural landscapes were his preferred countryside. Mountain landscapes were still very much a minority taste in Defoe's day. Westmorland was 'the wildest, most barren and frightful of any [country] that I have passed over in England, or even in Wales.'[3] The Welsh mountains were made worse by being barbarously named and inhabited by the Welsh. The district of Lochaber in the Scottish Highlands, not surprisingly, was 'mountainous, barren and frightful'.[4] Even the tamer Peak District was a 'howling wilderness'.[5] Samuel Johnson, whose tour of the Highlands in 1773 was even more famous, was scarcely more enamoured of rugged mountain landscapes and was clearly relieved to return to civilization. Both Defoe and Johnson, however, were Londoners, whose impressions of the remoter upland areas of Britain were almost bound to be unfavourable. Defoe even found some of the heaths within 32 km (20 miles) of London barren and horrible. We need not believe that the people who were born and lived in the upland areas of Britain and Europe viewed their surroundings with similar revulsion. Contemporary topographical descriptions of areas such as the northern Highlands of Scotland, written by local people, emphasized, by contrast with Defoe, the richness of the pastures, the numbers of livestock and the wealth of game. Their perceptions are altogether different, as are those of contemporary Scottish Gaelic poetry, which shows a remarkable sensitivity to, and delight in, wild upland landscapes, as in Duncan Ban Macintyre's 'Song to Misty Corrie'.[6]

Defoe's view of pastoral uplands as poor, backward and unattractive reflected the traditional distrust and misunderstanding of arable-oriented lowlanders for hill and mountain areas, their landscapes and their inhabitants, seen throughout Europe and indeed worldwide.[7] As Angus Winchester has pointed out, the tendency among historians has been to see upland areas as deficient and backward by lowland standards, through focusing on what they lacked in terms of extensive areas of good arable soils, rather than emphasizing the positive side of their resource base.[8]

Elite attitudes to landscape in early-eighteenth-century Britain are also reflected in the work of contemporary artists such as the Cumbrian painter Mathias Read (1669–1747). He painted estates and their mansions, and prospects of the rapidly-growing planned industrial town of Whitehaven. The Lake District fells served only as a distant backdrop to his views rather than a focus of interest in themselves. When he painted the lake of Bassenthwaite he stood with his back to the mountains and depicted the scene looking towards the lowlands.[9]

Attitudes to landscape at this time were codified by Edmund Burke in his *Philosophical Enquiry into the Origin of our Ideas of the Sublime and Beautiful* (1757). Burke claimed that man had two fundamental instincts, which underlay all human passion and emotion: self-propagation and self-preservation. Attractive things – soft, smooth and harmonious – appealed to the instinct for self-propagation and were considered beautiful. Those that gave rise to apprehension or fear affected the instinct for self-preservation and were sublime. Sublime landscapes included elements that were huge, vast, uniform or threatening – such as mountains, deserts and the sea – and that generated a sense of awe or terror in the observer. Burke's ideas had an important influence on landscape aesthetics in Europe and America in the later eighteenth century, and influenced both the Picturesque and Romantic views of landscape. There was a strongly gendered element to Burke's ideas: beautiful landscapes were soft, rounded, feminine; sublime ones, rugged and masculine. In artistic terms Beauty was associated with the gentle, calm landscapes of Claude Lorrain, the Sublime with the darker, more violent scenes of Salvator Rosa (1615–73).[10]

The agricultural changes that transformed the landscapes of so many parts of England in the later eighteenth century attracted little attention from landscape artists, despite all the contemporary debate in prose and even poetry.[11] There are no pictures of newly enclosed fields, new farmsteads or the plough-ing up of commons. Towards the later eighteenth century, the fashion for landscape art turned away from cultivated land towards wilder, more picturesque scenes. John Barrell has sug-gested that artists addressed the impact of agricultural change indirectly through their depiction of social relations.[12] Landowners did, of course, commission pictures of their man-sions and parks, and even their prize livestock, while the new enclosed landscape appears as a background in many hunting scenes. Hugh Prince, looking at the iconography of a sample of landscape paintings, emphasized that the patrons who commis-sioned them, in some cases notable improving landowners such as the Dukes of Bedford, preferred idyllic Classical or pic-turesque views to the reality of landscape change.[13]

Outdoor conversation pieces, in which landowners and their families were portrayed in informal poses and dress in the midst of their parks, to demonstrate their status and taste, were popular in the mid-eighteenth century.[14] Thomas Gainsborough's painting of *Mr and Mrs Andrews* (1748) is unusual in that, instead of a park, it depicts in the background an agricultural landscape with many features of improvement: crops of drilled wheat surrounded by well-laid hawthorn hedges and, in the distance, sheep of an improved breed that could have been fed only upon turnips or sown grasses. Mr and Mrs Andrews were not separated in the picture from their source of income, but the landscape behind them is curiously empty of the people who worked in it. Many landowners, in the design of their parks and the location of their mansions within them, were at this period distancing themselves from the actual means by which their lifestyles were maintained. Gillian Rose has pointed out that the responses of the two figures to the landscape around them are markedly different, highlighting the contrasting roles of husband and wife in contemporary landed society, and their

Thomas Gainsborough, *Mr and Mrs Andrews*, *c.* 1748, National Gallery, London.

differing freedom of activity within the landscape.[15] Mr Andrews's stance is an active one: he seems poised to stride off into the landscape with his gun. Mrs Andrews, by contrast, sits passively contemplating it. He is the landowner; she is not. Mrs Andrews is almost as much her husband's prize possession as the livestock behind her. Landscape painting, Rose argues, involves gender as well as class relations.

LANDSCAPES OF ENCLOSURE AND IMPROVEMENT

The rational approach of the Enlightenment, the sense of struggling with and overcoming Nature with the aid of science, is well seen in the ethos of the agricultural improver in England, and even more notably in Scotland, where the landscape was so much wilder. To seventeenth-century Scottish topographers, peat bogs were a source of fuel and a manifestation of God's providence. To eighteenth-century improvers, they were an affront to civilization, a challenge. When Lord Kames reclaimed the carselands – peat-covered estuarine clays – in the upper Forth valley at Blair Drummond by bringing Highlanders in to remove the thick peat cover from 1767, a contemporary writer compared his achievement with that of David Dale's creation of the factories and industrial community at New Lanark.[16] Improvement of the landscape could also be related to patriotism. During the Napoleonic Wars, the reclamation of upland waste in Britain was seen to be at once a conflict with nature and a blow against the French.

Much of the eighteenth-century British countryside was a monument to the domination of the powerful over the power-less. By the turn of the nineteenth century, not just country houses and their parks but the whole fabric of the countryside embodied the hegemony of the landed elite, their aesthetic preferences, their economic interests and their leisure pursuits. One of the most important factors in the creation of this hegemony was large-scale enclosure, an expression of power in the landscape in its most stark and striking form. The eighteenth-century Enlightenment, with its emphasis on order and the control of nature, became stamped on the British landscape. Its largest scale and most widely spread manifestation was Parliamentary enclosure in England and Wales, which was undertaken mostly during the later eighteenth century, especially the 1770s, and during the war years from 1793 through to 1815. More than 2,900,000 ha (7,000,000 a) of land were affected.[17]

Parliamentary enclosure transformed open-field arable land, especially in the wide belt of country running from south-central England to east Yorkshire, as well as extensive areas of open heath and common and large blocks of upland waste. Although enclosure awards were made at parish level, and local surveyors and commissioners accomplished the work of planning and fashioning the new landscape, they worked to a fairly standard blueprint. Landscapes of Parliamentary enclosure in lowland areas are characterized by regular patterns of square or rectangular fields, surrounded by hawthorn hedges, accessed by wide, straight roads and dotted with new farmsteads. In upland areas, the grids of stone walls, constructed in a similar way in each area, created even more regimented landscapes. Differing allotment sizes and the need to fit in with existing administrative and topographic boundaries sometimes reduced this extreme regularity, but landscapes created by this process are instantly recognizable across the country. The scale of the upheaval at a local level aroused some opposition from smallholders, cottagers and squatters, who stood to lose more from the extinction of their traditional common rights than they gained from the small portions of land allotted to them in lieu. Nevertheless, while John Clare mourned the passing of the open fields and the communities that had worked them, the face of the landscape was transformed with remarkably little unrest.[18]

Some of the Parliamentary commissioners who undertook a lot of enclosure work were among the most efficient agents of landscape change ever in terms of the amount of land they transformed and the scale of the alteration involved.[19] The visual and social changes that Parliamentary enclosure caused were major ones. The poet John Clare, who lived at Helpston, Northamptonshire, was appalled by the scenic and social consequences of enclosure. In 1821 he wrote in one poem in *The Village Minstrel*:

> There once were lanes in nature's freedom dropt,
> There once were paths that every valley wound –
> Inclosure came and every path was stopt:
> Each tyrant fix'd his sign where paths were found
> To hint a trespass now who cross'd the ground:
> Justice is made to speak as they command,
> The high road now must be each stinted bound:
> 'Inclosure, thou'rt curse upon the land,
> And tasteless was the wretch who thy existence plann'd'.[20]

More recent agricultural historians have seen Parliamentary enclosure as less of a class conspiracy, but at every stage of the process the wealthy and influential were advantaged, and the poor disadvantaged. Enclosure had various unintended effects: for example, it changed fox hunting from a pursuit across open country to one that involved jumping hedges, while the power of the elite gained new visual expression with the planting of fox coverts of between 0.8–8.09 ha (2 and 20 a).[21] Parliamentary enclosure also affected artistic representations of landscape by encouraging the taste for wilder, unplanned countryside.[22]

The transformation of the Scottish landscape proceeded on an equally large scale at much the same time as Parliamentary enclosure in England and Wales. The pace of change was faster in Scotland than south of the Border, because so much more land was held in leasehold tenancy as part of large estates. Major Scottish landowners had even more power than their English counterparts and could undertake the enclosure of their estates at will, without reference to any higher authorities. The transformation of the landscape of Lowland Scotland in the two generations from the 1760s was even more dramatic than in the main belt of English Parliamentary enclosure, because a greater proportion of the land was affected and in Scotland there was no tradition of earlier, piecemeal enclosure. The pre-improvement landscape was one of areas of open field surrounded by extensive wastes and areas of ill-drained peat moss. Some Scottish proprietors had been undertaking limited amounts of enclosure around their castles and mansions since the later seventeenth century, but the first main wave of activity came in the 1760s, contemporary with the start of large-scale Parliamentary enclosure in England.[23] A gradual process of holding amalgamation and a reduction in the number of tenancies in the late seventeenth and early eighteenth centuries was an important preparatory stage. It created a class of more prosperous and commercially-minded tenant farmers, who participated in the process of enclosure with their landlords and who often provided much of the labour required to enclose, drain and improve the land. Open fields were enclosed, large areas of waste improved and taken into cultivation, and much of the wetter land drained and brought under the plough.[24]

During the same period there was a revolution in the standards of construction for farmsteads in Lowland Scotland. The old single-storey biggins – thatched, with stone-and-clay walls – gave way to two-storey farmhouses with proper lime-mortared walls and tiled or slated roofs, sash windows and chimneys. At the same time, the increasingly large farms required a growing range of outbuildings, which, in the more arable areas, were organized into various courtyard layouts. From the late eighteenth century, these included threshing machines powered by horses, wind, water and eventually steam, with central courtyards for feeding livestock, the epitome of rationality and efficiency. Many of the new farmsteads, built in a plain Georgian style, provided better accommodation for farmers than their landlords had enjoyed half a century before. A second phase of rebuilding in the early nineteenth century led, on some estates, to even more impressive farmsteads, where even the outbuildings were designed in Classical or Gothic styles.[25]

The process of improvement in Lowland Scotland removed many small farmers and cottars, or sub-tenants, from the land. To accommodate them, from the mid-eighteenth century, landowners began to create planned estate villages, in which cottars and small tenants displaced from the land could set up as tradesmen with smallholdings. This generated local markets for agricultural produce, provided a range of services for the new large farms and created foci for industrial development. Some 300 planned villages were established throughout Scotland in the later eighteenth and early nineteenth centuries. Settlement plans were mostly based on regular rows or, in more ambitious schemes, grids of streets with central squares. Housing was sometimes financed by the landowners, but was more normally provided by the developers, who worked within tight building guidelines to ensure quality and uniformity of design.[26] Some existing settlements were relocated as the result of settlement clearance, due to the enlargement of the parks around new mansions, as at Fochabers near Gordon Castle in Aberdeenshire.[27]

In Ireland, landowners did not have quite as much freedom or resources as their Scottish counterparts, but many estate villages were nevertheless laid out for a combination of utility and show.[28] Improvement in Ireland involved the large-scale reclamation of peatlands, which extended to 1.2 million ha (2.9 million acres) according to the first survey of 1810–14, almost certainly an underestimate. Much of the reclamation and drainage came late, though, and was associated with the increase of population on the eve of the Great Famine of the mid-1840s.[29]

One of the most unobtrusive yet ubiquitous changes in the British landscape was the development of efficient systems of undersoil drainage. Before the nineteenth century, arable land was either drained by ploughing into ridge and furrow or by crude underground stone drains. The development in the early nineteenth century of machinery capable of turning out standard-gauge tile pipes allowed effective undersoil drainage systems to be used for draining everything from prime arable land to marginal moorland.[30] There was a positive mania for field drainage in mid-nineteenth-century Britain.

The eighteenth century also saw a change in attitudes to woodland, with the birth of scientific forestry. Traditional systems of woodland management, such as coppicing and pollarding, were increasingly seen as damaging and uneconomic and were abandoned in favour of plantation forestry.[31] Estate owners were concerned to improve their woodlands for a variety of reasons: economic, patriotic and aesthetic. Timber was just one of a range of resources on an estate that could be exploited more commercially as part of a package of improvement.[32] This did not prevent a continuing attack on European woodlands, though: between the mid-eighteenth and mid-nineteenth centuries the area of forests in France was reduced by about one half, resulting in increasing floods and soil erosion, as well as a shortage of timber.[33]

COUNTRY HOUSES AND LANDSCAPE PARKS

As well as enclosure, the eighteenth century in Britain witnessed an astonishing burst of country-house building and rebuilding, and the improvement of their grounds.[34] In England, analogies were frequently made between the running of rural estates and the kingdom as a whole, between the power of landlords and monarchs. Successful management of an estate and its community, scaled up, could be translated into successful management of a nation. At this period, the links between landscape and political ideology were especially evident in the design of country houses and the increasingly extensive landscape parks that surrounded them.

Estate landscapes were used to proclaim the wealth, power and success of their owners, as well as demonstrating the ruling elite's beliefs and ideology, as a statement of their tastes and knowledge. A 'national style' of landscape design emerged after 1688, associated with the rise of constitutional liberty and the greater security of property, which stimulated a growth in wealth and attempts to 'improve' landscape.[35] Throughout the eighteenth and much of the nineteenth century, arguments about the aesthetics of landscape were almost always arguments about politics. Intervention in the landscape was understood as making statements – sometimes explicit and easily read, in other cases more coded – about political history, the political future of England and the relations that should exist between its citizens. Political statements and personal opinions were made by statuary and the design of garden buildings, while, more generally, gardens could be gigantic statements of their owners' affiliations, designed to impress supporters and overawe opponents.

In the eighteenth century, designed elements in the rural landscape, particularly country houses and their surrounding landscape parks, came to reflect the political split between Whigs and Tories. The Whigs had benefited from the Glorious Revolution of 1688 and the Hanoverian succession of 1714. Between 1714 and 1742, Robert Walpole's Whig administration dominated Britain. They included many of the largest landowners, those with important interests in finance and commerce whose values were associated with 'progress' and religious toleration. The Tories, in the early decades of the eighteenth century at least, often supported the Stuart succession and were associated with more traditional, conservative values, High Church Anglicanism, minimal involvement in trade and more paternalistic attitudes towards the lower classes.

These political differences were given visual expression in the designs of houses, gardens and landscape parks. The great Whig mansions, such as Holkham in Norfolk, were set in vast parks, distanced from any activity that related to the economic base that supported them. In the Whig idea of landscape, it is often hard to distinguish ideas of taste from the assertion of private property and the control of territory. The revival of neo-Classical architecture in the style of Palladio (it briefly flowered first under Inigo Jones in the first half of the seventeenth century) began early in the eighteenth century, brought to prominence in England by Colen Campbell under the patronage of Richard Boyle, third Earl of Burlington. From the 1710s a group of Whig politicians fostered Palladianism as a style of architecture that claimed to be a more faithful interpretation of ancient Classical buildings than those of the seventeenth century or the contemporary Baroque forms favoured by leading Tories and decadent Continental monarchies.[36] Such a style was deemed appropriate for the rulers of a nation claiming to be the true heirs of republican Rome. Campbell's multi-volume *Vitruvius Britannicus* (1715–) spread enthusiasm for the new designs widely throughout British landed society. For half a century, Palladianism dominated almost every aspect of polite architecture.[37] As Palladianism took over country-house design, it spread into the park with Classical-style temples and other garden buildings, although Gothic buildings and grottoes also featured on some estates.

The Walpoles' family seat at Houghton in Norfolk reflected this. In the early eighteenth century, an intricate geometric garden was laid out around the old hall and then a new neo-Classical mansion was built. In the 1730s the park at Houghton was redesigned by Charles Bridgeman (*d.* 1738). He eliminated the intersecting avenues and replaced them with a starker, sparer geometry of parkland and blocks of woodland, so that the expanded park complemented the austere majesty of the house.[38]

Classical ornamentation in an 18th-century English garden: Studley Royal, Yorkshire.

Only slowly through the eighteenth century did attention turn towards medieval as well as Classical architecture, and it was the end of the century before Gothic styles began to acquire some status. In much early Gothic building, medieval-style detail and ornament were merely added, somewhat incongruously, to basically Classical-style buildings with little sense of period or accuracy, as at Inveraray Castle in the West Highlands.[39] The growing interest in Gothic was encouraged by Horace Walpole's house at Strawberry Hill in Middlesex, from 1748 onwards, and Sanderson Miller at Lacock Abbey, Wiltshire.[40]

Tory landowners were excluded from power during the Whig ascendancy. They were often smaller squires crippled by high land taxes imposed to support the centralized Whig bureaucratic and military machine. Few of them could afford large geometric gardens: more often they opted for rides and avenues through gardens, extending them visually into the surrounding farmland. The more traditional Tory pattern of landscape involved not an isolated mansion but one forming part of a community, with the village and parish church adjoining. The Tory view of landscape stood apart from the fashionable economic theories of Adam Smith and his characterization of humans as self-seeking individualists; by contrast, it valued tradition, continuity, obligation and sensibility.[41]

Landscape parks were a uniquely British contribution to landscape design, expressing many aspects of the lives of their owners in complex and subtle ways.[42] Seventeenth-century English gardens had been highly regimented, enclosed by high walls, geometric in layout, dominated by clipped hedges and topiary, sometimes with mounts (artificial mounds) for viewing the symmetry. Late-seventeenth- and early-eighteenth-century formal gardens, such as those at Blenheim, Chatsworth and Longleat, were modelled on those of André Le Nôtre (1613–1700), especially his work at Versailles, which involved much use of elaborately patterned parterres, water features, statuary and long, straight avenues. In the seventeenth century, France and the Netherlands were strongly influenced by Italian garden design, but in different ways. Dutch gardens were smaller, reflecting patterns of land ownership: they were rigidly symmetrical, defined by hedges and lines of trees with immaculate topiary and water features, such as canals and moats. In France, under garden designers such as Le Nôtre, much larger gardens were created, with avenues radiating out through ornamental woodland towards vistas. Houses and gardens rarely formed components of an integrated design. During the early eighteenth century, the popularity of such gardens declined with a gradual change towards greater naturalism. It has been suggested that, as society's dominance over nature increased, more 'natural' landscapes came to be valued more, but landscape parks were nevertheless highly artificial and controlled environments. In a competitive, capitalist, commercial society, landowners developed parks not only for their own pleasure but with a keen eye for what neighbouring proprietors were doing.

On the other hand, it is easy to misjudge the pace of change by focusing on a few well-known, innovatory estates. For much of the eighteenth century, most English landowners were content with the geometric garden layouts they had inherited. Indeed, the early eighteenth century saw the peak of such geometric designs with more simple, less fussy layouts, less topiary and more woodland.[43] These styles dominated until the 1730s. In the 1740s, existing styles were taken to their conclusion in larger, more magnificent layouts, as in Robert Walpole's gardens at Houghton. Other landscape gardeners, such as Charles Bridgeman and Stephen Switzer, (1682–1745), created a simpler, more sombre style with vistas framed by blocks and clumps of trees rather than avenues. Parks were increasingly expanded to isolate their mansions. The adoption of the ha-ha or sunken fence, first used in Britain by Bridgeman, allowed landscape parks to be extended visually even further into the surrounding countryside.

William Kent (1684–1748) moved towards more irregular, less geometric layouts. By the 1790s, there were more than 4,000 parks in England: thanks to the work of Lancelot (Capability) Brown (1715–83), they were mostly 'landscape parks' – open, irregular, with grass and scattered trees, surrounded by belts with serpentine drives and lakes with curving margins, a much more sparing use of garden buildings, with grass sweeping right up to the walls of the mansions, and outbuildings banished to a distance. Brown's aim was to make it appear as if the mansion had been planted straight into the park with grass coming up to the walls on all sides. He may have had a direct hand only in about 200 parks, perhaps 5 per cent of the total number, but his principles were widely adopted by other landscape gardeners, and by the stewards and land agents who designed many smaller parks. His three main elements – grass, trees and water – gave an illusion of eternal tranquillity. His parks were enclosed by belts of trees broken in places to show more distant prospects. Many parks used pre-existing woodland, but in arable areas most of the woodland was often new with exotic conifers as well as native species. A lake in the middle distance was a crucial feature. Small clumps and individual trees on carefully shaped mounts added to the effect.

The scale of landscape parks in England increased greatly during the eighteenth century. In the early eighteenth century, French formal gardens rarely exceeded 12–16 ha (30–40 a) in extent. By the later eighteenth century, some lakes in English landscape parks were as large as this, such as the one at Blenheim in Oxfordshire, landscaped by Capability Brown. The style of park created by Capability Brown could be stretched over a landscape as far as funds and property allowed. Such parks cost a good deal less to maintain than the more formal geometric gardens that characterized the later seventeenth and early eighteenth centuries.[44] The change from the smaller formal gardens on Dutch and French models in the later seventeenth century to more informal, extensive ones in the eighteenth was due in part to the relative cost of maintenance. But while landscape parks may have been relatively cheap to maintain, they could be expensive to create, their more 'natural' appearance sometimes being achieved only by earth-moving on a heroic scale, a rationale that Ann Bermingham has seen as parallel to that of Parliamentary enclosure.[45]

Capability Brown's parks offered affordable magnificence. The grass was kept short by grazing animals, often superior breeds with agricultural and landscape improvement going side by side. Thinnings from the woodlands provided an additional income for the estate. Mature timber could always be felled in a time of financial crisis, or national need. The planting of oaks was seen as especially patriotic, while there were clear parallels between the longevity and stability of oaks and landed families.[46] Parks were also useful game reserves, sources of venison but especially reserves for game birds. In the second half of the eighteenth century, shooting then changed from a casual activity to a highly organized sport.

In asserting control over territory, landowners sometimes removed villages that were close to their mansions when extending their parks; they evicted the inhabitants but often relocated them in model estate villages. The Sweet Auburn of Oliver Goldsmith's poem *The Deserted Village* (1770) is believed to have been Nuneham Courteney, destroyed in 1761 to make way for a park for Lord Harcourt.[47]

The process of creating and enlarging parks had a significant impact on the countryside. In Northamptonshire alone, eight villages were destroyed and 25 significantly altered as a result of emparking.[48] Roads were closed and diverted, lodges and perimeter walls built. Some landscape parks were converted from medieval deer parks, which were already partly wooded with coppices and pollards. Landscape parks should not be considered in isolation from the landscape around them. Ancient landscapes with many hedges and areas of woodland were more amenable to the creation of parks than recently enclosed landscapes. On the other hand, the increasing control over land made possible by the removal of open fields and the consolidation of land into more compact blocks often permitted the creation of parks. The creation of landscape parks was an affirmation of wealth and status, since it involved taking substantial areas of countryside out of production. The payback in higher rents from land enclosed under Parliamentary Acts more than offset the loss of revenue on many estates, though.

In the late eighteenth century the greater landowners increasingly came to play down differences in status between themselves, the gentry and the rising professional classes, who were seen more and more to merge into a single 'polite society' with shared aesthetics. By this time, Capability Brown's parks were starting to go out of fashion. They were criticized for their scale, their blandness and the way in which they were dissociated from the surrounding countryside. Humphry Repton (1752–1818) gradually developed a style that restored gardens round the house, making a greater contrast with the park. Repton's parks were more in sympathy with Tory perspectives. To him, a Capability Brown park symbolized the exclusivity of the landed elite and their rejection of paternalistic involvement in local communities. He saw this as increasingly dangerous after the French Revolution of 1789. By the end of the century, however, economic conditions were less ideal for landscape gardeners. Repton, who had begun his career landscaping large parks for aristocrats, ended it doing smaller commissions for social-climbing manufacturers on the outskirts of industrial towns such as Leeds, with views from the park framing their factories.[49]

In Scotland, there was some shift from formal gardens to larger, less regular parks, as at Gordon Castle in the 1760s and 1770s, but Capability Brown's style made much less of an impression north of the Border. Temples, obelisks, bridges and grottoes were also rare in Scotland, although the Hermitage at Dunkeld, built for the fourth Duke of Atholl, was an exception.[50] In Ireland, neo-Classical mansions spread, especially in the 1730s and towards the end of the eighteenth century, with similar patterns of parks, or demesnes, home farms and estate villages. This was an exercise in image building that emphasized the cosmopolitan style of the Irish landed gentry, and was based on the efficient commercial reorganization of the Irish rural landscape. As in England, the style of gardens in the late seventeenth and early eighteenth centuries was formal, with radiating avenues of lime, elm and chestnut and 'wilderness' areas of woodland between networks of paths and clearings. By the mid-eighteenth century, the new informal style of English park design was being adopted in Ireland and was universal by the end of the century. Classical-style garden buildings – temples, hermitages, grottoes and summerhouses – were popular, later giving way later to obelisks, pyramids and sham Gothic ruins. Demesnes occupied up to 6 per cent of the country with more than 2,000 country houses having parks of 4 ha (10 a) or more. They still form an important component in the Irish landscape.[51]

The eighteenth century saw the spread in many parts of Britain and Europe of rural landscapes that were dominated by dense concentrations of domestic industry, most frequently textiles but also including activities such as nail making or the manufacture of clocks. Such industries were often concentrated in pastoral areas, wood and pasture zones or upland districts. In the case of woollen manufacture, such locations were influenced by ready access to raw materials and the need for water power for fulling the cloth, but such areas were also often attractive because of the weakness of landlord control. This created the possibility of squatting on portions of land taken in from the waste, combining domestic industry with small-scale agriculture.[52] Such proto-industrial landscapes were often characterized by patterns of dispersed but dense settlement. This is a feature of parts of the southern Pennines, where the importance of handloom weaving in the local economy was emphasized by the construction of purpose-built weavers' cottages with loomshops in the cellar or, more commonly, on the first floor, where they were lit by a long set of mullioned windows. Such industrial landscapes in west Yorkshire also include wool warehouses in larger villages such as Heptonstall and mansions built by prosperous merchant clothiers.[53]

Mining lead, copper, iron and sometimes other minerals such as salt was another activity that, for geological reasons, was often located in remote upland areas. Mining companies sometimes had to provide company housing to attract workers, and intensive agriculture, sometimes at quite high altitudes, was encouraged to reduce the need to buy in food from the lowlands. In remote areas, skilled workers had to be brought in from a distance, creating little colonies of aliens, as with the English lead miners at Strontian in the western Highlands of Scotland.[54]

In other cases industry was drawn to such areas by the availability of charcoal for fuel. The charcoal iron-smelting industry in England, having expanded to the limits of its fuel supply in the Weald, sought more remote locations where charcoal was available – in the Forest of Dean or the Lake District, where land was converted from sheep pasture to coppice woodland to meet the demand. When the industry reached the limits of its fuel supply here, the ironmasters turned to even more remote sources of charcoal. Cumbrian firms set up charcoal blast furnaces in the western Highlands at sites such as Bonawe, on Loch Etive, sending ore from Cumbria to be smelted and bringing the iron back south.[55]

Coal mining was still being undertaken on a relatively small scale wherever seams outcropped or lay close to the surface, using levels or shallow shafts and bell pits. Seams of coal that were too thin and too remote to be worth working in later times were exploited for local use, to burn lime for improving arable and pasture for instance. The small-scale activities of this era of mining have generally been obliterated in the main coalfield areas by later, large-scale workings, but they still survive in more marginal locations.[56]

In Britain, the improvement of transport was an important feature of the eighteenth-century landscape. Turnpikes, where a group of investors put up the money to have a stretch of road properly constructed and maintained, recouping their costs by charging tolls on traffic, proved to be much more effective than the previous statute labour system of road maintenance, which used unskilled, unwilling labour in each parish for a few days every year. In the second half of the eighteenth century, the mileage of turnpikes expanded dramatically, with 389 new trusts established between 1751 and 1772, to create the basis of the modern road system in many areas.[57] In some districts, the turnpikes were crucial catalysts of landscape change; for instance in bringing coal from the St Helens area to the rapidly growing but fuel-starved port of Liverpool.[58]

The first British canals were another product of the need to transport cheaply bulk items such as coal. Early examples, such as the Bridgewater Canal, completed in 1765 to allow coal to be brought cheaply into Manchester from mines only a few miles away at Worsley, involved some of the most impressive engineering feats of their day. The Bridgewater canal had an aqueduct over the River Irwell and branches that led underground straight into the coal mines. By the end of the century, trans-Pennine canals had been completed, with major topographic barriers being tackled by flights of locks and even long tunnels. Industrial engineering, and its ability to modify the landscape, had entered a new phase.[59]

The Lancaster Canal, opened in 1819: British canals involved considerable engineering works but were still in tune with their surroundings.

LANDSCAPE AND ART IN EIGHTEENTH-CENTURY BRITAIN

Elite views of landscape and landscape art in Britain during the eighteenth century were strongly influenced by the institution of the Grand Tour, which had its origins in the sixteenth and seventeenth centuries, when many of the great Flemish and Dutch landscape artists spent some time in Italy. It can be considered to have ended with the outbreak of war with France in 1793. Its floruit, however, was during the eighteenth century, especially the second half. The Grand Tour involved the wealthy from France, the Low Countries, Germany and Sweden, but it was most strongly associated with the British aristocracy, who supplied by far the greatest number of travellers. The classic route of the British tourist took in France, the Low Countries, the Alps and parts of Germany, but the focus was on Italy and especially Rome, although Venice, Florence and other Italian cities also attracted attention. In the process, the landscapes of Italy, with their Classical and Renaissance architecture, became accepted as an ideal by the educated landowning elite, and by the artists they patronized. In the course of the eighteenth century, the areas visited by at least some tourists widened to include southern Italy: Pompeii was discovered in 1748. Visitors avidly bought up the works of Claude and other seventeenth-century Rome-based artists and took them back to Britain by the hundred.[60]

From serving as a backdrop to portraits, conversation pieces and historical subjects, and from the restricted genre of 'estate paintings',[61] British landscape art gradually emerged in the late eighteenth century, strongly influenced by the conventions of Claude Lorrain, Nicolas Poussin, Gaspard Dughet (1615–75; also known as Gaspard Poussin) and Salvator Rosa. The Dutch landscape tradition was not regarded as highly in England as the Italian one, because, instead of idealizing the landscape, Dutch artists appeared to present it as it really was. British landscape paintings were thus suffused with the light of the Italian Campagna, while hybrid British-Italian landscapes were created in reality in gardens such as Stowe and Stourhead.

In the second half of the eighteenth and the early nineteenth century, a 'correct' taste in landscape was seen as a test and vindication of the right to be a member of the governing classes. The possession of a commanding view of the country as the owner of an estate was very different from the view of 'private' men of narrow experience, locked in the countryside, unable to take a broad view, and was represented symbolically by cottages enclosed among trees.[62] Bermingham suggests that the emergence of rustic landscape painting in England from the 1780s, at the same time as the peak of Parliamentary enclosure, was no accident, and that new genres in art reflected profound contemporary changes in rural society.[63] Representations of nature in art, poetry and literature were used to clarify and justify social change. Bermingham's ideas may, however, be overstated in that she exaggerates the visual and social impact of Parliamentary enclosure at this time. The first big burst of enclosure, in the 1760s and 1770s, predated the artistic trends. Moreover, the areas heavily affected by the enclosure of open fields and lowland commons were concentrated in a belt from south-central England, through the Midlands into east Yorkshire. Areas outside this belt were often little affected; in many cases they had been enclosed in late medieval times or even earlier. Even in the main zone of enclosure, there were relatively few areas in which even half the parishes were affected.[64] Again, Bermingham exaggerates the degree to which social changes in the countryside were concentrated into the period about 1790 to 1815. The shift from paternalism to agrarian capitalism was already well underway by the start of the last decade of the eighteenth century, but was far from being complete by 1815.[65]

Rustic landscapes formed a sub-set of landscape art in general and are associated particularly with Thomas Gainsborough (1727–88) and John Constable (1776–1837). They differed from topographical landscape studies in that the intention was not to depict a particular spot or view, but to evoke the countryside and rural life more generally. As a landscape artist, Gainsborough was influenced by Dutch painters in his early days. His depictions of rural life are sunnier than those of John Clare or Oliver Goldsmith. It is interesting that both Gainsborough in west Suffolk and Constable in the Stour valley on the Suffolk–Essex border painted landscapes that had not been dramatically altered by eighteenth-century enclosure. In the case of Gainsborough this may have reflected deliberate choice, since landscapes of Parliamentary enclosure were not far distant from his home town, Sudbury. The figures in Gainsborough's landscapes seem to belong to a self-sufficient peasantry little disturbed by economic and social change.

The eighteenth-century 'discovery of Britain' by educated travellers led to British landscapes being viewed as cultural and aesthetic objects. Bermingham suggests that just as large areas of countryside were becoming unrecognizable as a result of enclosure, the countryside was being offered as something homely and stable, a process of 'active loss and imaginative recovery'.[66] This discovery of the countryside took many forms: travels by practical men such as the agricultural improver Arthur Young and natural historians such as Thomas Pennant, and an increasing interest in antiquarianism and the work of Picturesque writers (see Chapter 4).

CARTOGRAPHY AND LANDSCAPE IN THE AGE OF
ENLIGHTENMENT

The Enlightenment approach to mapping landscape is seen particularly well in the cartography of the Military Survey of Scotland, undertaken between 1747 and 1755 in the aftermath of the Jacobite Rebellion of 1745. In the later stages of the campaign that led to the Duke of Cumberland's decisive victory at Culloden, and in the policing of the Highlands after the battle, the Hanoverian forces were hampered by a lack of maps of the region. Colonel Watson was commissioned to undertake a survey, employing William (later Major-General) Roy. The survey covered first the Highlands and then the remainder of mainland Scotland at a scale of one inch to 1,000 yards (1:36,000). Lack of money to fund sufficient survey teams, the need for speed and the use of less than state-of-the-art surveying equipment meant that the maps were not as accurate as Roy would have wished. He modestly called the survey 'a magnificent military sketch', rather than an accurate map. The maps are notable for the high quality of their artwork, influenced by Paul Sandby (1725–1809), chief

The junction of Loch Eil ('Yeal') and Loch Linnhe by Fort William, from the 1747–55 Military Survey of Scotland.

drawing master at the Royal Military Academy at Woolwich and a noted early watercolour artist.[67]

The Military Survey was characteristic of eighteenth-century European cartography in that more peripheral parts of states, or their dependencies, were often better surveyed than core areas. The manuscript map of the Highlands was impressively detailed and remarkably accurate, considering the speed of the survey and the nature of the terrain. Its content was inevitably influenced by military requirements. Roads on which troops could be moved were marked prominently, while local tracks were ignored. Settlements were accurately located but, outside the towns, their layout was not shown in detail.[68] Roy's personal interest in Roman antiquities is evident in the exactness with which such sites were surveyed, notably the remains of the Antonine Wall. The survey's colour conventions were similar to the modern Ordnance Survey Landranger map at a scale of 1:50,000, of which it was an ancestor. The representation of relief by artistic brushwork anticipated the later technique of hill shading. Roy's work led directly to the foundation of the Ordnance Survey, which amalgamated the tradition of military survey with the best of contemporary civilian cartography. Similar or even higher standards of cartography were being developed by naval surveyors. Before being selected for his first Pacific voyage, Captain James Cook had surveyed the St Lawrence River in 1759 in preparation for the British assault on Québec and, between 1763 and 1767, he mapped extensive areas of the coasts of Newfoundland, Labrador and Nova Scotia.[69]

At the same time that the military survey was being undertaken, the Scottish Highlands were having other features of Hanoverian militarism stamped on the landscape. In the wake of the Jacobite rebellion of 1715, General George Wade produced a plan to open up the region with a series of roads linking government forts and outposts to each other and to the Lowlands. By 1745, 400 km (250 miles) of military roads and 40 major bridges had been constructed, including the elegant bridge over the Tay at Aberfeldy and the zigzag road over the Corrieyairack pass. After 1745, a further 1,200 km (750 miles) of roads were constructed by Wade's successor, Major William Caulfeild. Although the roads were often hastily constructed, and sections of them rapidly succumbed to floods and erosion, and they were not always well-routed for civilian purposes, they nevertheless represented a scale of military planning not seen in Scotland since the days of the Roman governor Agricola.[70]

Civilian cartography in Britain, which still focused on the county map, had broken free from the long period of plagiarism in the seventeenth century. Prizes of £100, awarded by the Royal Society for Arts from 1759 to 1808, encouraged the production of more detailed county maps based on new triangulation surveys at scales of one inch to the mile or greater. Such prizes, however, would have covered only part of the cost of a county survey. More important was the increasing demand for better maps from a public that was conscious of the increasing scale and speed of landscape change with Parliamentary enclosure, industrialization, urbanization and the spread of the turnpike and canal systems. Between 1765 and 1783, 29 new English county maps, based largely on new surveys, were produced. By 1800, only Cambridgeshire, among the English counties, had not been the subject of a new survey. While country houses and their parks were still as prominent as in Saxton's day, much more attention was given to the details of settlements and road networks, including the new turnpikes, to contrasts in land use between improved and unimproved land, and even to industrial sites, notably on Yates's map of Lancashire of 1786, which marked coal mines and water-power sites.[71]

The rapidity of landscape change also increased the demand for accurate large-scale estate plans. The eighteenth and early nineteenth centuries were the golden age of local surveys commissioned by individual landowners, as well as for Parliamentary enclosure maps and tithe surveys. In Scotland, where the pace of agricultural improvement was slow before the 1760s but accelerated rapidly thereafter, the speed of landscape change could be measured by the number of private land survey-ors at work at any time. There were only about ten of them active in the 1750s, but around 70 by the 1770s, rising to a peak of about 85 around 1815.[72]

In France, between 1750 and 1780, Jacques Cassini (1714–84) first used triangulation for surveying an entire coun-try, based on a chain of triangulations running along the meridian passing through Paris. This projected an image of France that emphasized national unity rather than local and regional diversity, and showed the concerns of central government, such as roads, fortification and the exploitation of natural resources.[73] The linking of the British and French triangulation systems in 1790 was a major achievement.

LANDSCAPE EVOLUTION IN NORTH AMERICA

In North America, landscape elements from the two initial core areas of British settlement, New England and Pennsylvania, were transported across the Appalachians during the eighteenth century. The landscapes of early colonial America had not been a duplication of those of Britain, although some distinctive elements did persist. Immigrants from areas where stone-built houses were normal, such as Cornwall, Wales and Scotland, sometimes continued their building traditions in America where geological conditions were favourable. The nature of housing, however, was affected by the abundance of wood, something that had long ceased to be a characteristic not only of much of Britain but also many other parts of Europe from which the immigrants came. Ways of organizing the landscape that had worked in Britain did not necessarily suit the American environment. Nor was the human impact on the landscape always sustained. In New England in the early nineteenth century, as inhabitants abandoned the thin, infertile soils and moved in search of better opportunities, depopulation occurred on such a scale that a major reversion of cleared land to woodland occurred. This process produced wilderness landscapes whose atmosphere has been exploited by writers such as H. P. Lovecraft and Stephen King. Much of the modern woodland may seem original, virgin territory, but this view is often betrayed by remains of walls, settlements and cemeteries deep among the woods.

Ethnic influences in the North American landscape are particularly evident in vernacular building styles. In Pennsylvania, the tradition of vernacular architecture was more conservative than in New England, and as settlers moved inland they took English traditions of building in brick with them. German-speaking immigrants brought designs of barns that reflected those of areas such as the upper Rhineland and northern Switzerland. Classical architectural styles began to spread in the United States soon after the Revolution, and particularly from the 1790s for mansions, court houses and eventually even farmhouses. Such styles, and the wealth of Greek and Roman place names, symbolized America's break with the British monarchy and its embracing of republican ideals. A major difference between European and American landscapes was the early rejection by American settlers of the ideas of living in European-style villages. The dispersed farmstead or house, on its own lot and set back from the road, became the ideal for rural areas and, later, American suburbia.

The continuity of society, and with it housing styles, settlement patterns and farming systems, was particularly marked when large groups of people from the same area emigrated together, as was the case with Scottish Highlanders in the later eighteenth century. This was emphasized by Samuel Johnson, who commented that the Highland emigrant's departure, 'was no longer exile ... He sits down in a better climate surrounded by his kindred and friends ... they change nothing but the place of their abode ... this is the real effect of emigration, if those that go away together settle on the same spot and preserve their ancient union.'

The Age of Enlightenment in the American landscape was dramatically reflected in the township and range system into which most of the country outside the original thirteen colonies and Texas was divided. The idea of a grid fitted in with the rational, scientific philosophy of the Enlightenment, controlling boundaries from the level of the individual field to that of the state. Based on north–south/east–west survey lines, divided into townships of 10 x 10 km (6 x 6 miles), each subdivided into 36 sections, in turn divided into quarter sections of 16 ha (16 x 40-acre) lots, it stamped a grid plan across much of the United States, which is still strikingly reflected in field patterns, road alignments and settlement distribution and layout. Proposed by Thomas Jefferson in 1794 and started in Ohio in 1796, it was a powerful expression of a desire to master and tame the wilderness. It also reflected the idea of rural American society as composed of self-governing communities of independent farmers. Land was sold on the basis that half of it would be released as complete townships and half in individual lots, but market forces and the activities of land speculators soon began to disrupt the pattern, as did individual settlers who often improved their lots, sold out at a profit and then moved on. As a result the survey did not always produce neat chequerboard landscapes of square 64.7 ha (160-acre) farms divided into 1.6 ha (4 x 40-acre) fields.[74] The system may seem over-regimented, but it undoubtedly avoided much litigation over boundaries by enabling easy, precise descriptions of the location of areas of land.

As European colonization spread, there was increasing awareness of the scale of landscape change and environmental damage that was being caused in many areas. A small, but significant example was St Helena, an important staging point for vessels en route to and from the Cape of Good Hope that required fresh water and provisions. Deforestation was caused by the depredations by the goats of the original Portuguese settlers, then the establishment of plantation agriculture in an area of high relief and variable rainfall following the first British settlement in 1659. By 1700, soil erosion and fears of drought on the islands were causing concern, while goats and rats were major pests. A few years later, a new governor began a programme of tree planting, which, sadly, was not followed by his successors. By the later eighteenth century, this produced an island of ravaged landscapes that contrasted with the more effective management of Dutch settlers at the Cape. In the course of the eighteenth century, the link between deforestation and climatic desiccation became better understood, particularly by the French, whose stewardship of Mauritius, in the face of worries about deforestation, emphasized a conservation programme for the protection of the remaining forests, a policy that was drastically reversed after the British took control in 1810.[75]

PICTURESQUE LANDSCAPES

Interest in landscape in Britain culminated during the last thirty years of the eighteenth century, particularly the 1790s, with the cult of the Picturesque, a way of seeing landscape that has been considered quintessentially English. The Picturesque was not a single, coherent view of landscape, but a set of interconnecting themes embracing tourism, landscape, architecture, estate management, narrative and art.[76] Although interest in the Picturesque peaked during the 1790s, some views and descriptions of English scenery from the 1750s are very much in the Picturesque tradition. The poet Thomas Gray (1716–71), whose journal of a visit to the Lake District in 1769 was first published in 1775, has been considered to be one of the first Picturesque tourists in terms of the vocabulary he used to describe landscape. His descriptive prose graphically captures the excitement of the pioneer visitor.

At its simplest, in the sense used by William Gilpin (1724–1804), the great publicist of Picturesque tourism, a Picturesque landscape was one that would look good in a picture, but specifically a picture painted by one of the great neo-Classical artists of seventeenth-century Italy, notably Claude, Poussin, Dughet or Rosa. Picturesque was seen by Gilpin as a subset of Burke's category of Beauty. Picturesqueness was later defined more precisely by Uvedale Price as a category intermediate between Burke's Beautiful and Sublime. Its qualities included roughness, variety, irregularity and intricacy. Something that was beautiful pleased the eye in its natural state, but with something that was picturesque its quality could best be appreciated when it was depicted in a painting. Picturesque objects and scenes were better suited to painting than beautiful ones. The high, or romantic Picturesque of Price was also concerned with the time dimension in the landscape, particularly ruins and the process of decay.

From the 1780s, Gilpin encouraged Picturesque tourism and the appreciation of landscape by middle-class travellers. Originally from Cumbria, he took holy orders and pursued a successful career as a headmaster in the south of England. Early retirement to a parish in Hampshire's New Forest gave him enough leisure to undertake a series of tours and to write them up. His accounts of Picturesque tours to the Wye Valley (1770), the Lake District (1772), the Scottish Highlands (1776) and other parts of Britain circulated privately in manuscript form for some years before they were published, because of technical problems in reproducing satisfactorily his accompanying line and wash sketches.

Gilpin's most important theoretical essays on the nature of the Picturesque appeared in 1792, but he was less a serious thinker than a great popularizer who focused on the practicalities of Picturesque tourism.[77] His contemporary, Uvedale Price (1747–1829), was more concerned with the theoretical side of Picturesque landscapes and aesthetics and with its impact on the landscaping of estates. Price inherited an estate at Foxley, 11 km (7 miles) from Hereford, and improving it became his life's work. His *Essay on the Picturesque* (1794) criticized the work of landscape architects such as William Kent and Capability Brown for the dull, despotic character of their parkland designs, which he likened to a military invasion of the countryside. Instead of demolishing cottages on estates, he encouraged their retention as ornaments in the landscape.[78]

Picturesque tourism in Britain produced an explosion of descriptive travel literature in the last two decades of the eighteenth century, following the publication in 1782 of Gilpin's tour to the Wye Valley. Tourism at this time was greatly aided by the development of the turnpikes, which improved access to the favoured areas, and the improvement of local roads in areas such as north Wales and the Lake District, which made it easier for visitors to move around when they arrived. People had, however, been taking boat trips down the Wye to view Chepstow Castle, Tintern Abbey and other historic sites for at least twenty years before Gilpin's visit. Gilpin's published tours became extremely popular. The fact that, unlike the Grand Tour, Picturesque tourism focused on British scenery meant that Picturesque landscapes could be consumed by the middle classes as well as the aristocracy.[79]

Gilpin's published 'tours' were really instruction manuals on how to view the landscape in Picturesque terms rather than detailed guidebooks. They were grammars of the rules by which the landscapes of an area could be understood and appreciated, a programme of study for visitors, to show them how to see the landscape.[80] Gilpin was critical of the encyclopaedic nature of other contemporary tour guides compared with his tighter focus on landscape. The basic Claudean landscape framework with dark foreground, side screens of trees or ruins, a strongly lit middle ground often containing a plain with a river or lake, leading to a background of hills or distant mountains, was applied to each area. Gilpin analyzed scenery from particular viewpoints, comparing them (often unfavourably) with idealized yardsticks. Each view was dissected and its components considered: mountains were deemed picturesque when pyramidal or irregular in form, and merely lumpish and unattractive when they were not.

In the process, landscapes in areas such as the Peak District, the Wye Valley and even Snowdonia were converted into facsimiles of the Roman Campagna. Picturesque travellers carried Claude glasses to help them view scenery in the appropriate manner. These were small, round or oval convex mirrors. Observers stood with their backs to the landscape and held up their Claude glasses, which converted views of the scenery to frameable possessions, diminishing the scale of the background and expanding the foreground, while also reducing contrasts in tone and colour. Different coloured overlays could be used to convert the view into a sunset or moonlit scene. If this way of containing, controlling and altering landscape seems bizarre, one has only to think of the similarities with a modern wide-angle camera lens combined with coloured filters to realize that some aspects of Picturesque tourism are still with us.

Picturesque tourists went in search of 'unspoilt' landscapes and their 'unspoilt' inhabitants: Lake District statesmen, Highland clansmen and Welsh peasants, whose societies were rapidly changing as their regions were drawn more closely into the national economy – and which changed all the faster as a result of the commercialization brought by the visitors themselves, the eternal paradox of tourism. There were contradictions in how the Picturesque viewed certain areas and their inhabitants. The Lake District, with its sturdy farmers, might have epitomized Tory values of independence against the cultural dominance of Whig improvers, but the inhabitants of areas of extensive woodlands – and commons within the lowlands – in areas such as the Weald and the New Forest were often portrayed as lazy and idle, because their smallholdings provided them with a measure of independence that allowed them an element of choice concerning how much wage labour they undertook for the larger farmers.[81]

Picturesque tourism was a conservative, nostalgic way of looking at landscape. In an era of major agricultural change, characterized by Parliamentary enclosure and a great expansion of cultivation, it rejected the ethos of agricultural improvement, preferring pastoral to arable farming, unimproved to enclosed landscapes. It harked back nostalgically with a sense of loss to an older, paternalistic, rural order. In the process, however, it obscured the agencies of social change so that fate, rather than capitalist landowners, seemed responsible. It also generally ignored industry, although the iron foundries and charcoal burning on the banks of the Wye qualified as Picturesque. Suitable figures in Picturesque views were idle shepherds, beggars and gypsies, people who had little impact on the landscape, while industrious agricultural labourers were avoided. While Picturesque tourists found attractive the unimproved and unimprovable landscapes that had caused revulsion to Augustan observers, this did not necessarily mean that totally wild landscapes were automatically seen as Picturesque. The presence of a human imprint, in the form of ruins, was seen as a distinct asset. The Picturesque love of ruins and dilapidation matched the rather sombre and elegaic mood of the period.

Although Gilpin did not create Picturesque tourism, he gave it a tremendous boost and provided it with a clear set of objectives. His version of Picturesque theory influenced not just how artists interpreted landscape, but how all educated people reacted to it. Picturesque tourism within Britain has sometimes been portrayed as a middle-class alternative to the Grand Tour. In fact the two kinds of tour were complementary. Even the sons of wealthy aristocrats generally only ever made one Grand Tour, but the landscapes of Wales, the Wye Valley, the Lake District and the Scottish Highlands could be visited at any time and were appreciated all the more after acquaintance with the Alps and the Apennines. Among the more wealthy, Picturesque tours might serve as a reconnaissance for locating prospective sites on which to build the villas that were beginning to proliferate in the Lake District and parts of Wales. The curtailment of the Grand Tour and foreign travel generally at the start of the French wars in 1793 (a conflict that only ended with Waterloo over twenty years later) also helped to promote Picturesque tourism within Britain.

The Picturesque approach provided a rigid, restrictive, highly formalized, tightly controlled way of seeing landscape. Tourists in the Lake District, following Thomas West's *Guide to the Lake District*, which was first published in 1778, travelled on prescribed circuits, stopping at particular viewpoints or 'stations' to admire the scenery and, following Gilpin, deciding how far, and in what ways, each view fell short of the Picturesque ideal. It involved a limited vocabulary for describing landscape, which rapidly became over-used and cliched. In Norman Nicholson's words, it was 'a small, mean, self-satisfied manipulation of abstract landscapes'.[82] Nevertheless, the cult of the Picturesque was important in encouraging the landed elites and the middle classes to travel in search of attractive landscapes, even if they were taught to appreciate them only within a limited framework. By the early nineteenth century, the Picturesque tour had become the subject of satire, by Thomas Rowlandson in 1812 in his illustrations for *The Tour of Dr Syntax in Search of the Picturesque* (a thinly disguised caricature of Gilpin himself), in a play of 1798 entitled *The Lakers* and, more memorably, in Jane Austen's *Northanger Abbey* (1818). By this time, both writers and artists were beginning to react against the restrictive conventions of the Picturesque.

While the Picturesque idea dominated landscape aesthetics in the late eighteenth century, it was not accepted universally or uncritically. The writings of natural historians such as Thomas Pennant and agricultural improvers such as Arthur Young, and the contributors to the Board of Agriculture reports, demonstrated alternative approaches to topographical description. Towards the end of the eighteenth century, there seems to have been a shift of attitude within the Picturesque in favour of factories and industrial landscapes. Joseph Wright of Derby's painting of Richard Arkwright's mill at Crompton (1783), seen by moonlight, views nature and industry as coexisting: the mill does not look any more out of place than a Georgian mansion. In John Sell Cotman's picture of *Bedlam Furnace, near Madeley in Shropshire* (1802), however, nature seems overwhelmed, polluted and despoiled, a foretaste of the increasing rejection of urban and industrial landscapes that occurred over the course of the nineteenth century. The Picturesque, by contrast, celebrated a world of cottage industry and small farms that was already in rapid decline over much of England.[83]

Shilling

ROMANTIC LANDSCAPES

The Romantic Movement, which was well under way by 1800, placed landscape and nature at the heart of cultural interest in nineteenth-century Europe. The early nineteenth century, with the aftermath of the French Revolution and the rise of industrialization in Britain, saw the questioning of old certainties about society and an increasing focus on individualism – a growing preoccupation with the self, questioning and doubting by troubled individuals who became the heroes of their own personal epics, whether Wordsworth in poetry or Constable in art. There was a greater overlap between the various forms of landscape depiction, artistically and through poetry and prose, than in earlier periods. Through pictures, mass-produced engravings of romantic views, novels by writers such as Walter Scott, and poems by William Wordsworth, Percy Bysshe Shelley, Lord Byron and Alfred Tennyson, landscape appreciation became an element of middle-class, not just elite, education.

The Romantic Movement was the antithesis of the Age of Reason, a philosophical and artistic shift from seeing humans as social beings to individuals who sought their identity in nature. It involved a reappraisal of the roles of reason and imagination. A country churchyard had provided Thomas Gray with a landscape context conducive to measured reflection, in a setting where 'the rude fore-fathers of the hamlet sleep'. Forty years later, another rural churchyard at Alloway in Ayrshire gave Robert Burns the location for his Gothic tale of witches in *Tam O'Shanter*. No doubt superstitious tales had been told about country churchyards in Gray's day as well as Burns's, and for that matter in earlier times too, but for the first time they were allowed to become a central theme in literature.

Romanticism also involved a reaction against authority, a preoccupation with liberty and an upsurge of interest in the place of man in the natural order. The Romantic Movement was in part a reaction against the limitations and rigidity of Picturesque tourism, but at the same time it was a development of the more thoughtful Picturesque of Uvedale Price, with its stronger focus on the historical associations of ruins in the landscape. It was a reaction against natural sciences and economics, the guiding principles of industrialization.[84] Romanticism was also closely linked to the rise of national identities and nation states. It involved a rejection of industrialization and urbanization, though in few cases was this done as drastically as by Henry David Thoreau in his two-year retreat in 1845–6 from Concord, Massachussetts, to a hut beside Walden Pond. A distaste for urban life and a desire to escape to rural settings had long been a cultural convention, but the Romantics chose wild landscapes, not simply countryside.

Romanticism was a more personal, emotional response to landscape, nature and art than the attitudes of the Enlightenment era. It was opposed to the neo-Classical insistence on order and hierarchy, and championed individual freedom through man's relationship with nature. It was a reaction against authority and was preoccupied with liberty. The Romantics believed that nature possessed abstract qualities such as truth, beauty, independence and democracy. In the natural world, people could reclaim something of the lost innocence of their origins. Artists such as Turner and poets such as Wordsworth involved the spectator or reader as a participant in the dynamic experience of nature and landscape, instead of remaining objectively distant from it.

As we have seen, mountain landscapes were generally shunned by educated travellers before the mid-eighteenth century. Thomas Burnet, in *The Sacred Theory of the Earth* (1684), had suggested that the surface of the original earth had been smooth, like an egg, and that mountains were the result of the biblical Flood, and thus the product of human sin. Little wonder that such areas were popularly associated with the Devil, or with dragons and monsters.[85] The rise of the Picturesque changed this to some degree, but the landscapes of high mountain country were seen as Sublime rather than Picturesque. The Romantic Movement altered this.

In general, Picturesque travellers had been content to view mountains from a distance as suitable backdrops to their favoured landscapes, encountering them more closely, often with considerable terror of rock falls and avalanches, only when crossing the Alps by the high passes en route to Italy. A greater interest in the Romantic Sublime encouraged visitors to start exploring and climbing mountains. In the Lake District, early visitors tended to make the ascent of easier fells such as Skiddaw on horseback, accompanied by guides. The first recorded Lake District rock climb, however, on Broad Stand, Scafell, was undertaken, in descent, by Samuel Taylor Coleridge in 1802. In the Alps, from the early nineteenth century, an increasing number of the major peaks began to be ascended by their more straightforward routes: the Grossglockner in 1800, the Jungfrau in 1811, Monte Rosa in 1855 and, most famously, the Matterhorn in 1865. The Romantics were drawn, in particular, to mountain landscapes and to the societies that inhabited them: the sturdy Swiss peasant, the Highland clansman or the Lake District statesmen, like the world of Wordsworth's poem *Michael* (1800), were seen as being closer to nature than their lowland counterparts. Michael was presented as being totally at one with the wild landscapes in which he lived and from which he wrested a bare living as a shepherd.

WILLIAM WORDSWORTH AND THE LAKE DISTRICT

In Britain, one of the earliest and most influential Romantic writers, in terms of shaping attitudes to landscape, was William Wordsworth (1770–1850). Wordsworth appealed to the moral conservatism of the growing middle classes, and it is hard to exaggerate his influence on the nineteenth-century reading public. He was concerned almost obsessively with man's experience of nature. The young Wordsworth accepted the code of the Picturesque. His early works, such as *An Evening Walk* and *Descriptive Sketches* (1793), are poetic descriptions of Picturesque landscapes. In *Lines Written a Few Miles above Tintern Abbey*

(1798), however, he firmly rejected the restrictive framework of the Picturesque in favour of a more individual and personal identification with nature.

Wordsworth has been criticized for failing to portray the real causes of social change in the Cumbrian countryside. In *Michael* (1800) he linked the downfall of the independent peasant farmer to circumstances that were individual and specific, rather than to the broader processes of developing agrarian capitalism and its effects on the rural poor. In a letter to Charles James Fox, however, he hinted that Michael's fate was indeed designed to symbolize such changes among the statesmen farmers of Lakeland. Some writers have expressed surprise that he did not take a stronger anti-enclosure stance, as did John Clare, forgetting that in the early nineteenth century Parliamentary enclosure affected mainly the fringes, not the heart, of the Lake District. Even there they benefited small farmers rather than drove them out.[86] Clare, in a lowland, arable parish, saw the direct impact of enclosure in displacing labourers and cottagers and depriving them of their livelihoods, as well as destroying the landscapes familiar to them.

Wordsworth's *Guide to the Lakes*, originally published in 1810 though not reaching its definitive form until the fifth edition of 1835, demonstrates clearly the poet's decisive break with the superficial focus of the Picturesque approach to landscape. In the *Guide*, Wordsworth considered that landscape and nature should be viewed for themselves and not adapted to some ideal framework. His Guide was not a detailed description of the Lake District, but a manual designed to help the visitor to observe the landscape analytically and understand its complex structure. It began with his famous three-dimensional evocation of Lake District topography as seen from an imaginary viewpoint above the mountain summits, over Esk Hause between Scafell and Great Gable, with all the major valleys radiating out like the spokes of a wheel. It was at the same time both excellent regional geography and a perceptive landscape history. Its approach was holistic, covering not merely scenery but geology, landforms, climate, natural history, the society and economy of the inhabitants, their impact on the landscape and their influence on the environment. It was primarily an essay about how visitors should

Grasmere from Loughrigg Terrace: Wordsworth's Lake District, a unique fusion of physical environment and human activity.

see the landscape of the Lake District, but in the process it provided a vehicle for Wordsworth to air his concerns about the kinds of contemporary landscape changes in the area that he considered undesirable. He realized that the landscapes of the Lake District were substantially the product of human agency over thousands of years. They created an essential harmony between society and nature, man in partnership with the environment, as expressed through, for example, vernacular building styles. This realization was tempered by the knowledge that the pace of contemporary landscape change was accelerating and that some of the recent changes were undesirable.[87]

THE CELTIC ROMANTIC WORLD

The origins of Romantic interest in the mountain landscapes of Wales and the Scottish Highlands lay in the eighteenth-century fashion for Celtic mythology and literature. Thomas Gray wrote *The Bard* in 1757, the Revd Richard Evans's *Some Specimens of the Poetry of the Ancient Welsh Bards* dates from 1764, and Edward James's *Musical and Poetical Relicks of the Welsh Bards* from 1784. James MacPherson's *Fragments of*

Ancient Poetry Collected in the Highlands of Scotland and Translated from the Gaelic or Erse Language, published in 1760, was a clever invention, and not based on original manuscripts, as the author claimed, but along with *Fingal* (1761) and *Temora* (1763) it was immensely popular and influential. These Ossianic poems expressed very effectively the melancholy grandeur of the landscapes of the Scottish Highlands. Copies of the 'works' of mythology. The way in which they influenced perceptions of landscape is shown by the creation of Ossianic place names: Ossian's Cave at the poet's supposed birthplace in Glencoe, and Fingal's Cave on Staffa, named as late as 1772 by Sir Joseph Banks.

One achievement of the Romantic movement was the reinvention of Scotland as a Celtic nation by popularizing the landscapes of the Highlands. In the seventeenth and eighteenth centuries the Scottish Highlands had been viewed by Lowland Scots, as well as English visitors, as a wild country, inhabited by barbarous, warlike savages speaking an unintelligible language. The combined structures of clanship and feudalism in the Highlands made it easy for pro-Jacobite landowners and clan chiefs there to raise armies of trained fighting men. This meant that the Highlands were the focus of rebellion in 1715, 1719 and, most spectacularly, in 1745, when a Jacobite army, largely Highland in origin, marched as far south as Derby then returned to Scotland, almost unopposed. After the final defeat of the Jacobites at Culloden in 1746, the Hanoverian government took decisive steps to disarm the Highland clans and rob their inhabitants of their sense of identity by banning Highland dress and bagpipes. The penetration of the forces of commercialization into the region in the second half of the eighteenth century probably had an even greater impact in destroying traditional Highland society than Hanoverian military activity. The Highlands and their inhabitants were steadily integrated into mainstream British society, especially through the recruitment of Highlanders into the British army on a large scale during the Seven Years War (1756–63) and later Anglo-French conflicts. Just as visitors like Samuel Johnson in 1773 were beginning to open up the region to early tourism, the traditional pastoral, warlike clan society that they had come to see was vanishing under the impact of Improvement.[88]

The pacification of the Highlands and the improvement of roads encouraged a growing number of visitors. English Picturesque tourists often found the Scottish landscape empty and barren, lacking trees and hedges. Many were critical of the wildness of the landscapes and the poverty of the people, but others saw the Highlanders with their traditional pastoral economy as noble savages. In the late eighteenth century, the traveller in search of the Picturesque often preferred the more varied, less dramatic and sublime landscapes in the southern Highlands or the Tay valley. The contrast between mountain and lowland scenery at Luss, beside Loch Lomond, where many visitors entered the Highlands, was particularly valued.[89] Many eighteenth-century visitors to the Highlands used adjectives such as 'desolate', 'gloomy', 'horrible', 'hideous' or 'melancholy' in contexts that make it unclear whether they are meant to express appreciation or distaste.

Sir Walter Scott (1771–1832), more than any writer, helped to rehabilitate the Highlands as part of Great Britain and to develop romantic interest in its landscapes and culture. First came his poem *The Lady of the Lake* (1810), set in the Trossachs, an area of the southern Highlands conveniently accessible from Stirling or Glasgow. Then the first of his novels, *Waverley* (1814), was set partly in the Highlands, as was *Rob Roy* (1818). Although the Trossachs already attracted tourists, the impact of *The Lady of the Lake* in encouraging travellers to visit its locations was immediate. Sir John Sinclair's carriage, in the autumn of 1810, was the 297th to visit the area that season, where previously around 100 carriages had been usual.[90] It was Scott who stage-managed George IV's visit to Scotland in 1822, rigging out the fat king preposterously in tartans. The modern paraphernalia of clans, kilts and tartans, which took over as a form of identity for the Anglo-Saxon Scottish Lowlands as well as the Highlands, was essentially a nineteenth-century invention aided by Romantic landscape art, especially in the works of such painters as Horatio McCulloch (1805–67) and Edwin Landseer (1802–73), and continuing royal interest in the Highlands by

Queen Victoria. She visited the Highlands in 1842, 1844 and 1847. In 1848 she spent her first holiday at Balmoral. During this period, many parts of the Highlands were suffering from large-scale depopulation, the result of landlord policies and the failure of the economy of the area to cope with the stresses of a more commercialized world. Ruined cottages in glens empty of all but sheep might have made the region seem more romantic, but the causes of desertion were both recent and prosaic.

Romanticism about the Scottish landscape and traditional Scottish culture was often tinged with nostalgia for the doomed Jacobite movement, seen as respectable antiquarianism now that Jacobitism was no longer a serious threat to the security of the House of Hanover. In 1807 Lord Byron wrote *Dark Lochnagar*, in which the romantic landscapes of the Highlands are contrasted with those south of the Border:

> England thy beauties are tame and domestic
> To one who has roamed over mountains afar
> Oh for the crags that are wild and majestic
> The steep frowning glories of dark Lochnagar

He was happy, in this setting, to embrace the Jacobite cause:

> Ill-starred now the brave did no vision foreboding
> Tell you that fate had forsaken our cause?
> Yet were you destined to die at Culloden
> Though victory crowned not your fall with applause.

There were different strands within the Romantic Movement, just as there had been within the Picturesque. Sir Walter Scott's view of landscape, for example, was very different from that of Wordsworth. Where Wordsworth focused on nature, Scott emphasized the power of historical association. Scott made topographical context an integral part of romance. This was evident in his first major work, *The Minstrelsy of the Scottish Border* (1802), a collection of traditional (and sometimes re-worked and edited) ballads from the Scottish Borders with rich and often violent historical associations. It was even more clear in his epic poems such as

The Lay of the Last Minstrel (1805) and *Marmion* (1808), where places are located and experienced primarily through their historical associations. Thus in *The Lay of the Last Minstrel*, Sir William of Deloraine's night ride from Branksome Hall to Melrose Abbey is described in terms of the string of tower houses and other historic sites that he encounters on the way:

> He passed the peel of Goldiland,
> And cross'd old Borthwick's roaring strand;
> Dimly he viewed the Moat-Hill's mound,
> Where Druid shades still flitted round;
> In Hawick twinkled many a light;
> Behind him soon they set in night;
> And soon he spurred his courser keen
> Beneath the tower of Hazeldean, ...
> He turn'd him now from Teviotside,
> And, guided by the tinkling rill,
> Northward the dark ascent did ride,
> And gained the moor at Horsliehill;
> Broad on his left, before him lay,
> For many a mile the Roman Way.

The elements of medieval chivalry and the supernatural in the *Lay of the Last Minstrel* sit rather uneasily and unconvincingly with the often brutal reality of Border life at this time. Scott's first novel, *Waverley* (1814), contains detailed descriptions of landscapes on the edge of, and within, the Highlands, seen through the eyes of an English visitor, but in his later novels the amount of landscape description was often relatively limited. His greatest novels contrasted continuity and change, tradition and modernity in both society and landscape, something particularly well seen in the landscapes of Galloway described in *Guy Mannering* (1815).

The central Tweed valley, focusing on the area round Melrose, had become, by the later nineteenth century 'The Scott Country'. This area had hardly been noticed by late-eighteenth-century visitors en route to the Falls of Clyde or the Highlands, and was considered too bare and open for

Walter Scott country: the Eildon Hills and the central Tweed valley near Melrose.

Picturesque tastes. The associations with Scott, however, who made his home at Abbotsford near Melrose, turned it into a popular area of pilgrimage, even during the writer's own lifetime, visitors who included Wordsworth. This particular identification of writer with place is all the more curious in that the area figures little in Scott's work after publication of *The Lay of the Last Minstrel*. He never produced a major novel with a sixteenth-century Border setting.

Romantic ideas also produced other myths about the Scottish landscape, which are still perpetuated in print. Christopher Smout has shown how the myth of the 'Great Wood of Caledon' arose.[91] The story of a native pine forest covering much of the Scottish Highlands, which survived largely intact into late medieval times and was then destroyed by impoverished clan chiefs to supply greedy English ironmasters following the Jacobite defeat at Culloden, is a good one, but unfortunately it is not true. In fact, much of the deforestation of the Highlands was pre-Roman and the myth of its late removal owes much to Romantic tales of the forests of central Europe transmitted by the Sobieski Stuarts, whose claim to be descended from Prince Charles Edward Stuart was as false as their notions of Scotland's Gaelic past.

'Celtic' mythology, language and culture were associated with landscapes that were remote, rugged, wild and mysterious.

Within Britain the Celts, while British, could also be seen as an ethnic 'other', more primitive than their 'Anglo-Saxon' neighbours. One area that discovered its Celtic heritage rather late was Cornwall, where the impetus came during the mid-nineteenth century rather than the later eighteenth, as in Wales and the Highlands, perhaps because of the disappearance of the Cornish language during the eighteenth century. Despite the prominence of the tin-mining industry and china clay extraction in the landscape, Cornwall became seen as an area where the landscape, as well as the people, remained untouched by modern changes – a timeless, primitive region of magic and romance with its dolmens and hut circles. In the later nineteenth century, however, the marketing by the Great Western Railway of the 'Cornish Riviera' as a well-to-do, health-enhancing tourist destination created very different landscape perceptions.[92]

ROMANTICISM AND SCIENCE

Attitudes to landscape in the nineteenth century were strongly influenced by developments in the physical and natural sciences. Geology, following the work of James Hutton (1726–1797) and John Playfair (1748–1819), abandoned the short biblical chronology for the age of the earth and began to consider geological changes over a far longer timescale. Developments in fieldwork and stratigraphy led not only to a greatly improved understanding of geological history, but also of the relationship between rocks and topography. Ideas about surface processes also developed, notably in the acceptance from the 1840s of the existence of past phases of widespread glaciation, and their impact on the landscape.[93] The Victorians were avid natural historians and collectors; local field clubs proliferated. Artistic and scientific observation were not seen as separate at this time. Wordsworth had a keen interest in geology and accompanied the geologist Adam Sedgwick on field trips, while the critic John Ruskin believed that accurate scientific observation and recording was an essential quality for an artist.

The end of the eighteenth century and the early years of the nineteenth saw striking changes in the depiction of British landscapes, as restrictive, formulaic approaches such as the Picturesque lost their influence and a more scientific approach to the study of landscape emerged with a growing interest in, and knowledge of, natural history. Apart from the Romantic movement, the great contribution of the nineteenth century to landscape was the development of scientific ideas and observation, such as the classification of rocks and landforms. In its various editions, Wordsworth's *Guide to the Lakes* bridged the eras of Picturesque tourism and that of Victorian science. It demonstrates that the poet was closely in touch with contemporary debates in geology, as well as the writings of geographers such as Alexander von Humboldt. He also seems to have absorbed Hutton's ideas about the evolution of the earth, possibly through Playfair's more readable work.[94] Wordsworth's interest in geology reminds us that the Romantic view of landscape was strongly influenced by advances in the physical sciences.

Attitudes to landscape were profoundly influenced by developments in geology in the late eighteenth and early nineteenth centuries. The biblical chronology of the evolution of the earth, with its timescale of the Creation in 4004 BC, was becoming increasingly incompatible with the growing body of geological evidence. At the start of the nineteenth century, there were two prevalent theories in Britain concerning the formation of rocks and land forms: the Neptunist ideas of Abraham Werner (1749–1817), who considered that all rocks had been physically deposited or chemically precipitated in a primeval sea, and the diluvialist theory that the surface form of the earth was largely the result of the biblical Flood. Most nineteenth-century scientists believed in 'natural theology', that nature revealed the handiwork of God, a view also held by the numerous middle-class collectors of fossils and pressed flowers. William Buckland (1784–1856), one of Britain's most famous geologists, was a convinced diluvialist who cited evidence of fossils high in the Andes and the Himalayas as evidence of the Flood. This view was manifest in the titles of works by the self-taught Cromarty stonemason turned geologist, Hugh Miller (1802–56), whose books included *Foot-prints of the Creator* and *Testimony of the Rocks*.

A radically new perspective was put forward by James

Hutton in his uniformitarian *Theory of the Earth*, which was first published in 1795 but achieved recognition only with Playfair's more lucid exposition, *Illustrations of the Huttonian Theory of the Earth* (1802). It became more widely known in the 1830s with the publication of Charles Lyell's *Principles of Geology*. Hutton's ideas were based on careful field observation matched to a bold theoretical grasp. He proposed an endless cycle – 'no vestige of a beginning, no prospect of an end' – in which land was uplifted from the sea, mountain chains were formed, worn down and eventually submerged. Hutton could not explain the actual mechanisms involved in the process of rock formation and uplift, but the evidence of progressive landscape modification through erosion was clear to see, and the timescale that such processes required could not be fitted into the 6,000 or so years since the Biblical Creation. Charles Lyell (1797–1875) and Roderick Murchison (1792–1871), the two most influential British geologists of the mid-nineteenth century, were convinced that current processes in the landscape held the key to changes in the past.

Another important element in the understanding and interpretation of physical landscapes in nineteenth-century Europe was the development of the theory of glaciation. The Swiss geologist Louis Agassiz (1807–73) was not the first scientist to observe that in the Alps there was abundant evidence that glaciers had once been more extensive than they were at present. He was, however, the first person, in 1840, to identify similar landforms relating to glacial activity in areas such as Britain, where modern glaciers were absent. Previously upland glacial landforms such as cirques had been explained as the result of volcanic activity or marine erosion, while erratics – boulders that had been transported by glaciers or ice sheets, often a considerable distance from their areas of origin – were explained as having been carried by icebergs during former periods of high, cold seas.

ROMANTICISM AND FORESTS

Germany was an important cradle of Romanticism, which was fused with the emerging nationalism forged during the wars against Napoleon.[95] British romantic writers, such as Coleridge, Scott and Wordsworth, were strongly influenced by German authors. The brooding forest and mountain landscapes of Caspar David Friedrich (1774–1840), while strangely atmospheric, nevertheless drew on careful scientific observation of nature. In America the Romantic movement took hold from the 1820s, with writers such as James Fenimore Cooper (1796–1851) showing the clear influence of Scott in the structure of their novels. Romanticism in America was particularly characterized by the celebration of the simple life and the concept of the noble savage. Cooper eulogized the pioneer, yet regretted the passing of the wilderness. The artist George Catlin (1796–1872) was a recorder and defender of the West and its native peoples. Ralph Waldo Emerson (1803–82) and Henry David Thoreau stressed the need for contact with nature. It was nevertheless hard in some respects to assimilate European Romanticism to American landscapes, because the ideal European landscape was defined so much in terms of association with ruins, relics, myths and legend. The Catskill Mountains in upstate New York became an American Lake District, an idealized American primeval landscape. Asher Durand's *Kindred Spirits* (1849) showed the artist Thomas Cole and the poet W. C. Bryant in a romantic forested landscape in the Hudson Valley.

If most of the people in Europe and America still saw forests as something to be conquered, some at least saw them as a source of freedom, beauty and purity, their scale and extent a matter for patriotic pride. By the end of the eighteenth century, England was one of the least wooded countries in Europe. Despite this, or perhaps because of it, there was a great enthusiasm for trees and woodland, especially in appropriate settings. A continuing association of unregulated woodland with outlaws, lawlessness and poaching is seen by the reaction of writers such as Gilpin to the New Forest; they loved the treescapes but deplored their shiftless inhabitants. Woodland needed to be enclosed and planted, which emphasized ownership and control. This was reflected in increasingly tough legislation designed to protect plantations from wood-gathering by the rural population at large.[96] On the other hand, there was no better way of showing dissatisfaction with a landowner than by

Caspar David Friedrich, *Traveller Looking over a Sea of Fog*, c. 1818, Kunstalle, Hamburg.

cutting green wood in their plantations, something that seems to have had a long-established tradition of indirect protest in Scotland.[97]

While planting helped to demonstrate the power of an estate, large-scale felling of mature timber to pay off debts or make a quick profit was widely condemned. In the mid-eighteenth century, the clearing of areas of woodland on the shores of Derwentwater in the Lake District on land owned by Greenwich Hospital was widely condemned by locals and visitors for its detrimental impact on the landscape. Such views partly reflected the symbolism of trees – sturdy, long-lived oaks were metaphors for England's landed families. The country was defended from the French by its 'wooden walls' and 'hearts of oak'. The shortage of good-quality oak and other hardwoods for shipbuilding, more apparent than real, was a constant matter for concern.[98] Beech, the wood of which was suitable for high-quality furniture, also had patrician associations, while elm was linked more with hedgerows and the working countryside of farming. Conifers were welcomed by landowners with extensive areas of poor, marginal soils. On the Atholl estates, millions of trees were planted in the later eighteenth century, the plantations being seen as a considerable ornament to an otherwise bare countryside. In the Lake District, the introduction of plantations of larches by landowners such as John Christian Curwen and the Bishop of Llandaff was condemned by Wordsworth as an alien visual intrusion. Humphry Repton came to associate conifers not only with the wartime conditions that threatened his own livelihood but also with the nouveau riche landowners for whom he was reluctantly forced to execute commissions.[99] Repton contrasted such an estate with an old aristocratic one. The latter was a landscape of connection, where the boundaries between park, road and common were not clearly defined and were softened by the shade of the deciduous trees. The parvenu landscape was one where regimented conifers had replaced the deciduous trees. The park had been separated and hidden away by a high fence. The common, enclosed and fenced off from the road, was being ploughed up under the direction of the new owner. Money had severed the linkages on which Repton's idea of landscape was based.

LANDSCAPES AND ROMANTIC ART

The conventions of the Picturesque influenced the early careers of the two greatest British landscape artists, John Constable and J. M. W. Turner (1775–1851). Some of Turner's early views have a classical structure drawn from the works of Claude, but in 1798, following a visit to the Lake District, he appears to have rejected the clear lines and sharply delineated forms of picturesque landscapes for a murkier, more Romantic view, as seen in pictures of Buttermere and the Coniston fells. Turner saw new potentialities in the nature of colour and light. His painting of farm workers ploughing up turnips near Slough (1809; Tate Britain, London) depicts the harsh reality of rural labour but, with its exaggerated silhouette of Windsor Castle on the horizon, it also linked the workers' efforts to the patriotic task of feeding the country during wartime.

Constable's landscapes emphasize the elements of continuity rather than change in the English landscape. Constable revolutionized the attitude of the landscape painter to the process of converting observation into expression. In the early days of his painting, he was torn between his own feelings for landscape and the conventions of the Picturesque, which he seems to have adopted with reluctance, temporarily and only partially. Constable's career and family background, which are well known and well-documented, provide a good example of the danger of ignoring the purely personal elements in an artist's relationship to landscape in favour of generalizations about social and economic trends. Constable's almost obsessive focus upon the landscapes around the village of East Bergholt, where he was born, and the Stour valley can be understood only in

J.M.W. Turner, *Buttermere Lake: A Shower*, c. 1798., Tate Britain, London.

relation to his complex, often difficult, relationships with his father, his family and local society more generally. His pictures of places such as Flatford Mill and Dedham Mill are seen in a different light when it is appreciated that they were owned by his family, that his father, a wealthy miller, expected Constable to take over his wide-ranging business interests, and that, in determining to make a career as an artist, Constable was opposing his parents' wishes. These were landscapes rich with associations for Constable, but also full of personal tensions and conflicts.

Constable's later work, particularly his series of large landscape canvases painted from 1819, has been seen as involving increasing nostalgia for the landscapes of his childhood, which had changed markedly since then. It is by no means certain, however, that landscapes in this area had changed so dramatically, any more than had the rural society portrayed so ambivalently by Constable. The elements of continuity in English rural society in the later eighteenth and early nineteenth centururies have probably been underestimated, and are brought out, albeit nostalgically, by Constable. On one hand, the figures in his well-known 'six footers' are engaged in work that was traditional in many ways. On the other, they were connected with commercial agriculture and the production and transport of food to meet the demands of the huge London market. Constable was ultimately the painter of non-Picturesque England, the landscape of intensive, commercialized cereal farming. His pictures capture the order of this landscape and the regimented, highly stratified rural society that worked it.

Along with a passionate interest in wilderness, Romanticism included a fascination with medieval times, a period whose achievements had been marginalized by Renaissance and Enlightenment thinkers. The Romantic movement and its mysticism of place was also a strong influence on the shaping of nationalism in the nineteenth century (see Chapter 4). The Gothic revival involved a dream of social harmony of the Middle Ages, a time when everyone, supposedly, knew their place and were united by simple Christian faith. In the late eighteenth and early nineteenth centuries, Gothic architecture was a style favoured by eccentrics. Horace Walpole (1717–97), son of the prime minister, Robert Walpole, and author of the Gothic novel *The Castle of Otranto* (1764), had Strawberry Hill in Middlesex built. William Beckford (1760–1844), author of *Vathek* (1786), had an even more extravagant – and structurally unstable – house built at Fonthill Abbey, Wiltshire (the great central tower repeatedly collapsed). By the mid-nineteenth century, however, the Gothic style had acquired seriousness and stature, encouraging the 'restoration' of many medieval churches as the Victorians thought they ought to have been built rather than as they actually were.

In the later eighteenth century, the nature of landscape aesthetics had changed rapidly from the Enlightenment view through the Picturesque gaze to the Romantic view. In Britain, this was paralleled with, and influenced by, important changes in economy and society that were also impacting on the landscape. The focus of Romanticism on wild countryside was in part a reaction to the growth of industrialization and urbanization. In the next chapter we will look at their impacts on landscape in more detail.

FOUR

Industrial and Imperial Landscapes

INDUSTRIAL LANDSCAPES

The Industrial Revolution, which gathered momentum in parts of England and central Scotland during the late eighteenth century, created some distinct landscapes. Early textile factories depended on water power and were sited wherever a suitable head of water was available, sometimes in relatively remote rural locations. Because of the need to attract and retain a workforce in such areas, factory owners frequently provided relatively good-quality housing for their workers, creating model communities. New Lanark, beside the Falls of Clyde in southern Scotland, and Styall, south of Manchester, are good examples. Other industrial areas developed on the basis of coal and other resources as well as water power, such as Ironbridge in Shropshire, with its iron-smelting and pottery works.[1] Industrialization was also associated with improvements in road transport with the system of turnpike trusts, and with the construction of canals for moving bulky items such as coal, cotton, grain and stone. By the end of the eighteenth century in England, trans-Pennine canals had been constructed, using flights of locks, aqueducts and tunnels to overcome the topography.

Before the nineteenth century, industry, whether urban or rural, had been relatively small in scale and had affected only limited areas. Now it spread over entire coalfields, often in an unplanned sprawl of mines, factories, waste heaps, workers' housing and transport arteries. In northern France and southern Belgium, a belt of country, the *pays noir*, some 241 km (150 miles) long, developed with large areas of blighted landscapes but few sizeable towns, the character of which is well captured in Emile Zola's novel *Germinal* (1885). The landscape of England's Black Country was similar. In upland areas, mining for iron, copper and lead ores also produced blighted areas, especially where the fumes from smelting poisoned the vegetation.

Developments in industrial technology also affected other aspects of the landscape. Coppice management of woodlands declined with the switch to coal for smelting iron and as a domestic fuel, and the shift from wood to metal for many manufactured goods, as well as a fall in demand for bark for tanning leather in the face of cheaper supplies and alternative chemicals from abroad. Although the need for wooden bobbins for the Lancashire cotton industry kept up the demand for coppicing in Furness in the southern Lake District, imports of Scandinavian softwoods undercut local producers, and by the 1890s coppicing was in rapid decline. More and more woodlands were converted to high forest.[2]

Increasingly, as the nineteenth century went on, early factory locations in rural areas gave way to urban ones on coalfields or beside canals, where coal could be brought in cheaply. Industrialization spread more slowly on the Continent, but had affected Belgium and northern France profoundly by the mid-nineteenth century. Germany was industrialized a little later. In these countries, the railway played the role in industrialization that canals occupied in Britain.[3]

Developments in transport technology affected people's perceptions of landscapes. Canals, despite the amount of engineering involved, fitted into the landscape rather than disrupting it; river navigation had been a feature of transport for centuries and canals were not very different, except where flights of locks, aqueducts or tunnels added novel elements to the landscape. Nor did the speed of canal transport alter travellers' views of landscape. The fastest passenger boats could manage little more than 18.5 km (10 miles) per hour, no more than the quickest stage coaches, so that people still moved through the landscape at a sedate pace. Travellers had been involved in the passing landscape before the coming of the railways, but trains were faster and noisier than previous forms of transport. Railways distanced their passengers from the landscape, which they went past rather than through. Railways were seen by many as unnatural and at odds with the established order typified by the rural landscape.[4]

The impact of the railway on the countryside: a viaduct near Melrose, Scotland.

The railways were different from previous forms of transport in many other ways. First, they were much more flexible in their construction. The Leeds–Liverpool Canal, hugging the contours, followed a serpentine course through south Lancashire. The Liverpool–Manchester Railway of 1830 linked the two cities by a direct route. When, in 1846, the west-coast main line between Lancaster and Carlisle over Shap was completed without any tunnels, the flexibility of railway over canal engineering was clearly demonstrated. Early reactions to the railways, and descriptions of them, tended to polarize into strongly pro- and anti-groups. Some early illustrations dramatized the new railways, but many early prints show them as relatively unobtrusive features of the landscape. William Wordsworth, in his unsuccessful opposition to a proposed line to Windermere, asked in a poem of 1844: 'is then no nook of English ground secure from rash assault?'. In the same year Turner's famous picture *Rain, Steam, Speed – The Great Western Railway* seems to be more ambivalent about the new form of transport, celebrating the achievement of the Great Western Railway in building the longest railway line in Europe.

The railway boom in Britain of the 1840s mainly involved a race to connect Britain's major towns and cities. A later phase of branch line construction, culminating at the end of the nineteenth century with the construction of light railways,

J.M.W. Turner, *Rain, Steam, Speed*, 1844, National Gallery, London.

really opened up more remote areas of countryside, such as the Pennine dales, and isolated industrial sites, such as the mines at Leadhills in the southern Uplands of Scotland. In France, to an even greater extent than in Britain, the coming of the railways in the later nineteenth century ended rural isolation and initiated change in the landscape, as economies shifted towards more commercial production.

If the early large-scale industrial sites of the eighteenth century seemed exciting to many observers, the thrill rapidly palled. Urbanization and industrialization were soon seen as twin evils that produced not only blighted landscapes but also affected adversely the lives of the people who lived in them. A similar process of rejection and repugnance occurred in the eastern USA slightly later.

THE IMPACT OF INDUSTRIALIZATION ON THE LANDSCAPES OF PERIPHERAL REGIONS IN EUROPE

Industrialization and urbanization in the core regions of Europe produced various impacts on the landscapes of peripheral areas.

In the early nineteenth century, population still continued to grow in areas such as the Scottish Highlands, western Ireland and the Alps, despite seasonal and permanent out-migration. The pressure of population on limited resources resulted in both an intensification and an expansion of peasant farming systems. In the west Highlands, the hand cultivation of raised lazy-beds for potatoes pushed higher up the mountainsides, while temporary shieling sites on the summer grazings were converted into permanent settlements.[5] Population growth would have resulted in a major crisis even without the impact of landlord involvement. In the later eighteenth century, however, landowners in the Scottish Highlands began to replace the existing small-scale mixed peasant farming systems on their estates with commercial sheep farming, in an endeavour to increase their incomes in order to maintain their increasingly expensive lifestyles. They were also keen to emulate their Lowland counterparts in agricultural improvement.[6] Sheep farming, to be profitable, had to be undertaken on a large scale. Unlike earlier cattle farming, it could not be easily integrated into existing farming systems. As a result, in a wave that rolled northwards and westwards – reaching areas beyond the Great Glen in the early years of the nineteenth century – existing smallholding tenants were cleared off their lands in the interior glens to make way for commercial graziers. The aim of landlords was not to force the existing population off their estates, but to resettle them in coastal locations, where they could make a living from combining smallholding agriculture with fishing or industrial work. The relocated families were often given land that had not been previously cultivated, set out in large, regular townships with rectangular lots running back from straight roads. Thus was born the crofting landscape, not an ancient form of agriculture as some modern visitors to the west Highlands suppose, but a landscape that was contemporary with, and in many respects the result of, the steam engine and the textile mill.[7]

Groups of former farming townships in the glens, with their cultivation ridges and enclosures, were replaced by single, better-built farmsteads and shepherds' cottages. Where the land has not been disturbed by later afforestation, these landscapes of pre-clearance agriculture still remain remarkably intact. Such

A crofting landscape, Garenin, Isle of Lewis: a landscape created as a result of clearance and resettlement.

landscapes are thus of major importance in European, not merely Scottish, terms, because they provide a direct link with a pre-improvement landscape. Although far from unchanging since prehistoric times, as has sometimes been supposed, they were at least the end product of very gradual, organic landscape changes, until they were finally fossilized by abandonment, which often took place within a single year. So widespread are such landscapes that it is only relatively recently that they have started to be surveyed and studied in detail.[8]

The aims behind the Highland Clearances were misguided, and the execution of the evictions was sometimes heartless and brutal. The success of the new crofting townships and the planned fishing settlements that were established in the western and northern Highlands in the early nineteenth century was undermined by the post-1815 economic slump, which affected the kelp, textile and fishing industries.[9] Ironically, the fortunes of sheep farming soon began to deteriorate too. By the mid-nineteenth century, it was no longer profitable. In many places in the Highlands, farmsteads and shepherds' cottages lie derelict beside the peasant townships they replaced. The rise of industrial society in the south, however, had created an increasingly large class of manufacturers and professionals who had the money and leisure to indulge in rural sports. From the mid-nineteenth century, many Scottish estates in the Highlands and Borders turned to deer stalking, grouse shooting and salmon fishing as the mainstay of their income. This resulted in the construction of shooting lodges, boathouses and networks of stalkers' tracks, as well as lines of grouse butts on hillsides.[10]

In Ireland, despite rising emigration, the population continued to build up to even higher densities in the early nineteenth century, with a proliferation of lazy-bed cultivation on more and more marginal land, especially in the west. The population cuts caused by the Great Famine of the 1840s, and the ensuing flood of emigration, encouraged a major reorganization of the landscape over large areas of countryside, with clachans or hamlet clusters of smallholding tenants being replaced by larger farms or individual crofts. Only in parts of the west, as at Iar Connacht, did the pattern of clachans continue into the post-Second World War period. Here, abandoned ruined settlement clusters are still visible among the networks of tumbled stone walls.[11]

Similar trends, of marked population growth leading to an expansion of cultivation on to more and more marginal lands, followed by the collapse of the traditional economy, massive out-

A deserted Irish clachan, Formyle, Co. Clare.

migration and abandonment of extensive areas of improved land, were a feature of other peripheral areas of Europe. The expansion of cultivation was associated with techniques that were essentially those of the pre-industrial era, supported by immense investments in labour. Population pressure led to deforestation and increased soil erosion. In some areas, such as the Sierra de Gador in south-east Spain, large-scale mining created a temporary economic boom and large-scale environmental damage.[12] In addition to landlord policies and growing poverty, if not famine, the undermining of local industry by outside competition with the spread of the railway network and improvements in roads, as well as more information about alternative opportunities, encouraged emigration to core industrial areas and across the Atlantic. In the Alps, the process termed *hohenflucht* had led, by the 1930s, to the abandonment of a third of the farms in some areas, a trend paralleled in the Apennines.[13] In Corsica, the cultivated area fell from c. 200,000 ha (49,420 a) in 1890 to 12,000 ha (29,652 a) in 1960.

Although the population of many peripheral areas was in decline in the later nineteenth century, there were still pioneer fringes of colonization in Europe. In eastern Europe, the growing demand for timber and grain from western Europe led to large-scale forest clearance in Lithuania and Poland. Deciduous trees, which grew on the richer soils, were cleared preferentially, leaving behind conifers on poorer soils.[14] The improvement of the heathlands of west Jutland is another example. This had been a thinly populated area of moor and bog, but the loss of Schleswig-Holstein to Prussia turned attention to the conquest of a natural enemy. In 1866, the Danish Heathland Society was formed, large areas of peat bog began to be drained and soils were improved. An area almost equal to the size of Belgium was reclaimed. In Sweden, there was also a move to settle internal areas with a spread of population into Norrland between the River Dal and the Arctic Circle. Colonization of the northlands of Sweden continued into the early twentieth century; the population of some areas more than doubled between 1850 and 1900, with population peaking in south Norrland around 1920 and north Norrland in about 1940.[15] The economies of some areas were diversified by the development of industries using local raw materials. In Scandinavia, the introduction of steam-powered sawmills from the 1840s heralded the start of a phase of peripheral industrialization. Later in the nineteenth century, the development of hydro-electric power encouraged a switch from timber to pulp and paper production. Some industries had quite specific locational requirements that attracted them to such areas. In the late nineteenth century, in Scandinavia and the Scottish Highlands, the aluminium smelting industry, which required abundant supplies of cheap electricity, was associated with hydro-electric power schemes, regardless of how remote the site.[16] Medieval transport technology continued in some remote areas. In Scandinavia, the use of sledges on frozen lakes continued to the end of the nineteenth century. In the Apennines and Sierra Nevada, roads reached remote villages only in the 1930s, in parts of Greece in the 1950s.[17]

In the later nineteenth century, branch railways were important in opening up many remote areas. In France, they began to penetrate Brittany, the Massif Central and the Alps in the 1860s and '70s.[18] In Brittany, the railway reached Brest in 1865, but the interior of the peninsula was really opened up only with the construction of branch lines in the 1880s and narrow gauge lines in the 1890s. This enabled lime to be brought in for agricultural improvement, encouraging the large-scale reclamation of moorland.[19] Improved transport stimulated the commercialization of agriculture: the cultivation of subsistence crops such as buckwheat declined and the area under wheat increased. Railways came even later to Scandinavia.[20] The Bergen–Oslo line was not completed until 1909, and the Oslo–Trondheim line across the Douvre massif only in the 1920s. Steamships were also important in opening up the north of Norway and the Western Isles of Scotland, although across Europe the construction of better roads was probably the most significant change.

NINETEENTH CENTURY ART, LANDSCAPE AND NATIONAL IDENTITY

Landscape painting of the late eighteenth and early nineteenth centuries has been seen as a denial of industrialization and a celebration of landscapes that were being rapidly lost. From the 1770s Joseph Wright of Derby (1734–97), whose patrons included Richard Arkwright, Samuel Oldknow and Josiah Wedgewood, used dramatic contrasts of light and shade, echoing the techniques of seventeenth-century Dutch artists such as Rembrandt, to depict men working in iron forges and other forms of manufacturing. He later painted Arkwright's mill at Cromford, already a popular subject for amateur artists, in a style that echoed his earlier paintings of volcanoes such as Vesuvius, which emphasized the parallels between man-made and natural energy. He has been seen as the first artist to capture the spirit of the Industrial Revolution. Philippe de Loutherbourg (1740–1812), in a similar style, painted *Coalbrookdale by Night* (Science Museum, London) in Shropshire in 1801. The popularity of industrial areas as tourist attractions and subjects for painting was short lived, though: artists increasingly shunned such scenes, while Uvedale Price, in his essay on the Picturesque in 1794, found Richard Arkwright's mills at Cromford disgusting. Much of the concerns of Picturesque tourism may be seen as a reaction against industrial and urban growth. Turner was one of the few artists who captured industrial landscapes with detail and precision, and who depicted industrial towns as being seamlessly linked to their rural surroundings, with foregrounds filled not with agriculture but with activities linked to manufacturing.[21] Despite the scale of the landscape transformation associated with urbanization and industrialization, most artists refused to register the change. The early Picturesque depiction of factories by Joseph Wright of Derby had few followers apart from Turner.[22] The Industrial Revolution vanished almost completely from landscape art, and the great achievements of Victorian engineers such as Isambard Kingdom Brunel failed to provide artistic inspiration, although it should be remembered that rural activities such as the boat-building captured by Constable continued to epitomize the character of industrial work over much of Britain.

By the late eighteenth century, tours of Britain were being undertaken increasingly by the middle as well as the upper classes. Owners of famous sights on private estates were increasingly interested in displaying them to genteel visitors. Drawings and paintings of such places, initially commissioned by owners for their own viewing, became mass-produced for a wider public. By the early nineteenth century, books of views of English landscapes were available for potential or vicarious tourists, giving them visual access to the land, a gesture towards inclusion by landowners who were still politically dominant. The possession of paintings or engravings of national landscapes could buttress claims of belonging to that nation. Turner's *Picturesque Views of England and Wales*, issued in parts between 1826 and 1835, provided the ascendant urban middle classes with the means to 'own' England visually, to claim membership of the meaningful national community.[23]

Landscape art in England peaked in Ruskin's day. Ruskin saw landscapes as texts in a way that is familiar today, and his *Modern Painters* (1843), initially designed as a defence of Turner's work, aimed ultimately to set landscape painting within a broader context than merely the history of art. He was a critic of the demoralizing, alienating effects of industrialization, and considered late medieval Venice the perfect society.[24] In nineteenth-century England, a succession of novelists and commentators increasingly saw industrial cities as diseased and unhealthy. There was a sense of the failure of the city in social terms as a community by people such as William Morris and Ebenezer Howard. Similar concerns were articulated in America by Nathaniel Hawthorne, Henry James, Herman Melville and Edgar Allan Poe. The rejection of industrialization reached its peak at the end of the nineteenth century, when the gentrified middle classes who had absorbed the conservative values of the aristocracy increasingly condemned urban environments. The rapid increase in the reading public, whose nostalgia for the countryside was fuelled by authors such as Richard Jefferies and W. H. Hudson, was accompanied by a widespread interest in natural history.[25]

In the process of rejecting the city, some rural areas were elevated to a kind of cult status, notably the Scottish Highlands. Various artists, but especially Edwin Landseer, helped to create the Victorian myth of the Scottish Highlands.[26] Landseer first portrayed the royal family in the Highlands in 1847, and was invited to Balmoral two years after Queen Victoria had leased it in 1848. His most important commission for the queen, started in 1850 but not completed until 1872, *Royal Sports on Hill and Loch*, identified the royal family with the Highlands, and with hunting and fishing. The first royal visit to Scotland since the days of Charles I was only 30 years in the past, and the image of the royal family surrounded by loyal Highland servants – Prince Albert himself wearing tartan – denied the tensions of the first half of the eighteenth century – the era of the Jacobite rebellions – and emphasized that the Highlands had been fully integrated and reconciled with the rest of Britain. Another of Landseer's paintings, *Highlander and Eagle*, depicts a striking image of sturdiness, but of a faithful servant, a Balmoral gillie named Peter Coutts, not a Jacobite clansman.

The tranquil image of the Highlands depicted in Landseer's work was at variance with contemporary social changes, particularly the clearance of much of the population to make way for commercial sheep farming, which had characterized the area in the recent past, the harsh lives of contemporary Highland crofters and the equally harsh urban, industrial reality of much of the Scottish population. Landseer's early commissions showed the royal family set among real, romantic, rugged Highland landscapes, but increasingly these backgrounds became more stylized and eventually virtually disappeared. Landseer's paintings were widely reproduced as engravings. The development of the steel printing plate allowed engravings to be produced in greater numbers and at lower costs, but at a price that, even so, made them accessible mainly to the middle rather than the working classes. It was to this group that the 'Highland myth' was largely targeted. While T. R. Pringle suggests that the myth was not consciously created by the royal family, the way in which the queen specified in great detail the composition of paintings such as *Royal Sports on Hill and Loch* indicates active rather than passive involvement.[27]

Constable's landscapes and his attempts to capture natural light had a far greater influence in France than in Britain. His work has been seen as a precursor of Impressionism, a style that began to emerge during the 1870s and which involved a more objective study of nature than the subjective approach of Romantic artists. While many works by Impressionist artists are associated with the cafés, theatres and boulevards of Paris, rural landscapes were also important subjects. With their emphasis on painting in the open air rather than in the studio, the climate of the Paris Basin was a relatively favourable one. The landscapes they chose to paint were not the dramatic mountain scenes favoured by Romantic artists, but the tranquil, more subtle ones of northern France, especially small market towns and rivers on the outskirts of Paris. Their 'unfinished' style represented an attempt to capture fleeting effects of movement and light. Artists such as Claude Monet (1840–1926) often painted an identical scene many times at different seasons and under varying atmospheric conditions. The Forest of Fontainebleau, particularly the village of Barbizon, was the focus for a group of artists in the mid-nineteenth century whose work led directly to the achievements of Impressionism. Easily accessible from Paris, yet unspoilt, the Forest provided artists such as Jean-Baptiste Corot (1796–1875) with inspiration. The later Impressionists chose places such as Argenteuil, Louveciennes, Marly and Pontoise, on the outskirts of Paris but not yet overwhelmed by suburban expansion. The Normandy coast provided another important focus for Impressionist work. The so-called post-Impressionist artists such as Vincent van Gogh (1853–90) and Paul Cézanne (1839–1906), while working in an Impressionist style in the early part of their careers, were attracted by the brilliance of the colours of the landscapes of the south of France.[28] The contrast between the sombre tones of van Gogh's work in the Netherlands and northern France, and the bright, vivid canvases that he painted in Provence is striking.

Pre-Raphaelite artists such as John Everett Millais (1829–96), Arthur Hughes (1830–1915), Charles Allston Collins (1828–73) and William Holman Hunt (1827–1910) tried in their art to imitate photography, producing landscapes painted in tremendous detail and colour, but with themes that were symbolic or very sentimental and contemporary. They turned their back on the real Victorian countryside and its social tensions.

In the nineteenth century, artists made important contributions to the development of national iconographies, sometimes quite consciously. Eighteenth-century depictions of New World landscapes were largely projections of European ideas. American landscapes were moulded into formats created by people such as Burke and Gilpin, and depicted using artistic conventions developed in English landscape painting. Such conventions often showed American landscapes and their native inhabitants in Picturesque and Romantic styles, which contrasted markedly with the real new landscapes of frontier settlement. The work of many landscape artists in mid-nineteenth-century Canada, such as Robert Whale (1805–87), emulated British art. They produced Canadian landscapes with a curiously English look to them. In the later nineteenth century, new artistic images were needed to foster nationalism, and there was an increasing focus on regional differences in landscape in both Canada and the United States. The American West was recorded and idealized by artists such as Frederic Remington (1861–1904) and Charles Russell (1864–1926). In Australia, artists such as Tom Roberts (1856–1931), Arthur Streeton (1867–1943) and Charles Condor (1868–1909) helped to create an iconography of the Outback, with scenes of work on sheep and cattle stations, and mining claims. In Canada, during the period 1860–90, wilderness landscapes became a major symbol for artists, especially after 1867, when Canada became a single nation, and its expansion to the Pacific Ocean by 1871. Frances Hopkins (1838–1919) depicted canoe travel, while Tom Thomson (1877–1917) and the 'Group of Seven' firmly rejected outmoded European influences and promoted landscape painting that was distinctively Canadian in spirit. They focused on the sparsely inhabited wilderness, and contributed to the development of a national sense of identity through paintings of Canada's far north. They were influenced by the Symbolist landscape movement in Finland, Norway and Sweden, in which the North became a focus for nationalist feeling. Such Northern images were, however, foreign to many people in a country as big and as regionally varied as Canada.[29]

Landscape art in Australia followed similar patterns to North America. Early nineteenth-century Australian landscapes were painted in the style of Claude Lorrain. White visitors to Australia at this time produced two artistic responses: the Romantic and the neo-Classical. Aborigines were sometimes depicted as noble savages in a Garden of Eden, a counterpoint to corrupt and effete Western society. Long-term settlers saw things differently. Their presence in the landscape was considered a mark of progress, as demonstrated by John Glover (1767-1849), who depicted the Australian vegetation accurately, but the aborigines poorly. Glover was an established artist in England who followed the tradition of Claude. In 1831, aged 64, he emigrated to Tasmania and bought a 2,834 ha (7,000-a) estate at Patterdale. He was one of the first artists to treat Australian vegetation seriously, capturing the effects of light on gum trees. His aborigines, added at best for artistic effect, were not the noble savages of Captain Cook but a mere touch of romantic interest, lacking human individuality. He produced pastoral views of the Australian landscape – sheep and shepherds, views of estates, areas of improvement contrasting with wilderness – but these were sanitized landscapes with no signs of the convict labourers who did so much of the work. Eugen von Guerard (1812–1901) arrived in Australia in 1852. He came from a Viennese family of artists and was trained in the early nineteenth-century German Romantic tradition of landscape art. He travelled widely in Australia and New Zealand, his career coinciding with the agricultural boom, and painted pictures of prosperous steadings, like those of eighteenth-century English estates. Tom Roberts, who was born in Britain but emigrated to Australia in 1869, was influenced by Monet and Whistler. His humanized Australian landscapes, particularly sheep-shearing on outback stations, helped to define a national identity different from that of Britain, particularly the myth of the bush as the 'real' Australia.

Another form of nineteenth-century landscape depiction, which owed its development to new technology, was photography. During the 1830s, various people, including William Fox Talbot in Britain and Louis Daguerre in France, were experimenting with chemical processes that would permanently fix the images generated by a camera obscura. When Daguerre announced his invention in Paris in 1839, the artist Paul Delaroche is said to have commented: 'from today painting is dead'. The rapid development of technology in the mid-nineteenth century took photography out of the studio and into the landscape, especially in the USA, where it began to capture the landscapes of a country still coming to terms with its new-found nationhood. As a new medium in a new country it was rapidly accepted. The first generation of American landscape photographers, in the 1840s and 1850s, were dependent on pictorial conventions in terms of the subjects they chose and how they were composed, but there was a growing demand for landscape photographs from a middle-class clientele. Photography developed at a time of great economic, social and landscape change in both Europe and America. Travel photography appeared as early as 1840, when collections of callotype and daguerreotype images of Italy, Greece, Turkey and Japan began to be produced. Maxime Du Camp, (1822–94) a friend of Gustave Flaubert, was photographing ancient Egyptian sites as early as 1849. In the 1860s, images of landscapes of imperial possessions, especially India, were becoming commonplace in Britain, bringing home to people the vast, exotic character of the sub-continent. Photography of the American West began in earnest after the end of the Civil War in 1865. Photographers such as Carlton Watkins (1829–1916) and E. J. Muybridge (1830–1904) were attached to official expeditions along with artists such as Thomas Moran (1837–1926). Watkins was a member of the California State Geological Survey's expedition to Yosemite in 1866.

From its earliest days, photography was heralded as the ultimate means of capturing reality. To the Victorians, photography was a means of revealing the realities of far away and exotic landscapes. Yet photographic collections such as that of the Royal Geographical Society say as much about the imaginative landscapes of imperial culture as they do about the physical spaces depicted in them. From the late 1850s, photographic equipment was increasingly included in the baggage of British expeditions. They took photographs of major geographical features, but also ones that reflected the cultural assumptions and political aspirations of particular expeditions. For example, photographs of tangled, impenetrable vegetation in central Africa fitted in with perceptions of the 'Dark Continent', a place of barbarism and savagery.[30] The introduction of lighter, mass-produced hand-held equipment in the 1880s, and the mobility offered to amateur photographers by the bicycle, led to a great increase in landscape photography in countries such as Britain and France. Individuals and photographic clubs began to record historic scenes and buildings in their local areas. During the First World War, collections of photographs of the English countryside became particularly popular for patriotic reasons.

REGIONAL LANDSCAPES AND REGIONAL NOVELS

Novels as a form of literature started to replace epic and drama as the main literary form only in the early eighteenth century. In English literature, place specificity emerged slowly: in the eighteenth century it was generalized in novels by writers such as Henry Fielding (1707–54) and Samuel Richardson (1689–1761), often only in an urban–rural dichotomy; it became more specific and detailed with early nineteenth-century writers such as Scott, the Brontë sisters and Jane Austen. In the second quarter of the nineteenth century, the English regional novel developed,[31] exploring the character of landscape and society in specific areas. Thomas Hardy's Wessex novels are the most famous in this genre, but there were many others. A feature of many regional novelists was that they had been separated from the areas they described before they recreated them in print, while in other cases tensions were developed between home and distant, often foreign, landscapes. In many cases their approach was nostalgic. Scott's novels were also consciously set in the past – a medieval one in novels such as *Ivanhoe* (1820) – but his best work was concerned with the relatively recent past, remembered by adults whom he had known in childhood. The subtitle of his first novel, *Waverley*, set at the time of the Jacobite rebellion of 1745, was *'Tis Sixty Years Since*. Yet such had been the pace of landscape change in both the Scottish Highlands and the Lowlands that his descriptions of such places as the castle and village of Tully-Veolan have a distinctively archaic air about them.

Other regional novels sought to portray more contemporary settings and landscapes, including those of the rapidly-expanding industrial areas. Mrs Gaskell's *Mary Barton* (1848) and *North and South* (1855) successfully captured the distinctiveness of the industrial North. Arnold Bennett's novels about the Five Towns of the Staffordshire Potteries district were equally atmospheric. Regional novels have continued into more recent times, with novels such as those by Alan Sillitoe, (*b.* 1928) set in Nottingham. The setting of novels in a particular region does not always guarantee a strong identification with landscape, though. Hugh Walpole's *Herries Chronicles*, set in the Lake District in a period spanning the mid-eighteenth to the early twentieth century, have little sense of place.

Perhaps the epitime of the nineteenth-century English regional novelist was Thomas Hardy (1840–1928). Hardy's Wessex novels are set mainly in the earlier decades of the nineteenth century, around the time that the author was born. They describe a rural peasantry that had vanished by the time he was writing, so that an element of nostalgia is involved here too.[32] Hardy emphasized the links between his characters, the societies they lived in and the landscape that they worked in. Although he manipulated the landscapes of Dorset in creating his fictional Wessex, his characters, as 'insiders', inhabit identifiable landscape regions, or pays, and are conscious of the visual changes that occur when they move out into adjacent ones, as with Tess and the Vale of Blackmoor in *Tess of the D'Urbervilles* (1891). John Barrell has emphasized Hardy's skill in giving Tess, aged 16, only a child's sense of place.[33]

Maps in literary guides of British regional novelists are thickly dotted with names, but it is possible to view broader features in common among groups of writers. D.C.D. Pocock has analyzed novelists' images of the north of England, drawing on a range of regional writers.[34] These consistently conform to a harsh stereotype in terms of the landscape and climate they describe, characterized by mines, industry and deprivation, with smoke the most obvious, ubiquitous single indicator of the North. Pocock emphasizes the power of such literary images in affecting popular perceptions of places that were otherwise little known to outsiders. Images of conflict in such novels could reflect man against the environment, as in the crofts of the Howe of the Mearns in Lewis Grassic Gibbon's *Sunset Song* (1932), as well as conflict between the farmers and their landlords in this novel and William Alexander's *Johnny Gibb of Gushetneuk* (1873).[35]

In previous chapters we have looked at the landscape impact of the European colonization of North America. It has sometimes been suggested that the effects of European imperialism in transforming the landscape were confined mainly to North America, the southern part of South America, Africa, Australia and New Zealand, and that in Asia and Africa the scale of change was much reduced.[36] But while Europeans did not settle in the tropics in such great numbers as in the areas mentioned above, they nevertheless drastically altered the landscape with irrigation, deforestation, afforestation and the introduction of plantation agriculture, although R. H. Grove has put forward a case for the existence of more sensitive approaches to landscape modification by colonial authorities in some tropical areas from the eighteenth century onward.[37]

Edward Said has urged the critical reading of 'imaginative geographies', figurations of place, space and landscape that dramatize distance and difference in such a way that 'our' space is divided and demarcated from 'their' space.[38] Said's concept of Orientalism has demonstrated that the representation of the 'other' to the world, and even to those being represented, has been at least as powerful in destabilizing and radically altering societies as major economic, technological and political changes. The Orient was constructed as a stage onto which the Occident projected its own fantasies and desires. This is well seen by recent research on western European, especially British and French, reactions to the landscapes of Egypt in the nineteenth century.

Egypt was seen by nineteenth-century travellers as a text to be read and the object of a gaze. Visitors looked at the landscape and read about it, rather than interacting with the local population, whose languages they could not speak. Nineteenth-century Orientalism focused on textual associations; the Orient was seen less as a place rooted in history and geography than as a chain of literary references. Travel guides recommended a miniature library of scholarly works on Egypt for travellers to take with them. They voyaged on the Nile with these texts beside them, writing their journals and letters, framing Egypt as a picture.

European attitudes towards the landscapes and peoples of Egypt are well displayed in the volumes of the *Description de l'Egypte*, a remarkable piece of collaborative research produced by the savants who accompanied the Napoleonic expedition of 1798–1801. Published in 22 volumes between 1809 and 1828, the research was, in most cases, at the frontiers of knowledge in each respective subject, which included archaeology, landscape description and cartography. At the time, no part of contemporary France had been studied or portrayed at this level of detail. The maps were inextricably tied to imperial conquest in their conscious and unconscious representation of Egypt. The *Description* was part of the 'Enlightenment Project', and reflected the values of the scholars who compiled it. They believed that the world could be controlled and rationally ordered if it could be properly pictured and represented.

The mapping and technological transformation of Egypt provided a rationale for conquest, and the primary instrument for the social, economic and political restructuring of the country. The links between Egypt and France were stressed by the use of the same scale (1:86,400) as Cassini's topographic survey of France, and identical cartographic symbols. Large-scale topographic mapping of an entire country, especially outside western Europe, was a relatively new phenomenon in the early nineteenth century. The maps carried the greatest authority in the *Description* because they best embodied its ideals in producing a complete, detailed and standardized survey. One of the main aims of the expedition and the *Description* was the association of France and French culture with ancient Egypt. Egypt, under the rule of the Mamelukes, was seen as being in need of rescuing by French culture and science. European, and especially French, civilization was seen as superior in every way. The *Description* paid little attention to modern Islamic Egypt, focusing instead on the country's antiquities. Ancient Egypt was seen as the only true Egypt, imbued with meanings and values of far greater significance than those of the modern country and its inhabitants. The period of Islamic rule was viewed as a barbarous decline from a former state of splendour. Modern Egypt and its people were ignored except as stereotypes. This was reflected in the topographic maps, where antiquities such as those at Luxor were depicted in great detail, while the street plans of modern settlements were highly generalized. Illustrations showed French scientists actively examining and recording the ruins, while their Egyptian guides occupied subservient positions, staring vacantly and indifferently into space, oblivious to the significance of the monuments they leaned against.[39]

Derek Gregory has examined mid-nineteenth-century imaginative geographies and how they brought Egypt within European horizons of intelligibility and visibility.[40] When travellers ventured beyond Europe, they took their preconceived images with them. How did their physical passage through other landscapes and cultures affect their writing and their representations of these spaces? Florence Nightingale (1820–1910) and Gustave Flaubert (1821–80) both visited Egypt in the mid-nineteenth century, when they were in their late twenties, and have left accounts that enable reconstructions of their imaginative geographies. Not surprisingly, given their backgrounds, they held in common a number of assumptions and responses, but there were also significant contrasts caused by differences in their gender and nationality; some experiences were open to Flaubert that were denied to Nightingale.

Nightingale, travelling with friends, visited Alexandria and Cairo before embarking on a houseboat for a river cruise. For European visitors, such cruises were becoming extended house parties, with their own conventions and rituals. She experienced great difficulty in coming to terms with, and even finding terms for, the Egyptian landscape. Her sense of astonishment and wonder was tempered by the sense that, compared with the familiar landscapes of Europe, this was a colourless, unnatural, dead landscape dominated by tombs and temples, an inversion of the ordered, Christian world of Europe, inhabited by a debased, barely human population. She saw Cairo as the city of the Arabian nights: Arabian not Egyptian. Her view of ancient Egypt was that its inhabitants must have been very like modern Europeans, very different from the barely human Arabs who lived among the ruins. She was appalled by much of what she saw of modern Egypt, and especially the position of women, although she also appreciated that the construction of the pyramids represented an equally bad oppression. Without the past, she concluded, Egypt would be utterly uninhabitable. She liked the solitude of the great temple at Abu Simbel because of the absence of modern Egyptians. For her, the achievements of ancient Egypt and their contrast with the squalor of the modern country called into question the notion of progress and the long-term future of the British Empire.

Flaubert was seeking to escape the conventions and boredom of bourgeois Europe. He had read widely in the literature of Orientalism before his departure, and these texts clearly influenced his reaction to the Egyptian landscape. Following a broadly similar itinerary to Florence Nightingale, he claimed not to be particularly interested in either Egypt's landscape or its antiquities, but his images of particular moments, such as sunrise viewed from the top of one of the Pyramids, were highly evocative. He was more bored with the incorporation of ancient sites into a discourse of tourism than with the atmosphere of the sites themselves. Alexandria disappointed him because of the scale of Western influence; Cairo fascinated him.

Nightingale's representations of Egyptian landscapes are hard, angular, desiccated, mortified and seen with an abstracted gaze, while Flaubert was able to distance himself from some of the conventions of Orientalism and to see the inhabitants of Egypt as people rather than sub-humans, partly due to the greater freedom of action available to him as a man. Even so, his journey was influenced by many of the assumptions of colonialism in which Egypt was commodified. Flaubert constructed his Egypt in Europe before he left. Once he arrived, his idealized, exoticized view of the Orient did not disappear, but he was realist enough to see that his imaginative geographies were very vulnerable.

There had been a revival of interest in Egyptian art and architecture during the eighteenth century with the Enlightenment, but this increased dramatically after the Napoleonic expedition to Egypt and the publication of the *Description de l'Egypte*. Egyptian styles became popular in Britain and the USA for some kinds of public buildings and in the iconography of death, with obelisks and pyramid-shaped mausoleums decorating expanding urban cemeteries. The massiveness and horizontality of Egyptian building gave an air of solidity to bridges, railway stations and even the domestic buildings of some Scottish lighthouses.[41] The Egyptian revival peaked in England around 1830, but reached its climax in Scotland rather later, between 1830 and 1870, being characteristic of a number of churches designed by Alexander Thomson in the 1860s and 1870s.

Imperialism involved an expansion of European landscape conventions and ways of seeing landscape – and often elements of European landscapes themselves – into other parts of the world. Exotic environments like the Pacific islands were quickly assimilated into the conventions of European landscape aesthetics. Tahiti was presented by early European visitors as a Claudean-style paradise, New Zealand as a romantic wilderness complete with exotic banditti (Maoris). Early explorers saw the Pacific as a society living in a golden age of innocence, but the death of Captain Cook in 1779 was the Pacific's original sin for which the inhabitants needed to atone. Nineteenth-century views were polarized between those who saw the Pacific islands as a heavenly paradise and those who viewed them as a region ridden by disease, especially leprosy. Influential books included Herman Melville's *Typee* (1846), a semi-fictional account of his stay in the Marquesas, R. M. Ballantyne's *The Coral Island* (1858) and Harriet Martineau's *Dawn Island* (1838). The views of the British and French in the Pacific have been presented as highly polarized between utopian/empiricism and romance/realism. Yet influences also worked in the opposite direction. The landscapes of imperial homelands were diversified and enriched by the introduction of exotic plant species such as sequoias, Chile pines and rhododendrons, as well as building styles from colonial areas, such as bungalows. Images of imperial landscapes were transmitted through popular culture by a variety of media: art, newspapers, photography, prints, posters and postcards, school geography textbooks, illustrated periodicals, children's stories, even music hall and, later, film.[42]

Imperialist expansion produced a need for more accurate maps of wider and wider areas. Cartography was still strongly associated with the military tradition. In the early nineteenth century, Napoleon's conquering armies were accompanied by military geographers, *ingénieurs-géographes*, who undertook surveys of the lands conquered by victorious French armies. Apart from the maps that accompanied the *Description de l'Egypte*, they produced tens of thousands of maps of areas ranging from Spain to Russia and Greece.[43] The spread of large-scale standardized government surveys during the nineteenth century began to depict colonial as well as European landscapes in greater detail than ever before, imposing a sense of order and control on them. The development of such surveys fitted in with the increasing desire for accurate statistical information, in its original sense of information about the state, a trend also manifested in Britain by the start of the official census in 1801.

Major-General Roy had made proposals for an official survey of Britain in 1763, 1766 and 1783, but they were dismissed on grounds of cost and on account of the increased production of civilian county maps at a scale of one inch to one mile (1:63,360) By the time of Roy's death in 1790, London and Paris had been linked by triangulation and there was scope for using this method as the basis for further survey work in Britain. The success of Cassini's survey in France indicated that Britain was in danger of falling behind her traditional rival in the cartographic representation of landscape. In 1791, the Ordnance Survey was established, and surveying was gradually extended from the south-east, the area most vulnerable to French invasion, over the rest of the country. Its first maps, of Essex, were surveyed in the 1790s and issued in 1805.[44] At the start of the nineteenth century, privately surveyed county maps were still the cartographic norm in Britain. The increasing control of industrial societies over landscape was demonstrated by the development of national surveys, which mapped entire countries and their colonies at uniform scales. Over the course of the nineteenth century, the Ordnance Survey moved from mapping at scales of one inch to one mile to surveys at six, twenty-five and even sixty inches to one mile. Just as the Cassini survey had done in France, the new government surveys displayed new dimensions of national unity and centralized authority. In Britain the first six inch to one mile survey (1:10,560), of Ireland in the 1840s, was a deliberate exercise in control.[45] Even the ways in which the Ordnance Survey authorized landscape by the recording of place names reflected the authority exerted by a colonial power. In North America and elsewhere, native names and even native peoples were excluded from the mapped representations of new, colonial space. In Gaelic-speaking areas of Ireland and Scotland, the Ordnance Survey field officers chose local 'authorities', generally property owners and the professional middle classes, as reliable people to provide information on local place names. Gaelic-speakers were chosen from these groups to interpret and evaluate information provided by people of lower status. The level of accuracy in recording names in circumstances where only a small percentage of the population was literate, and orthography and spelling were variable, is questionable.[46] The work of the Ordnance Survey was extended in the mid-nineteenth century to include other aspects of landscape, such as geological survey, for economic rather than academic purposes. By the middle of the nineteenth century, the six-inch survey of Britain was well under way, and attention began to turn towards the more systematic and accurate mapping of the Empire, although relatively little was actually achieved at this time.

Across North America and Australasia, too, new place names were being coined as settlement expanded. Sometimes indigenous names were continued; more often new ones were created, and these soon settled into regular usage. In the Arctic, however, a phase of naming physical features occurred in an area in which the sparse Inuit population was hardly likely to use them.[47] Some of the names, like the cape named after Tennyson, proved to be short lived, because inaccurate charting prevented them from being securely located again.

The perceptions of European colonists, developed in rela-tion to European landscapes, often failed to match up with the environmental conditions in the landscapes they moved into, sometimes with disastrous results. In some cases, too much faith was placed in the ability of European technology to overcome environmental problems. French efforts in the 1870s and 1880s to create a huge new inland sea in the Sahara of Algeria and Tunisia, using canals to bring water from the Mediterranean, fall into this category. The aim was to create a sea of 6,700 square kilometres (2,587 sq miles) in area, between 20 and 30 m (65–98ft) deep, from a series of natural depressions. France, self-styled inheritor of the Classical tradition, would recreate the environmental conditions that the area had enjoyed when it had been the 'granary of Rome', reversing centuries of degradation by Arab and Turkish rulers. French engineering works would transform the landscape into sea, and this, in turn, would alter the climate. The sea would provide a new gateway to the interior of Africa and open up what were imagined to be rich mineral deposits. Perhaps fortunately, there were those who foresaw that the project would result merely in the creation of a huge salt marsh, and a cautious French government refused to provide the necessary funding for the work to go ahead.[48] Sometimes landscapes were misrepresented by organizations whose aim was to encourage settlement, such as the railway companies that tried to attract farmers to settle on the Great Plains. Early nineteenth-century explorers such as Meriwether Lewis and William Clark had less favourable perceptions of this region, and the name Great American Desert began to be used on maps. Such an image was hardly likely to encourage profitable colonization, though. Settlement promoters over-estimated rainfall and underestimated its variability, encouraging farmers to plough up the prairie sod in the mistaken belief that 'rain follows the plough'. It was unfortunate that the settlement of the Great Plains in the late nineteenth century coincided with a relatively moist period. In fact, periodic drought, massive loss of soil by windblow and the bankruptcy of farmers was a cyclical feature of this region that would be repeated into modern times.[49]

At a global scale, the most significant change in the late nineteenth and early twentieth centuries was the tremendous expansion of cultivable land at the expense of natural ecosystems. It has been estimated that, from 1860 to 1920, 432 million hectares (1,069 million a) of land worldwide was taken into cultivation.[50] Even in India, already well populated and exploited when the British arrived, colonial rule led to the large-scale conversion of grassland and forest to arable land, and instead of intensifying production on the existing acreage, the cultivated area was expanded. Colonial administrators were also prone to write off indigenous systems of cultivation and other forms of land management as inefficient and wasteful, rather than ecologically balanced. In central India, slash and burn agriculture and the grazing of cattle in the teak forests were seen as backward practices by administrators who wanted a sedentary, controlled peasantry. In humid tropical areas, slash-and-burn agriculture was suited to an environment in which the vegetation had a higher nutrient capital than the soil. In India, however, colonial officials saw the system as wasteful and destructive of the forests, a basically disorderly system. Shifting agriculture was made illegal and the forests were reserved as a state resource. New systems of agriculture had to be developed with permanent fields and ever-shorter periods of fallow, which led to declining yields and erosion.[51] In traditional Indian society, hunting, whether at the aristocratic or the subsistence level, had been carefully controlled. British attitudes, deriving from a country in which large predators had long been exterminated, were to try to eliminate wolves, wild dogs and big cats systematically in order to protect the local population. The removal of the predators disrupted local food chains and caused an upsurge in the population of herbivores such as deer, until they, too, began to be shot for sport on a large scale.

As had occurred in the Caribbean in the seventeenth and eighteenth centuries, plantation agriculture expanded rapidly in many parts of Asia in the nineteenth century, transforming the landscape. In India the crucial date was 1833, when the East India Company's new charter allowed foreigners to own rural land. Tea began to be cultivated in Assam and Sikkim from the 1830s. By 1900, there were 764 tea plantations in Assam, producing 66 million kg (145 million lb) of tea a year for export.[52] At the end of the nineteenth century, rubber provided an equally profitable crop in Ceylon, Singapore and especially Malaya.[53]

British hill stations in India came to symbolize the imperialists' view of the British Empire and their part in it. Around 80 were established, away from the worst of the heat and disease of the monsoon season. Some aspects of imperial rule still survive in stations like Simla, Darjeeling and Poona, such as European-speaking public schools and exclusive clubs. Such areas were originally relatively sparsely settled and could more easily be refashioned into a British-style landscape, with English garden landscapes, English flowers and trees, English churches, schools, parks and clubs. There was a physical separation between rulers and ruled based on altitude, with the governor occupying the

Imperial landscape: the former British hill-station of Simla, India.

most splendid mansion high on the slope and the natives living low down where the drainage was poor.[54] For the rest of the year, in the cantonments inhabited by colonial administrators and officers, gardens, often laid out in Capability Brown styles, acted as cultural icons. Lawns, roses, fruit trees and other reminders of England were tended by Indian servants but overseen by British memsahibs, with borders that were designed to keep the reality of the everyday life of the ordinary Indian population at a distance and, as far as possible, out of sight.[55]

In more temperate areas of North America, southern parts of South America, South Africa, Australia and New Zealand, more extensive efforts were made to recreate European landscapes. Here the introduction of familiar British species led to the alteration of much of the local flora and flora, a form of biological imperialism. In New Zealand in the later nineteenth century, the pace of landscape change was rapid as woodland was cleared for farms and pasture. Many settlers brought with them an almost obsessive Victorian interest in natural history, but also the confidence to initiate large-scale landscape change. They deliberately introduced new flora and fauna for aesthetic and recreational as well as economic reasons, while other species arrived accidentally, for example in earthen ballast. By the end of the nineteenth century, some 500 species of plants had been introduced and the New Zealand flora had been profoundly altered, not least by the introduction of European sheep and goats. Trout and deer were brought in for recreation, skylarks to provide familiar birdsong, gorse and broom for hedging fields.[56] The inevitable result of such large-scale, rapid environmental modification was soil erosion, which had become recognized as a major problem by the early twentieth century. Soil conservation in New Zealand was initially seen in terms of waging war on the environment, using hard engineering solutions rather than modifying land use, and putting the blame on nature rather than man for the problem.[57]

In Australia, areas such as South Australia and parts of New South Wales had been sold off in large estates, but from the 1860s, as more land was sold off in smaller units, the model of a rural squirearchy was replaced by that of the independent yeoman farmer, especially in newly settled areas like Queensland. The colonization of South Australia demonstrates the speed with which the landscape was transformed. The first settlement, near Adelaide, was in 1837. By 1845, there were more than 1,200 farmers and 10,572 ha (26,000 a) of cultivated land. By 1859, this had increased to more than 7,000 farmers and 146,097 ha (361,000 a). By 1866, more than 202,339 ha (500,000 a) were under wheat, and by 1872 the acreage had increased to 303,508 ha (750,000 a). Land was laid out for occupation on the basis of regular surveys, although the detailed pattern evolved over time, under the impact of changing social, economic, technical and political conditions. Areas were laid out in increasingly large lots, especially as settlement pushed into drier, more marginal areas. Large areas of woodland, scrub and eucalyptus savannah were cleared, and in the eastern part of the region some extensive drainage operations were undertaken in areas of poor drainage and swamp. Nevertheless, in the later nineteenth century, the monoculture of wheat, with insufficient fertilizers, and expansion into more and more drought-prone areas led to rapidly declining soil fertility and yields.[58]

A major miscalculation occurred in Australia in 1859, when a landowner in Victoria released two dozen wild rabbits from England for sport. In a country without serious predators or parasites their numbers increased rapidly. By 1880 they had severely damaged the vegetation on 809,356 ha (2 million a) of land in Victoria and were spreading into neighbouring states at a rate of 120 km (75 miles) a year, converting scrub woodland into poor grass and forcing livestock farmers to move their herds into more marginal areas, further increasing the ecological damage. The impact of drought in the 1890s, on top of this damage, added to the problem. It generated soil erosion on an unprecedented scale and led to the death of more than half the country's sheep.[59]

Nineteenth-century women travellers, though not recognized as 'geographers' by the geographical establishment, nevertheless made significant contributions to contemporary popular geographies, creating images of colonial landscapes for mass consumption. The complexities of their representation of landscape is highlighted in G. McEwan's study of the travel accounts of Victorian women in West Africa.[60] This area had been portrayed as an unspoilt wilderness, almost a paradise, in the early nineteenth century by anti-slavery supporters, but the failure to convert the inhabitants to Christianity, and the high mortality rate from disease among the Europeans who went there, produced a more negative 'Dark Continent', 'White Man's Grave' stereotype, a view that influenced most Victorian writers on the area. Such authors catered for a growing market among middle- and upper-class British women who were fascinated with the empire. Women travel writers described landscapes in different terms from contemporary male counterparts, in particular not using the sexual metaphors of penetration, conquest and domination that were a feature of the writings of many male authors. They saw themselves as observers rather than conquerors. Women travellers were more concerned to describe landscapes than to make scientific observations or political comments. Differences in the timing of their journeys, and in their backgrounds, influenced what each woman wrote. Their views often challenged the 'Dark Continent' image of West Africa. Writers such as Mary Kingsley (1862–1900) described the landscapes of this region in strongly romantic terms as wild and chaotic, in contrast to the ordered landscapes of Europe. Kingsley identified emotionally with the landscape through which she travelled. Other women adopted a more colonial gaze, with a greater attempt at scientific objectivity. They recognized order in the physical environments that they saw. In trying to convey impressions of landscapes to their readers, they often used European artistic and literary allusions and parallels.

Some landscapes resisted imperial conquest and, at the same time, captured the imagination of the public. Images of the Arctic had been fashioned from the later sixteenth century with the voyages of Tudor explorers in search of a North-West Passage, or an eastward route through the Barents Sea. Lack of British interest in the region in the eighteenth century meant that geographical textbooks were often very inadequate and frequently inaccurate. In the early nineteenth century, from 1818 to the 1840s, a series of British expeditions in search of the North-West Passage rekindled popular interest in the region and led to a wide range of representations of Arctic landscapes in the media, including paintings and engravings. Perceptions of Arctic landscapes were influenced by the fact that trained artists rarely sailed on expeditions there – as they had with Cook – so that representations, both of the landscape and its Inuit inhabitants, were often poor and misleading. Even photography came late to this region, because of the technical problems of using cameras and processing pictures in such cold conditions. In the mid-nineteenth century the disappearance of Sir John Franklin's expedition and then the evidence brought back by search parties generated a more sombre realization that Arctic landscapes were dangerous and inhospitable. Portrayals of the fate of the Franklin expedition,

Edwin Landseer, *Man Proposes, God Disposes*, 1864. Royal Holloway Collection, University of London.

especially Landseer's *Man Proposes, God Disposes* (1864), conveyed powerful images of a hostile, unforgiving environment. By the later nineteenth century, images of icebergs, ice-bound ships and dog sleds had become iconic and were being used in advertisements and cartoons.[61]

By the end of the century, however, British interest in the Arctic was fading and attention was turning to the Antarctic. When James Cook discovered South Georgia on his second voyage of exploration, he considered that claiming it for Britain was no more than a gesture: it did not seem possible that anyone would benefit from the discovery. The development of whaling in the Antarctic in the later nineteenth century, however, brought ships and even industry to the area. When Sir Ernest Shackleton (1874–1922) landed on South Georgia in 1916, at the end of his epic voyage to bring help to the stranded crew of the *Endurance*, the whaling settlement and factory there employed some 700 workers.[62] Antarctic exploration benefited from improvements in photography that had not been available to early generations of Arctic travellers. Images of the *Endurance*, beset by ice, her rigging festooned with frost, have become icons of the Antarctic.

CHANGING LANDSCAPE AND LANDSCAPE PERCEPTIONS IN NINETEENTH-CENTURY AMERICA

As the settlement of America continued during the nineteenth century, the differing impact of various cultural groups on the landscape became evident. A good example is the contrasts in the areas of the Ozarks settled by German-speakers and the 'Scotch-Irish', from Ulster. The Germans, coming directly from their homeland, were relatively well-funded and settled in substantial, regularly planned colonies on better-quality soils round the margins of the Ozarks near the Mississippi and Missouri rivers. Their settlements tended to be more nucleated, their farmsteads better built, their economy more arable-oriented than the Scotch-Irish. The Ulstermen mainly moved from other parts of the USA, such as Kentucky and Tennessee, rather than directly from their homeland. They were a less homogeneous group, with an economy geared more to pastoral farming, especially open-range herding. Poorer than the German settlers, they moved on to lower-quality land in more remote areas of the central Ozarks, settling in more scattered patterns. Their more ramshackle farmhouses rarely survived into modern times, while quite a number of the solid nineteenth-century German ones remain. Already geographically mobile, the Scotch-Irish tended to view land as a commodity to be exploited before moving on, rather than as a resource to be developed, as did the more sedentary Germans.[63]

The cultural differences between different groups of immigrants are reflected in the American landscape, especially in the character of traditional farm buildings, although patterns are complex in areas such as the Mid-West, where relatively few settlers moved directly from Europe to the frontier before the construction of the railways.[64] In many parts of the eastern USA, barn types are closely linked functionally to differences in agricultural systems, which sometimes have cultural as well as economic dimensions. So there are few barns in the cotton-producing areas of the South, because cotton, rice, peanuts and sugar cane did not require them. Early settlers in New France and New England built three-bay barns similar to those they had known in Europe, but they began to modify their designs as their farming systems became better adapted to the climate, with less emphasis on cereals and more on hay. In areas such as Wisconsin and upstate New York, which moved from cereals into dairying, raised barns were built with cowsheds on the ground floor and haylofts above, accessed by a ramp. In areas settled by Swiss farmers, such as south-east Pennsylvania, they introduced the idea of keeping animals and crops under the same roof, and the two-storey bank-barn design may have influenced the construction of outbuildings in other regions by different immigrant groups, being taken up by Scotch-Irish frontier settlers.[65]

European settlers had two basic views of the American wilderness: one was as a place of savagery and temptation that threatened to corrupt civilization, the other as a garden that would flourish with proper cultivation. Early settlers in the New World were not Americans but transplanted Europeans who saw the land as a spiritual and physical void that had to be conquered and civilized in the name of Christianity and progress. Early New England literature, art and folklore presented the wilderness as a place where reason was liable to succumb to passion and the Devil could seduce and corrupt. In the wilderness of Pennsylvania and Virginia the image was more of a garden to be tamed and cleared; nature was to be used, not feared.

A major obstacle to assimilating European ideas on landscape aesthetics to American conditions was that European landscapes in the early nineteenth century were defined substantially in terms of their rich associations with ruins, relics, myths and legends, features that America conspicuously lacked, a point often emphasized by contemporary European travellers in America. They suggested that America had plenty of wilderness but not much landscape. In America, early colonial settlers had been saddened, even appalled, by the lack of human history in the landscape, but they became accustomed to it, and after the Revolution the 'newness' of the landscape began to be seen more positively, rather than merely tolerated. The lack of historical remains came to be seen as a plus factor; Americans were in the process of shedding the links that bound them to their British origins. The magnificence of the natural landscape more than made up for the lack of historical associations. The worship of nature was a significant feature of the early decades of the Republic. The historical landscapes of Europe were diffuse and heterogeneous because of the complexity of their historical features. American landscapes, on the other hand, were unified, coherent and integrated. Americans looked to a more remote, natural past rather than to a more recent historical one. They dismissed history and invoked prehistory. The historical past of Europe was considered degenerate. The primitive nature of America was strong, savage, pure and free.[66]

In eastern America, European settlers created landscapes that eliminated native peoples in favour of large-scale agriculture and long-distance trade. It is here that white Americans now locate their heritage landscapes. There are nevertheless problems in trying to locate the origins of frontier landscapes in the eastern USA, in the presentation and representation of disputed pasts within modern landscapes, because the landscapes of the colonial eastern seaboard were geared to imperialism, slavery and environmental exploitation.

In the early nineteenth century, landscape perception in America was strongly influenced by European Picturesque and Romantic models. No longer was wilderness seen as the abode of the Devil and of savage Indians – it began to be appreciated as a precious and shrinking cultural asset.[67] The landscapes of Samuel Morse (1791–1872), who was working in New York state in the 1820s, are hard to distinguish from those of the Roman Campagna, while George Loring Brown (1814–1889) was known as 'Claude' Brown for his adherence to neo-Classical models of composition. Increasingly, though, Romantic ideas of sublimity in nature and freedom from a rigid tradition enabled American artists and writers to discover their own response to American landscapes. By the 1820s and '30s, ideas about romantic landscape had given the American wilderness a special significance as a place that demonstrated the great forces of nature and the hand of the Creator. American landscapes may have been criticized by Europeans for their lack of historical and legendary associations, but, in response, the newly-independent Americans could claim that their panoramas were not stained by the crimes of history. The American wilderness came to be seen as an experience not available elsewhere, with a moral force all of its own, spiritually pure, superior to decadent Europe.

As the nineteenth century went on, American writers and artists relied less on European models for their themes and images. At first American painters and writers favoured the wilderness landscapes of the Appalachians and the mountains of New England. As a symbol of Romantic landscape, the Catskill Mountains became the American equivalent of the Lake District.[68] Two interest groups developed. One was the Concordian, based in Concord, Massachussetts, which embraced writers such as Emerson, Hawthorne and Thoreau, who emphasized the qualities of a more tamed, civilized countryside, like the eighteenth-century English pastoral and Georgic models. By contrast, the Hudson River School stressed sublime wilderness landscape. From the later 1820s, the valley of the Hudson River became a focus of scenic appreciation and artistic inspiration, grander in scale, more impressive in topography than European rivers like the Thames, the Seine and even the Rhine.[69] Thomas Cole (1801–48) emigrated from England to the USA at the age of 17. In 1825 he made his first sketching trip up the Hudson Valley, developing a style that found favour with urban middle class patrons in New York and landowners in the surrounding area. On a trip to Europe between 1829 and 1832, he was unimpressed by English landscape artists such as Constable and Turner, but was captivated by Claude. Cole's painting *The Oxbow on the Connecticut River near Northampton* (1836; Metropolitan Museum of Art, New York), part Claude, part Salvator Rosa, illustrates the tension between wilderness and garden, savagery and civilization in the contemporary American landscape. He used European conventions of landscape painting to comment on the American environment; the savagery of the storm clouds over the wilderness, which is retreating from the advancing, cultivated landscape. Would the wilderness disappear due to civilization or would the two co-exist? Already the wilderness was disappearing among the eastern hills. In 1837 Cole was commissioned to paint a view of Catskill Creek, a largely wooded area with only a few pioneer settlements. In 1843 he painted the scene again, with a lot less woodland, more farmsteads, recently reclaimed fields with cattle and cut stumps, symbol of the settlers' attack on the wilderness. A railway runs prominently through the rapidly changing landscape.

With the increasing pace of industrialization in the mid-nineteenth century, Americans began to re-examine their relationships with the environment. The Hudson River School was signalled by George Innes's *The Lackawanna Valley* (1856), which married wilderness and civilization in the depiction of prosperous, pastoral rural communities. Authors such as Washington Irving and James Fenimore Cooper also turned to the still-wild woods of upstate New York for inspiration. Cooper's Leatherstocking Tales, beginning with *The Pioneers* (1823), celebrated the sublime character of the American landscape. While his hero criticized the 'wasty ways' of the settlers, he was clearly in favour of the process of civilization. More penetrating examinations of changing landscape emerged in the 1850s and '60s in the writings of Emerson and Thoreau in an

American Renaissance that was influenced partly by British Romanticism. Some artists of the Hudson River school, such as Asher Durand (1796–1886), continued to paint the Hudson. One of the most famous of his works, *Kindred Spirits* (1849; New York Public Library), depicts the artist Thomas Cole and the poet W. C. Bryant surveying a picturesque 'Hudsonian' landscape. Others, like Albert Bierstadt (1830–1902), went further west in search of landscape subjects. After the American Civil War the focus was firmly on the West. Nature was again seen as a suitable subject for American art and literature, but there was a new concern with change in the landscape: rather than seeing nature as an obstacle to the establishment of civilization, American authors and artists were beginning to see it as a source of the animating spirit behind the American character. Wild nature became a source of national pride, as a creator of character traits in the American national identity. The American wilderness was filled with the undiminished majesties of God. Artists such as Thomas Moran, Albert Bierstadt and Frederic Church (1842–1924) painted the uniqueness of the American wilderness for its own sake, their work being largely devoid of any contribution by indigenous inhabitants.

Settlers were surprised by the emptiness of the interior of the USA, by the violence of the landscape and the harsh extremes of climate. They expected monotony from the ocean, but not the land. Analogies with the sea often occur in accounts of early travellers in the West, especially the prairies, including writers such as Captain Marryat (1792–1848) and Charles Dickens (1812–70), as well as from later films like *The Big Country* (1958).[70] The Lousiana Purchase of 1803 added some 2,354,310 sq km (909,000 sq miles) of territory to the USA, doubling its area. Explorers were sent to report on the extent and character of this largely unknown territory. At first, the gap between perception and reality was so wide that the Rockies were not even seen as a barrier. Images of the West were rooted in optimism rather than fact, and information from known areas was transposed to unknown ones.[71] The predominant idea was of a fertile garden with a gentle climate. Immense plains were not seen as barren and semi-arid, but as lush, teeming with game, and suitable for the spread of agriculture. This view was replaced by more pessimistic assessments. M. J. Bowden has played down the idea that, throughout much of the nineteenth century, there was a widespread notion of a Great American Desert.[72] This, he suggests, is a recent academic construct that was not widely held at the time, and held sway for only a relatively short period. This image, however, was at its height around 1850–60, just at the time when the tide of settlement rolled up to the Great Plains and then leapfrogged over them to the west coast, leaving the plains thinly settled. Settlers from the East thought that a lack of trees indicated infertility. They were used to the availability of large amounts of cheap timber for building, fuel and fencing. False perceptions of the American West did not just belong to the pioneering age, though. The desert image of the Great Plains was reinforced by images of the dust bowl era of the 1930s. On the other hand, the wet prairies of Illinois, today some of richest corn and soya-bean land in the USA, were originally dismissed as malarial swamps. This kind of landscape distortion, once established, was plagiarized by others. The area was characterized as 'wet' regardless of reality, and erroneous landscape notions were more persuasive than real ones. It suffered from adverse stereotyping long after particular wet features had been drained.

Popular images of the American Mid-West focus on it as the cultural core of the nation. Its small towns with their Main Streets form a powerful symbolic landscape, with images of a sober, sensible, practical people, the home of the average or 'middle' American.[73] Even critics who labelled this image as materialistic and xenophobic never doubted its importance.[74] In fact, the term 'Middle West', with Kansas and Nebraska as its core, was first adopted as a regular label as recently as the 1880s, distinguishing it from the pioneer West and culturally different South-West. Soon after the start of the twentieth century, writers extended the area embraced by the label to include the states of the northern plains as well. The term was tied in with a pastoral, small-town ideal. So when industry and cities developed in Michigan, Indiana and Ohio, the perceived core region was shifted west, instead of altering the stereotype image to include major urban centres and manufacturing.

British travellers found the landscapes of the American Mid-West in the mid-nineteenth century both ugly and formal:

ugly in terms of the tree stumps, dead trees and litter-strewn yards, formal as a result of the straight roads and rectilinear field boundaries. It has been suggested that something of the rigidity yet impermanence of these landscapes was caused by the revivalist Christian beliefs of many of the settlers – who viewed life as transitory and had little interest in building large, permanent houses – allied to the mobility of at least some of them.[75] As the American frontier moved west, the spread of the railway network played an even more important role in landscape change than in Europe, creating new settlements and pushing forward the frontiers of improvement. This was shown dramatically in Frances Palmer's print of 1868, *Across the Continent – Westward the Course of Empire Takes its Way*, which shows the railway as the creator of settled, civilized landscapes, making the slow, meandering wagon train obsolete. The first trans-continental railway was completed in 1869.

The artist Albert Bierstadt accompanied Colonel Frederick West Lander's expedition of 1859 to survey an overland route to California and painted some striking views of the Rocky Mountains. Even more influential was the work of Thomas Moran. Born in 1837 in Bolton, Lancashire, his family emigrated to America when he was aged seven. He became one of America's greatest landscape artists. He was strongly influenced by Turner in his early years, and in 1861 travelled to Britain to study his works. Later he came to be known as the 'American Turner'. In 1871 he joined a government survey team exploring Yellowstone. In 1872 he produced one of his most famous paintings, *The Grand Canyon of the Yellowstone*, which now hangs in the Capitol, Washington, DC. In 1873 he joined Major John Wesley Powell's expedition to the Grand Canyon, producing another major canvas, *The Chasm of the Colorado*. His work was widely used by publishers and railway companies to promote tourism in the West. The Atchison, Topeka and Santa Fe railway, which for many years had the only direct route to the Grand Canyon, used his pictures in their brochures. Moran felt that American artists should paint their own country. His pictures were an important influence on the development of national parks in the United States, since they brought images of western landscape to an eastern public, and especially to influential politicians. More than any other artist, he made Americans aware of the West and its dramatic landscapes. Like Ruskin, he was a careful observer, studying the geology of areas such as Yellowstone and the Grand Canyon carefully. Yellowstone was created a national park in March 1872, with an area of 890,290 ha (2.2 million a), thanks in part to Moran's paintings. His *Grand Canyon of the Yellowstone*, which was purchased by Congress in 1872 for the unheard of price of $10,000, illustrates the complex relationship between Americans and their landscape at this period. On one hand the wilderness was seen as the true spring of American democracy, culture and national identity, while on the other it also provided an exploitable wealth of natural resources.

The most influential interpretation of the significance of land and landscape in North America was by Frederick Jackson Turner (1861–1932), who claimed in 1893 that the advancing American frontier was a source of democratic society, a blend of European Romanticism and American vernacular culture. He believed that contact between people and nature could be a positive, national character-forming experience. The challenge of the frontier was the prime medium of American society's transformation from a European to a new way of thinking. It was at the frontier, with its individualist, optimistic view of social and economic change, not the east coast, that a new American identity emerged. Turner claimed that the obstacles provided by the wilderness fostered American traits of independence, ingenuity, pragmatism, resourcefulness, democracy and equality. He wrote: 'the American character did not spring full-blown from the Mayflower ... it came out of the forests and gained new strength each time it touched a frontier.' His ideas were simply an extension of the European pastoral and are no longer accepted, but wilderness has nevertheless played a deep, fundamental role in reshaping American consciousness and has struck chords even in recent times, as demonstrated by the popularity of the American western film, and of the TV series *Star Trek*, boldly exploring space, the 'final frontier'. Not all Americans viewed frontier expansion in such positive terms, though. In 1864 George Perkins Marsh, himself brought up on the frontier, brought out the first edition of his book *Man and Nature*, in which he emphasized the darker side of environmental and landscape change associated with European expansion. Where some saw a noble design bringing order out of chaos, he saw something irreplaceable being lost.[76]

As settlement spread west, a wide range of environments was encountered, not all of them mountains or desert. There were extensive wetlands in some regions. The attack on these American wetlands was generally successful: extensive areas of wet prairie in Ohio, Idaho, Illinois and Iowa were converted into the American corn belt. In the marshes of central Wisconsin, however, economic development went through a series of short-lived phases: trapping, logging and wheat growing. Efforts to drain the marshes and convert them to arable land were only partially successful, and after the First World War much of the area was allowed to revert to marsh as farmers gave up. It came to be valued more for conservation and recreation than for agriculture.[77]

Perceptions of the West were influenced by frontier artists such as George Catlin (1796–1872), explorers' accounts, letters from emigrants, and tales from those who moved between the frontier and settled areas. In exploring the popular visions of landscapes of the North American interior, we find layers of environmental perceptions, many of them at variance with reality and in conflict with each other. The main period when myths about the American environment and its colonists were created was the mid- to late nineteenth century, when the entire body of traditions was either invented or refashioned. The romantic image of the cowboy was one element of this. The heyday of the cowboy lasted only from the end of Civil War to the severe winter of 1886.[78] Much of the invented tradition of the cowboy came from American interpretations of European Romantic tradition, with roots in paintings and literature associated with the fur trade in Rockies in the early nineteenth century, the era of the Mountain Men. Much of the socio-cultural baggage of the Wild West originated in the East, while the material culture of the cowboy was borrowed from Mexico. Tombstone, Arizona, of Wyatt Earp fame, later a ghost town, is now a national historic site. The location of the gunfight at the OK Corral in

1881, portrayed in so many films, is commemorated as much as a fantasy as reality.

The American West as a historical and geographical entity spanned the nineteenth century and the age of modernism, something that the makers of such films as *The Wild Bunch* (1969), *The Shootist* (1976) and *Butch Cassidy and the Sundance Kid* (1969) have emphasized. Wyatt Earp himself lived out a peaceful old age, dying in 1929. In his later years he acted as an advisor to film companies making westerns, helping in the process to create his own legend. He takes us into the twentieth century and the tremendous, complex landscape changes of recent times, which will be examined in the next chapter.

FIVE

Modern and Post-Modern Landscapes

LANDSCAPE CHANGE IN THE TWENTIETH CENTURY: AN OVERVIEW

As we have seen, change has been a feature of landscapes in Europe, and areas settled by Europeans, from the sixteenth century onwards. At certain times and in particular areas, changes have been both rapid and extensive. The pace of landscape change almost everywhere accelerated dramatically in the twentieth century, however, under a wide range of influences. These included unprecedented technological developments that had the power to create new landscapes and also the ability to destroy existing ones, evidenced first on the Western Front during the Great War and, even more menacingly, at the end of the Second World War, with the advent of atomic weapons.

In the twentieth century, landscape change became a truly global process and a global concern. Change has been dramatic not only in the developed world but also in developing countries. For example, in India since independence, a series of five-year plans designed to modernize the country has resulted in the construction of huge dams, power stations and factories, which have transformed the landscape of many areas and have displaced at least 5 million people. By the mid-1970s, almost all India's major rivers had been dammed to provide water for drinking, irrigation and power generation. In the Narmada region alone, two super-dams, 30 other major dams and some 3,000 smaller-scale projects were undertaken for a population of around 20 million. The Sardar Sadovar dam, one of the super-projects, will submerge 37,000 ha (92,500 a) of land in three states with 75,000 km (46,603 miles) of canals and irrigation channels, displacing in the process some 152,000 people in 245 villages. Changes in agricul-

A major Indian dam and irrigation project under construction.

ture, such as the flooding of paddy fields in Orissa, Tamil Nadu and Andhra Pradesh for large-scale commercial prawn culture, have been as dramatic. Even the growing tourist industry has altered the landscape in states such as Goa. In the Himalayas, excessive logging has caused drastic ecological changes and severe erosion, which in turn has increased the speed of runoff and added to the risk of flooding in the lower courses of major rivers.[1]

Between 1920 and 1978 globally another 419 million ha (1,035 million acres) of fresh arable land was taken into cultivation.[2] By the early twentieth century, good-quality agricultural land was getting scarce even in the New World, and there was pressure to open up new land for agriculture in less favourable areas with greater environmental limitations than would have been acceptable before. Isaiah Bowman produced a map of potential areas for settlement in 1937 that included the southern steppes, parts of Canada, parts of northern and western Australia, and in South America a belt of country to the south and west of the Amazon rain forests. Such environments were more difficult and posed greater challenges than the classic pioneering frontiers of the eighteenth and nineteenth centuries, needing more government support and greater factual knowledge of environmental conditions. In New South Wales and South Australia, legislation reallocated land from pasture to wheat cultivation. The need to reward soldiers returning from the First World War with land was an incentive, but in many cases they did not receive enough land or sufficient support to survive.

Our ability to monitor changes on this scale has improved dramatically through remotely sensed satellite imagery. The clearance of tropical rain forests emphasizes both the scale of change and the degree of concern. The destruction of tropical forests has accelerated significantly since the start of the twentieth century and especially since 1945. The greatest relative losses have been in Central America (*c.* 66 per cent), Central Africa (*c.* 52 per cent), South-East Asia (*c.* 38 per cent) and Latin America (*c.* 37 per cent), an estimated global loss per year of about 100,000 sq km (38,610 sq miles), with an area of comparable size seriously damaged and partly cleared each year.[3] In Ethiopia, 40 per cent of the country was forested in 1900; by 1990 the figure was only 3 per cent.[4] The problem is of global significance, and the reasons for the landscape changes – the commercial logging of tropical hardwoods, plantation cash-cropping and, in Latin America, large-scale cattle ranching – are also global in character.

Landscape has become widely affected by the indirect as well as the direct impacts of human activity: global warming in the first half of the twentieth century (possibly a climatic response to increasing pollution associated with widespread nineteenth-century industrialization), and especially since the 1980s, has produced widespread changes such as the worldwide retreat of glaciers, a thinning of the Arctic sea ice, and the spread of vegetation in the Antarctic Peninsula. In the Alps, the skiing industry, which has already had a considerable landscape impact, is threatened if the warming trend continues. The year 2000 was the warmest in Austria since 1768. Over the past century, average annual temperatures in the Alps have risen by 2 °C. Since 1850, more than half the mass of Alpine glaciers has melted and at least 100 glaciers have disappeared entirely. Major avalanches are becoming more frequent and more unpredictable, their danger increased by the construction of housing and ski facilities in avalanche-prone locations. More variable weather conditions have also increased the incidence and severity of destructive flash floods and mudslides. Air pollution causing acid rain has led to widespread forest dieback in central Europe and Scandinavia.

Media coverage of landscape and environmental issues has increased markedly in recent years, so that people are much more aware of worldwide as well as local trends and of their present and future implications. Even so, some landscape changes have been less obvious and less well publicized. For example, with the growing commercialization of agriculture in many countries, and continuing depopulation and abandonment of cultivation in marginal areas, there has been an increase in the extent of forests. In the USA for instance, between 1910 and 1979, 24,500,00 ha (60,500,000 a) were added to the forest area with the abandonment of cultivation, first in the interior of New England, then further south. The area of US forests – c. 333–344 million ha (822–850 million a) in 1492 – had been reduced to about 190 million ha (470 million a) by 1920, but by 1977 had risen again to 195 million ha (483 million a) and is still increasing.[5] As early as 1840, farmland was being abandoned in New England and was reverting to forest. After 1880, the process spread to the Mid-Atlantic states, and in the early twentieth century to the Southern states, as old cotton and tobacco fields were left to revert to pine forest. Similar trends on a smaller scale have occurred in many parts of Europe.

Rapid population growth has increased pressures on resources and quickened the rate of landscape change. Equally, social and economic change, urbanization, rural depopulation, rises in living standards, increased mobility and improved education have affected not only landscapes but also how we relate to them. Such forces have engendered increasing concern about the pace and nature of landscape modification. This in turn has led to growing interest in how existing, valued landscapes – and individual features within them – have developed in the past, along with a desire to protect them from changes that are seen as undesirable. Public awareness of landscape change is unprecedented today: at a global scale, for instance, in relation to trends such as the reduction of tropical rainforests; at a national scale with the possible impacts of rising sea levels; and at a local scale with concern for the impact of the spread of modern housing estates, or the construction of new by-passes.

The post-Second World War mechanization and commercialization of agriculture, which transformed farming into 'agribusiness', have produced some of the most marked changes in the rural landscapes of western Europe. In France, *remembre-*

ment, the consolidation of land formerly held in scattered blocks and parcels, has transformed many rural areas, particularly in the western *bocage* country, where massive field boundaries, or talus, and the hedges on top of them, have been removed on such a large scale that soil erosion has become a serious problem in some districts. In southern and eastern lowland England, as Marion Shoard has shown, the loss of hedgerows, ancient woodlands, wetlands, ponds and natural hay meadows has been dramatic.[6] In addition, the pressures on lowland British landscapes resulting from suburban expansion, not just housing but business parks, industrial estates, out-of-town shopping and leisure developments, as well as expanding road networks, have also wrought major changes. Present policies for the expansion of the housing stock in south-east England over the next 30 years seem likely to transform large parts of the region into near-continuous suburbs.

Upland areas of Britain have not been immune to landscape change, although the pace of transformation has been slower than in the lowlands. From the later nineteenth century, the need for large quantities of drinking water led to the construction of reservoirs in most upland areas adjoining major conurbations. Other reservoirs were constructed to regulate streamflow and allow the abstraction of water for industrial uses. While the names of the builders of canals, railways and bridges are familiar, the Victorian water engineers have been forgotten, although their achievements were sometimes as great. Although some objections were made in the later nineteenth century against Manchester Corporation's proposals to raise the level of Thirlmere in the Lake District, the damming of the Elan valley to provide water for Birmingham, the creation of Lake Fyrnwy to supply Liverpool, and the tapping of Loch Katrine to meet Glasgow's needs, there was little real opposition to these large-scale Victorian engineering projects, which were often designed in dramatic rather than unobtrusive styles. The Thirlmere scheme required the construction of a pipeline 160 km (100 miles) long, gravity-fed all the way. Farms, and sometimes larger communities, were submerged in the process. Growing nationalist feelings in Wales led to more effective protests against further reservoir construction and, since World War Two, the building of large hydro-electric power schemes.[7] Post-war reservoir construction has been more contentious and contested. Environmentalists lost the fight over the construction of the Cow Green reservoir in upper Teesdale in 1967, which drowned a significant proportion of the area's rare arctic/alpine flora.[8] With the decline of heavy industry, the need to expand water supply facilities has been reduced. There has been a greater emphasis on recreation at new reservoirs such as Kielder in Northumberland, created to supply water to a steelworks that was never built. Other recently constructed reservoirs, such as Rutland Water, have been more low key and understated in the design of their dams and infrastructure.[9]

Lowland areas have gained a number of wetland sites, valued for recreation and wildlife, from the flooding of abandoned gravel workings, while in former coal-mining areas lakes created by mining subsidence have been used in the same way. In the twentieth century, the development of schemes to generate hydro-electric power have had a greater impact in some areas than those for providing drinking water. The aluminium works at Kinlochleven in the Scottish Highlands, opened in 1909, involved the creation of the 10 km (6 mile) long Blackwater Reservoir. From 1943, the North of Scotland Hydro Electricity Board constructed 53 dams and power stations, transforming river systems in many parts of the Highlands.[10]

Upland afforestation with non-native conifers had its origins in the late eighteenth and early nineteenth centuries, when landowners such as the Duke of Atholl planted them extensively on their estates.[11] Manchester Corporation established conifer plantations around Thirlmere to control runoff in the catchment and reduce silting. The First World War, however, highlighted the lack of a strategic timber reserve in one of the least wooded countries in Europe. In 1919, the Forestry Commission was established and began to buy up and plant extensive areas with a limited range of alien conifer species. Concern over afforestation took on strongly nationalistic tones, as with the historian G. M. Trevelyan's objections to the Forestry Commission's attempt to blanket the Lake District fells with 'German pine forest'.[12] Forestry Commission policies, especially their preference for the establishment of plantations on previously unforested land, the choice of quick-maturing conifers, and their planting in regularly spaced rows for efficient management and felling, emphasized the differences between new forests and traditional woodland. The visual impact of serried ranks of dark-green trees in huge geometric blocks, as well as concern over the interruption of access to the fells for walkers, led in 1936 to an agreement between the Forestry Commission and the Council for the Preservation of Rural England under which no further large-scale planting was undertaken in the central mountain core of the Lake District. This understanding, which still holds good, was an important early example of integrated upland planning.

Elsewhere, however, as in central Wales, the Scottish Borders and Galloway, the area under conifers was extended massively after the Second World War, totally transforming the appearance of the countryside. The impact of afforestation can be appreciated when it is realized that in Scotland, during the mid-eighteenth century, only about 4 per cent of the land was wooded; today the figure is around 20 per cent. In fact, the visual effect is even greater, since much semi-natural woodland has been replaced by plantation forestry.[13] There has been serious concern about the effect of conifer plantations on runoff and erosion, acidification of streams and lakes, the survival of moorland bird species, and the loss of heather moorland. The impact of mainly private forestry developments in the peat bogs of the Flow Country in Caithness, through extensive drainage that affected areas that were not even planted, led to belated protection measures, including designation of Sites of Special Scientific Interest (SSSIs), for a rare habitat.[14] Current trends favour the extension of woodlands in lowland areas. In 1991, some 518 sq km (200 sq miles) of the English Midlands were designated as a National Forest, provoking less negative public reaction than many upland plantation schemes. Similar schemes have also been launched in other lowland areas.[15] Schemes for extending Scottish native pine forests in the Cairngorms and for recreating the original mixed-deciduous wildwood in the Carrifan valley near Moffat in the Scottish Borders have also been received enthusiastically.

Reafforestation has been a feature of other parts of Europe in the wake of large-scale felling during the First World War, notably in Spain, where reduction of soil erosion was a further concern.[16] Ireland, one of the least wooded countries in Europe, now has 7 per cent of its area covered with forest, less than one per cent of it broad-leaved and much of it planted since the 1960s by the state, with private landowners becoming involved only quite recently.[17]

Distinctive habitats, such as heather moorland, have been reduced in the British uplands as the result of grazing pressures caused by higher stocking levels on hill pastures, but the continuing popularity of grouse shooting, a major source of income on many upland estates, has helped to maintain it. Meanwhile, the continuing unprofitability of hill farming has led to the amalgamation of holdings, a drop in the non-family labour force, lack of capital for investment and the deterioration of the landscape of stone walls and field barns in areas such as the Yorkshire Dales. Sheet erosion, affecting entire fellsides, has been identified as a problem in recent years, although there is disagreement as to whether the cause lies with overstocking of sheep or other environmental changes. It has sometimes been assumed that Scotland has been under less pressure than England and has experienced less landscape change, but even here the length of hedgerows has been reduced by half since the 1940s; the area of woodland (mainly conifers) has risen from 5 per cent to 14 per cent of the country; heather moorland has been substantially reduced and the area covered by bracken doubled. The impact of the outbreak of foot-and-mouth disease in 2001 on livestock farming in areas such as Cumbria and Yorkshire may well be to reduce stocking densities substantially and to encourage a return to a less open, more scrubby landscape.

Depopulation has continued in many poorer, more peripheral rural areas of Europe with an exodus of young people to the towns, to such an extent in areas such as the Cevennes in southern France that entire communities have declined and disappeared. Counter-urbanization, the increase of tourism and the development of niche markets for specialist food and craft products have begun to reverse decline in some districts.[18] The abandonment of rural landscapes has been most notable in parts of the Mediterranean, or on islands such as Madeira and Tenerife. Depopulation since the nineteenth century, caused by emigration or, more recently, employment opportunities in coastal tourist resorts, has led to the widespread abandonment of terraced agriculture, often on steep hillsides that were only colonized because of population pressures in the eighteenth and early nineteenth centuries. Such abandoned fields are rapidly colonized by scrub woodland.

While the broad-brush picture is well known, detailed quantitative studies of landscape change have been remarkably few. In Britain since the late 1940s, sets of aerial photographs have been an important source of information, supplemented by statistical, photographic and cartographic data, and the increasing sophistication of geographical information systems (GIS) makes possible the three-dimensional modelling of landscape change. Such studies, providing information on rates of landscape change, are time consuming and often relate only to very small areas. At the opposite extreme, continental-scale studies of regional landscape diversity, based on variations in land cover detected by satellite imagery, are still at an early stage of development as policy-making tools.

As landscapes change, there is, paradoxically, a tendency for them to become more alike. Globalization is most obvious in an urban context, where the logos of multinational firms like McDonald's 'golden arches' are found worldwide, but it is also evident in the countryside, for instance in the landscape of motorways and their increasingly uniform associated infrastructure of service stations and motels.

LANDSCAPE, IDENTITY AND NATIONALISM

Nationalism has been seen as the result of bourgeois liberation in the mid- and late nineteenth century, or as the result of processes operating in the eighteenth century, although it undoubtedly received a major impetus from the French Revolution.[19] Landscape could become a framework through which ideologies and discourses of nationalism were constructed and contested through the manipulation of depictions of landscape, or the sacred symbols of nationalism embedded in landscape.[20] Images of national landscapes may seem ancient and timeless, but in Europe they are usually creations of the nineteenth century. Nationalism and its links with landscape is a relatively recent historical phenomenon. National identities are closely linked with, and often defined by, landscapes and the legends associated with them.[21] As Geoffrey Cubitt has remarked, when we wish to describe or explain difference, we think of it in terms of nations: this applies to landscape as much as anything.[22] To imagine a nation involves differentiating it from others, and landscape provides one of the best shorthand ways of doing this, something that is constantly emphasized in tourist brochures and advertisements.

Landscape helps to focus loyalties and affections, and through the development of the ideas of typicality a particular landscape can come to symbolize national identity. Nationalistic images of landscape are characteristically drawn from only limited areas of national territories.[23] The other side of this coin is that landscapes that do not symbolize nationhood may be marginalized and ignored. National landscapes can also be evoked through music, notably in the great burst of nationalistic compositions of the later Romantic period, perhaps most notably by Sibelius in tone poems like *Tapiola*, a magnificent evocation of the atmosphere of the Finnish forests, but also by composers such as Dvořák, Kodaly, Janáček, Smetana, Elgar and Vaughan Williams, many of them tapping into rich veins of traditional folk music.[24]

The rise of nationalism from the nineteenth century has led to the identification of particular landscapes with national images. National identity is closely tied to landscape; the poetic tradition of 'la douce France' is a geographical as much as a historical concept, a well-ordered place where rivers, fields, orchards, vineyards and woods are in harmonious balance. Sometimes these images were ancient, enduring ones, deep-seated in cultural consciousness extending through the centuries, with a surprising power to shape the institutions we still live by.[25] Landscape may be linked to nationalism through mythology, as with sites such as Glastonbury and Tintagel, which are associated with the Arthurian legend.

Sometimes the origins of such landscape images are quite recent. In England, national identity has become strongly associ-

Heritage and legend: Glastonbury Tor, Somerset.

ated with the intensive arable countryside of the south-east, itself in many areas a relatively late creation following Parliamentary enclosure in the eighteenth and early nineteenth centuries. Despite this, such landscapes are widely seen as emphasizing the continuity of English history. The identification of Englishness with an idealized southern landscape, while very significant throughout the twentieth century, is not the only extant English landscape metaphor, though. An east–west divide also exists alongside the north–south one, separating mystic and spiritual Celtic traditions from more down-to-earth Anglo-Saxon ones.[26] J. R. Short has emphasized that in English there are two meanings of the word 'country', which results in images of nation and countryside being merged. Images of the idealized English countryside are of enclosed fields, churches and villages, but also country houses and their parks.[27] Large landowners may have lost some of their power but not their symbolism.

In Britain, a continuing and growing nostalgia for the countryside has been a powerful influence on how people view the landscape, producing the paradox that one of the most urbanized countries in the world, the cradle of the Industrial Revolution, now visualizes its national identity primarily in rural terms. In England, the conservation of 'unspoilt' landscape is widely supported, but such landscapes are seldom the creation of a single, distinct historical era, even landscape parks. Countryside of 'early enclosure' is especially favoured: landscapes of small, irregular hedged fields. Stephen Daniels has suggested that this image of England became increasingly popular from the 1880s, as Britain began to lose her industrial supremacy to Germany and the United States, with the north of England no longer being portrayed as 'the workshop of the world' and the Industrial Revolution starting to be seen as merely a short-term aberration.[28] This was encouraged in the early decades of the twentieth century by a wave of evocative topographic writing about the English countryside and its society by writers such as H. V. Morton. This nostalgia was also captured in such autobiographies as Flora Thompson's *Lark Rise to Candleford* (1945) and Laurie Lee's *Cider with Rosie* (1959), and in fiction from Evelyn Waugh's *Brideshead Revisited* (1945) to the novels of James Herriot. It was also lampooned in Stella Gibbons's *Cold Comfort Farm* (1932). Children's stories have also emphasized this nostalgic rural landscape from Beatrix Potter's tales through Kenneth Graham's *The Wind in the Willows* (1908) to A. A. Milne's *Winnie the Pooh* stories (1926). Arthur Ransome's *Swallows and Amazons* (1930) presented the Lake District as an idealized adventure playground for middle-class children.

In the late nineteenth and early twentieth century, poets and writers such as Hilaire Belloc, Thomas Hardy and Rudyard Kipling strongly reinforced the centrality of the landscape of areas like the Weald, the Sussex Downs or Wessex to English identity. Literary associations can help to protect certain types of landscape. A plan, aimed at rescuing the area known as Egdon Heath in Thomas Hardy's *The Return of the Native* (1878), has recently been launched as part of a programme aimed at conserving nearly 10,117 ha (25,000 a) of lowland heath. The landscapes of the south-east have also been especially cherished because of their proximity to London, and also for their nearness to potential invasion from Napoleon and then Hitler, the White Cliffs of Dover having become one of the most familiar landscape icons of Englishness. The music of Elgar and Vaughan Williams, together with a revival of interest in English folksong and an architectural turn towards vernacular styles, also influenced views of landscape in the late nineteenth and early twentieth centuries, as did magazines such as *Country Life*, launched in 1897.[29] These portrayals of English landscape and society are set in a period loosely from the early twentieth century to the 1950s, close enough to modern times to be readily understandable but predating the massive landscape and social changes of the post-Second World War period. More recently, television and film adaptations of such books have had a further powerful nostalgic impact, as have modern coffee-table books on the English landscape or specific elements of it, such as churches, country houses and villages. The values of rural society as a whole have become identified with the very different values of the dominant, privileged world of the country house, now often redefined as 'our' rather than 'their' heritage.

This idealized British landscape has a broad mythical structure with London at its centre. Beyond it lies the 'English' heartland, a 'mythological' English landscape drawn from a limited area of the south-east, stretching from 'Constable Country' through 'Shakespeare Country' to the Cotswolds. Beyond this zone lie the upland landscapes of the north and west, where most national parks are located.[30] Within this peripheral zone there are tremendous contrasts in landscape imagery between areas such as Devon, Cornwall and the Lake District, the scenery of which has made them places of periodic refuge for people from the south-east, and the industrial areas of the north of England and south Wales, descriptions of which are still often strongly negative, despite the landscaping of derelict areas and abandoned industrial sites, or their transformation into heritage centres.

The 'English village', with picturesque thatched cottages of timber-frame or Cotswold-stone construction, facing a parish church across a green or marketplace, has come to epitomize the landscape image of England, being widely seen as the true heart of England, still enshrined in the Ambridge of the radio programme *The Archers*. A limited number of such villages is regularly used as a backdrop for costume dramas that range from adaptations of the novels of Jane Austen to the crime puzzles of Agatha Christie. The same idealized settings are portrayed on calendars, postcards, chocolate boxes and in magazine travel articles. Despite conservation orders, the number of villages that preserve this 'timeless' atmosphere is fairly small. Because of the pace of recent landscape change, such places can also be hard to find elsewhere in Europe. Producers of a recent British television series, *Monsignor Reynard*, depicting France in 1940 under German occupation, had considerable difficulty in finding a village or small town that was sufficiently unchanged over the last 50 years not to spoil the 'period atmosphere'.

As with the American frontier (Chapter 4), particular perceptions of landscapes can persist despite mounting evidence of their inaccuracy and redundancy. The English countryside is still visualized by urban dwellers as being rich with wildlife, birdsong and flowers, long after modern farming has left much of it sterile and lifeless. The English village acts as a symbol of qualities of life such as continuity, stability and sense of community, which, if they ever existed, are long gone, yet are still craved by a rootless urban society. The myth of the idyllic village and its community is illusory but influential, a symbol of durability. Today the 'typical' English village is a settlement divided by tensions, with a declining rural working class at odds with affluent, influential middle-class incomers set within an ecologically and visually damaged landscape.[31]

The landscape imagery of England has also been strongly influenced by nineteenth-century landscape art, notably that of John Constable. His *Haywain* (1821) is such a visual cliché today that it is sometimes a surprise to realize how recent is the development of such images into icons for English landscape and nationality. Appreciation of Constable's work and its identification as representing a quintessentially English landscape did not gather momentum until half a century after the artist's death in 1837. In the 1850s and '60s, even enthusiasts of his work were often vague about the location of his subjects. By the 1890s, however, tours of 'Constable Country' were being organized by Thomas Cook. Reproductions of the *Haywain* were used during the First World War to symbolize what the troops in the trenches were supposedly fighting for.[32] From about the same time came the realization that 'Constable Country' was vulnerable to change, especially to rural decline and decay, although it was not until the 1940s that the National Trust acquired the key

John Constable, *The Haywain*, 1821, National Gallery, London.

buildings depicted in Constable's most famous paintings. The 'Constable Country' of the Stour Valley is now designated as an Area of Outstanding Natural Beauty.

Images of this idealized English landscape have frequently been used in advertising, particularly of food products marketed as good or wholesome, but also in classic railway advertisements, the artwork of Ordnance Survey map covers, and in recruiting posters during the First World War.[33] These sometimes incongruously placed kilted Scottish soldiers in the foreground of southern English landscapes, which would probably have been as alien to many of them as those of rural France.

Landscape images of Scotland, Wales and Ireland are equally artificial. Views of Glencoe, carefully composed to omit traffic on the modern road, or Buachaille Etive Mor with Black Rock Cottage in the foreground, continue the nineteenth-century trend towards the 'Celtification' of Scottish landscape images and Scottish culture. Irish images of remote cottages amid the rugged scenery of western areas such as the Aran Islands, the Burren and Connemara are similar in character. Scotland's long struggle for independence, however, and her eventual forced acceptance of Union with England, have tinged

The heartland of Irish national identity: the rugged west coast of the Aran Islands.

Scottish landscape imagery with a sense of things lost, most palpably in the nostalgia and romance of sites associated with the Jacobite rebellions, such as Glenfinnan and Culloden.[34]

In early twentieth-century Wales, the growing movement for a distinctively Welsh education, closely bound up with national identity, was expressed in schools through the appreciation of scenery, as well as Welsh language, culture and folklore.[35] In the case of Wales, travel writers, from Thomas Pennant in the later eighteenth century, had presented the country as a place of difference, with its own culture, history and legends woven into the landscape. Twentieth-century texts, such as H. V. Morton's *In Search of Wales* (1932), continued this tradition, while images of Celtic Wales and its landscapes were reinforced by contemporary academic writing by archaeologists such as Sir Cyril Fox and geographers like H. J. Fleure. Morton's book, aimed at the visitor touring by car, was the first travel book to tackle the landscape, and problems, of the South Wales coalfield.[36]

Irish landscape identity, like that of Scotland, has tended to focus on past glories and lost causes. Ideas of Irish national landscape were shaped quite consciously in the later nineteenth century, in the context of the growing nationalist political movement for Home Rule and later for independence, in which Britain was viewed as 'the oppressor'. The focus for Irish identity was seen to be in the 'unspoilt' landscapes of the West, where the Gaelic language survived and Anglicizing, modernizing influences on the countryside were least apparent. The imagery was of an ancient, rural cultural heartland, where Neolithic megalithic tombs, Iron Age forts and Celtic monastic sites emphasized continuity with a remote, independent past before the era of Anglo-Norman conquest.[37]

Conscious attempts to create an Italian national landscape failed, partly because of a lack of a dominant heroic context like the American frontier on which to focus. The late unification of Italy, the heterogeneity of the Italian physical environment and the cultural diversity of the population were major barriers. In France, by contrast, the multiplicity of *pays* focused identity with landscape at a more local level. In Germany, the image of regular villages, surrounded by fields, in turn closely hemmed in by forest, is again an idealized representation that applies only to certain parts of the state.[38] In the later nineteenth and early twentieth centuries, by the time that the German forest was being identified as a crucial element in the quintessential German landscape, it was under heavy attack from the axe. It was widely believed that many of the most obvious differences between the German and English national character were due to the fact that Germany, unlike England, still possessed large areas of forest. In the 1930s, a nature-based nationalism flourished that linked German culture to a forest heritage. As a result, Nazi Germany led Europe in progressive forestry. Allied to this was an Aryan style of art focusing on landscape and rural, peasant scenes, while the work of German Romantic artists such as Caspar David Friedrich enjoyed a revival.[39]

The adoption of landscape for patriotic purposes and the cultivation of a special relationship between landscape and nationhood was especially pronounced in the USA.[40] In the USA and Canada, there has been less of an identification with images of settled, farmed countryside as a landscape ideal, possibly in part because such countryside does not have the same time-depth as European cultural landscapes, and also due to the monotonous grid pattern of boundaries, roads and settlements over huge areas. Such landscapes tend to symbolize agricultural progress rather than aesthetic amenity. In America, the landscape focus is on wilderness instead, with its chalets, cabins and summer camps, its hunting, fishing, canoeing, camping and backpacking, pastimes that grew into mass activities from the 1920s with the spread of car ownership.

LANDSCAPES OF POLITICAL IDEOLOGY

If politics find expression in the landscape, then this should be most striking under authoritarian and totalitarian regimes. This can be seen clearly in the relationships between landscape and politics in Nazi Germany. Cultural influences originating in the landscape affected Nazi policy-making, while Nazi theoreticians had ideas about how landscape should be manipulated in accordance with their doctrines. The forest landscapes of central Europe inspired a mythology, which was developed and exploited by the Nazis, that went back to the Roman author Tacitus, who claimed that the isolated forest habitat made the Germans the least mixed, most racially pure of European peoples. This encouraged the Nazi idea of a biologically pure Aryan race. After the Nazis came to power in 1933, forest themes invaded German art and politics, with the somewhat ludicrous image of Hermann Goering as Reichsforstmeister.[41] The Nazis imagined a strange relationship between nation, landscape and nature. Germans were believed to have special abilities to commune with nature, and unique talents for landscape design, although the German idea that each race was associated with a particular landscape preceded the Nazis. In the east European territories annexed by Germany, landscape was to be given a more Germanic character to make German settlers feel at home, and to help them love and defend the new territory. The myth that only Germans had a mystical sensitivity and kinship with Nature, and could exercise a responsible custodianship of the environment, led to the displacement of untermenschen in eastern Europe. Other nations were considered to lack the Germans' intimate association with nature, having no sensitivity to landscape. This made them unfit to hold land and liable to be ejected from it. The aim of National Socialist landscape design was to emphasize specific characteristics as living spaces for Germans.[42]

The autobahns built in Germany during the 1930s have been seen either as embodiments of the ideology of fascism, or as a modernist project with technology triumphing over the landscape. Neither view explains their unprecedented sensitivity to landscape aesthetics, the way they blended and flowed into the countryside. The origins of autobahns reflected a complex interplay between Nazi politics, modern technology and environmental awareness. The first one was opened in 1933; by 1939, 3,700 km (2,300 miles) had been built. The idea did not originate with Hitler, but developed before he came to power. They were certainly not originally designed to provide mobility for the Nazi war machine, as has sometimes been thought, but developed as a result of motoring, industrial and municipal interests. The autobahn network symbolized the binding together of the state, creating employment and heralding the rise of a car-owning society. Alwin Seifert (1890–1972), their designer, was an architect and landscape gardener from Munich. In 1934 he began to assemble a team of landscape architects who influenced the choice of routes and supervised the rehabilitation and planting of the landscape after construction. The landscaping of the autobahns was seen as the first stage in a programme of national environmental reform. They favoured a design of sinuous curves; travel on the autobahn was conceived as the experiencing of a succession of unified spaces – valleys, basins, forests. The new highways were intended to emphasize such spaces by following their borders, not cutting across them. Great care was taken over the choice of the mix of tree species used in planting the strip between the carriageways. The aesthetic tradition was more that of an eighteenth-century English landscape garden than a purely modernist project.[43]

Memory is encoded in landscape implicitly in the survival of features from earlier times, but also deliberately through the construction of memorials. The idea of commemoration spread in Europe and America during the later nineteenth and early twentieth centuries. In Britain, memorials to soldiers killed during the Boer War predated the ubiquitous ones commemorating the far more numerous dead of the First World War. Before this period, statuary had been largely confined to churches, urban squares and landed estates. Increasingly, commemoration in the landscape reflected the glorification of the national pasts of nation states in order to legitimize modern political circumstances. Equally, the demolition of statues and monuments can symbolize a change of leader or regime, as with the removal of statues of Stalin in the USSR, or the toppling of ones of Lenin in Eastern Europe that followed the collapse of communism.[44]

Landscapes of commemoration are often contested, though. This can be seen on a large scale on the Western Front. Commemoration became a politically contested issue during, and especially after, the First World War. In previous conflicts, it had been more usual to commemorate national leaders and heroes, such as Lord Nelson, rather than the men they led. The unprecedented scale of losses during the war – more than a million dead from Britain, the Dominions and the rest of the British Empire – led to a different approach. The decision was taken not to allow the repatriation of bodies, but to commemorate the dead in cemeteries near the battle front with uniform, simple grave markers. By 1930, there were 891 cemeteries in the British sector of the former Western Front, with more than 540,000 headstones. There was also a debate about the desirability of additional battlefield monuments. The initial, understated, British view was that these were inappropriate, but in the face of demands from the Dominions for their own monuments, opinions changed, and British memorials, such as the rebuilt Menin Gate at Ypres, were also constructed. In the end, nineteen memorials were built in the former British sector from Dunkirk to Amiens.[45]

Similar processes of contested commemoration at a more local scale have occurred in the Scottish Highlands. A massive statue of the first Duke of Sutherland, erected in 1834, overlooks the small town of Golspie. The duke was responsible for the clearing out of thousands of tenants and their families in Sutherland during the early nineteenth century in the name of agricultural 'improvement'. The sense of injustice, loss and dispossession caused by the Highland Clearances is still a significant element of local people's memory and sense of place today. Moves have been afoot since 1994 to demolish what is seen by some as a hated symbol of former oppression. Other local people have been against toppling the statue, however, arguing that it is now a prominent local landmark and that it provides an icon that helps to focus attention and keep alive the memory of past injustices.[46] The most prominent ruins of the Clearances are the houses that the relocated families built in the coastal fringe of crofts to which they were moved; but the ruins of these houses are not viewed in such emotive terms as the much more poorly-preserved clachans from which they were expelled, the remains of which are much less easily interpreted on the ground. One of these sites, Rosal, in Strathnaver, Sutherland, has been mythologized as the archetypical pre-clearance settlement site simply because it was arbitrarily selected for excavation by the archaeologist Horace Fairhurst in the 1960s. It has been preserved as an isolated landscape relic in the midst of modern forestry plantations.[47]

The commemorative significance of monuments can change over time, as can their role in the landscape. The memorial to the Jacobite rising of 1745 at Glenfinnan is one of the most distinctive of Scottish national icons, widely reproduced in tourist literature. Yet, when originally constructed in 1815, it was a personal memorial by the spendthrift Alexander Macdonald of Glenalladale to the part played by the Clan Macdonald in the rebellion. On his death in that year it also became his own memorial. Only later in the nineteenth century, with the removal of a two-storey shooting box to leave a single tower, and the addition of a statue of a lone Highlander on top, was it transformed from a private to a public monument. Its location was inspired, with a backdrop of loch and retreating

Memorial to a lost cause: the Jacobite monument at Glenfinnan, Scotland.

lines of hills, and it was clearly designed to be viewed in Picturesque mode from a particular 'station' above the tower, looking down the loch, the angle from which it is almost invariably photographed today.[48]

Battlefields provide particularly interesting landscapes of commemoration. Battlefields are a part of a cultural heritage in which the memory of past events, rather than the reality, is important. It is relatively rarely that commemoration on a battlefield is achieved impartially, with equal fairness to both sides. The classic example used to be Waterloo, where the displays in the battlefield museum focused almost entirely on Napoleon, barely giving Blücher and Wellington walk-on parts. Today the balance is more even. The battlefield itself is commemorated not only by the Lion of Waterloo statue on a 40 m-high mound, but by a variety of memorials to the Belgians, Dutch, Prussians and the French Imperial Guard. Some of these were erected early in the nineteenth century, others as recently as 1990. In addition to these, there is a miscellany of memorials relating to individuals on both sides, and the farms of Hougoumont and La Haye Sainte, key strongpoints in advance of the Anglo-Dutch battle line, have been preserved as historical monuments.

Pre-industrial European warfare left enduring marks on

the landscape, including Iron Age forts and medieval castles, which today form an important part of heritage. Yet the impact of warfare on the wider landscape before the twentieth century was generally small-scale and short-term, although the scale of devastation in conflicts like the Thirty Years War was considerable. Battlefields were confined to relatively small areas, whose landscapes were rarely profoundly altered by conflict. This smallness of scale has encouraged their commemoration. At Culloden and Waterloo, it is possible to walk over ground that has remained relatively unchanged since the conflict, or has been sensitively restored. At Bannockburn, the battlefield landscape and topography have been more markedly transformed, but the need for commemoration amidst modern suburbia persists. Gettysburg was turned into a 2,428 ha (6,000 a) national historic park in 1895. Today the park has more than 1,400 monuments, markers and memorials, as well as a visitor and exhibition centre.

In the twentieth century, however, the First World War brought a change in the scale of warfare to something capable of destroying whole landscapes over a wide area. On the Western Front the official regions devastées covered 3,337,000 ha (8,245,727 a), including 620 settlements that were totally destroyed and 1,334 severely damaged ones. Prolonged heavy artillery bombardments, including the setting off of huge underground mines, altered the topography as well as the landscape. Despite this, the reconstruction of the devastated areas was achieved remarkably quickly. Much was accomplished within three years of the end of the war. In the departement of Meurthe-et-Moselle, by 1921, 268,000 ha had been cleared of shells and barbed wire; trenches had been filled in using labour gangs from French colonies, eastern Europe and, even before repatriation, German prisoners of war. Abandoned land was returned to cultivation, farmhouses and outbuildings reconstructed, villages re-planned and by 1930 rural recovery was virtually complete.[49] Eighty years later, little of the former devastation is immediately visible while driving through the former Western Front, although traces are clearer on aerial photographs. In addition, extensive areas are covered today with thousands of war cemeteries. Sections of the Western Front, such as Verdun, have become visitor attractions with restored trench systems and dugouts. The Second World War brought a more mobile form of warfare, in which battlefields were not fixed for such long periods and devastation was more widely spread, particularly with the mass bombing of cities, culminating in the atomic bombs dropped on Hiroshima and Nagasaki.

The interpretation of battlefield sites that are linked to the construction of national identities can be taken over by dominant elites. The way in which the commemoration of such sites can be biased is shown by the Alamo, the mission of San Antonio de Valero in Texas, site of the famous siege of 1836 during the struggle for Texan independence from Mexico. Badly ruined by the end of the nineteenth century, the Alamo is a modern creation, carefully managed for public consumption. The mission has been restored so that the main façade of the chapel is presented as the focus, whereas originally it was only a part of a larger complex of buildings. The façade itself has been rebuilt in a style that is almost certainly not original. The presentation of the Alamo emphasizes the role of the Anglos rather than the Latinos in the birth of Texas, reflecting their later domination of Texan society rather than the actual makeup of the Alamo garrison of 1836. Today, the Alamo serves as a focus for tourists – and channels them into the nearby commercial centre.[50]

The study and preservation of landscape remains of military activity from the Second World War are fairly recent. In Britain, remains include thousands of pillboxes and gun emplacements, hundreds of former airfields and extensive coastal defences. Many have been removed since 1945, but some surviving examples are now seen as making their own distinctive contribution to the landscape. The modern military, with its slimmed-down manpower and technological sophistication, impinges less on our lives today than the larger armies of the past, but still has an impact on landscape. In Britain, firing ranges occupy substantial areas of national parks such as Dartmoor and Northumberland, and Areas of Outstanding Natural Beauty such as the North Pennines, reducing access by the general public yet paradoxically, amid the littered shells, preserving some archaeological and ecological aspects of the landscape quite effectively. Low-flying military aircraft are a noisy, intrusive and contentious feature of upland areas of Britain.

Large-scale landscape planning predates the twentieth century. Parliamentary enclosure and the creation of landscape parks are examples (Chapter 3), but such movements did not occur as the result of national-scale planning applied uniformly. A desire to protect landscape for posterity goes back to eighteenth-century estate improvements made by landowners who knew that the benefits of their work would be fully realized only by their sons or even their grandsons. An early desire to protect landscape was voiced by Wordsworth in his *Guide to the Lake District* (1810), in which he remarked that he regarded the Lake District as 'a sort of national property', and to William Gilpin's even earlier comment that the owners of ruins like Tintern Abbey were only their guardians for posterity. While there was a desire in the eighteenth century to control landscape change (see Chapter 3), this did not extend to a desire to slow down the pace of it in order to protect particular features and areas. Wordsworth's unfavourable comments on the proposed construction of a railway to Windermere were widely circulated but ineffectual. The views articulated by him provided useful ammunition for a later generation of Lake District conservationists, however, supported by John Ruskin and publicized by Canon Rawnsley, one of the founders of the National Trust, who successfully opposed other schemes to extend railways into the heart of the Lake District. In the later nineteenth century, the desire to preserve landscapes, and elements in them, was pushed by an educated and influential upper-middle-class minority rather than by government.

In the 1920s and '30s, there was growing appreciation that the pace of landscape change in Britain was accelerating, with increasing concern that many of the changes were undesirable. This led to the foundation of organizations such as the Council for the Preservation of Rural England in 1926 and, at a more local scale, groups like the Friends of the Lake District (1934).

Unsightly development: a landscape of chalets and shanties near Carlops, south of Edinburgh.

The CPRE, established largely through the effort of the planner Patrick Abercrombie, was less concerned with the conservative protection of traditional landscapes than with creative attempts to plan for change.[51] The CPRE argued that laissez-faire attitudes in the nineteenth century had destroyed British towns and that the same approach in the twentieth century was threatening the countryside. The need to avoid chaos and inefficiency in landscape management prompted some admiration, for a time at least, of planning in Fascist Germany and Italy. Suburban sprawl, occurring at an unprecedented scale, was the aspect of landscape change that prompted most concern, although the construction of bungalows, chalets and shacks around seaside resorts and elsewhere was also seen as a major eyesore. More than four million houses were built in Britain between the First and Second World Wars; in the 1930s around 20,235 ha (50,000 a) a year were being developed for housing. There were those who celebrated the understated Englishness of inter-war suburbs, and their landscapes were certainly far less chaotic than the rash of individual *pavillons* that was spreading around Paris at the same period.[52] The Second World War brought major changes to the British countryside after decades of stagnation: 2.6 million ha (6.5 million a) were ploughed up, and the number of tractors increased from 56,000 in 1939 to 203,000 in 1946.[53]

During the twentieth century, especially since the Second World War, the pace of landscape change and the desire to control, halt or even reverse it has led to increasing government intervention in the landscape through planning policies. This has involved the creation of areas where landscape has been protected to a greater or lesser degree, as well as the application more generally of regulations and restrictions relating to land use. The creation of national parks began in America in the second half of the nineteenth century. Although areas such as the Adirondacks, the Catskills and the White Mountains, relatively close to the rapidly urbanizing North-East, had been visited and valued for their scenery in the early part of the century, it was mainly as European explorers and settlers moved west that they discovered some of the most striking natural wonders of the continent (Chapter 4). The desire to protect scenery and natural curiosities such as geysers and hot springs led to the designation of Yellowstone as the world's first national park in 1872, although as early as 1864 Abraham Lincoln had granted the Yosemite valley to the state of California to be preserved for public recreation. Other national parks such as Sequoia and Mount Rainier were established in the American West in the late nineteenth century. National parks were originally concerned to safeguard natural environments, but the need for national historic parks to conserve places of cultural significance soon became evident. National park agencies in America and elsewhere have been powerful tools in the creation of cultural heritage, through establishing the hegemony of Eurocentric images of place at the expense of views of landscape held by indigenous peoples.[54] The landscape view enshrined in the ethos of the USA's national parks is that of the WASP (White Anglo-Saxon Protestant). The landscape image of Yosemite as a wilderness national park was created by Europeans, who conveniently ignored the extent to which the parkland landscape of meadow and open woodland had been created by the deliberate management of Indian communities in the interests of increasing the density of game animals.[55]

A leading figure in the American national park movement was John Muir. Born in Scotland in 1838, he emigrated with his family to the USA in 1849. After a varied career, in 1867 he began a life of wandering that took him all over western America and many other parts of the world, though his heart was in the high country of the Sierras. From 1874 he developed a successful career as a writer, recounting his travels and expounding his own naturalist philosophy, encouraging people to visit the country that he loved. He focused public attention on the damage that was occurring to the landscapes of the American West due to unrestricted development, spearheading campaigns to protect Yosemite and the Sierras. He was instrumental in the creation of Yosemite, Grand Canyon, Sequoia, Mount Rainier and Petrified Forest as US national parks. His view of landscape was encapsulated in his statement that 'none of nature's landscapes are ugly so long as they are wild'. His comment that 'Everybody needs beauty as well as bread, places to play in and pray in, where nature may heal and give strength to body and soul alike' was an inspiration for later campaigns for national parks in other countries.

Canada established the Rocky Mountain (now Banff) National Park in 1885. National parks followed in South Africa. In the early twentieth century, parks were designated in Argentina, Mexico and Sweden (1909), Switzerland (1914) and Spain (1917). In parts of Europe, it was possible to designate national parks on not dissimilar lines to those in the USA, in thinly-settled upland areas where population was, in any case, declining. Timanfaya national park on Lanzarote, where recent volcanic landforms are preserved in a desert environment with only very limited visitor access, is a good example. The preservation of historic landscapes has been the rationale for some parks, such as the Klondike National Historic Park (1976) and the seventeenth-century whaling stations of north-west Spitzbergen (1973).

In Britain, the creation of national parks on an American model proved impossible. Upland areas had histories of settlement and human impact stretching back for some 5–6,000 years. There were very few true wilderness areas; the thin population of parts of the western Highlands was a relatively recent phenomenon following the nineteenth-century clearances. Patterns of land use and land ownership were complex, and areas such as Dartmoor and the Lake District had substantial resident populations. Whatever form they took, British national parks could never be the same as Yellowstone or Yosemite. Wildlife protection was easier to achieve than landscape protection because it often involved fairly small sites and could claim scientific objectivity, which the more subjective criteria for the evaluation and protection of landscape could not. As a result, the designation of areas in England and Wales for their scenic beauty, as National Parks or Areas of Outstanding Natural Beauty, did not confer the same degree of protection enjoyed by wildlife through Sites of Special Scientific Interest.[56] The institutionalization of certain kinds of habitat has occurred very rapidly. In the 1970s, 'ancient woodland', defined as woodlands that have existed continuously on the same site since the seventeenth century, was not widely recognized by foresters as a category, while by the 1980s they were not only clearly identified but widely protected, and managed with increasing care and understanding of their distinctive character.[57]

Despite their status, national parks were not safe from government interference, such as the upgrading in the 1970s of the A66 road linking the M6 motorway to industrial West Cumbria through the heart of the Lake District National Park. Equally, the Exmoor National Park authorities were unable to prevent private landowners from ploughing up thousands of acres of heather moorland within the park. Nevertheless, national park designation in England and Wales is now seen as conferring the highest possible protection on the landscape, the aim being that national parks should provide models for the sustainable management of the countryside as a whole.

The movement towards the creation of national parks in Britain began in the late 1920s, led by the CPRE. It gathered momentum in the 1930s and, after a delay due to the Second World War, parks were established under the National Parks and Access to the Countryside Act of 1949. Between 1951 and 1956 ten national parks were designated in England and Wales, with the Norfolk Broads being added in 1989. The aims of the parks were based on the protection of scenic beauty and the promotion of visitor access, followed rather later by a third aim, the promotion of the economic and social development of communities living within the parks. The Environment Act of 1995 updated these to emphasize the need to conserve and enhance natural beauty, wildlife and cultural heritage within the national parks, moving away from purely scenic aims to concerns with the cultural landscape and local society. The first ten parks were all in relatively remote upland areas in northern and western England, or in Wales, ignoring an original aim of designating areas such as the South Downs, which were close to London, because they were not considered wild enough. Currently, following the 50th anniversary of the passing of the 1949 legislation, the New Forest is about to be designated as a national park and one for the South Downs is planned.

In many respects, the three basic aims behind the national parks outlined above were incompatible. The protection of scenery conflicted with the provision of better visitor access, such as improving roads and providing car parks, and also with the maintenance of jobs for local communities in unsightly industries such as quarrying. In 1974 the Sandford Committee established the principle that, in cases of conflict between conservation and access or amenity, conservation issues should take priority. National parks in England and Wales had much less power and far slimmer finances than had originally been intended. A feature of British post-war planning in general was its limited control over rural land use, which gave farmers and foresters considerable freedom in what they did to the landscape. The slender financial resources of the national parks prevented them from purchasing land on anything other than a small scale. As a result, management within national parks involved trying to persuade landowners to undertake landscape-friendly management, rather than requiring them to do so.

Other areas of England and Wales were identified for protection on the grounds of their landscape quality. From the mid-1950s, 37 Areas of Outstanding Natural Beauty, covering 15 per cent of the country, were designated, ranging in size from the Isles of Scilly (16 sq km/6 sq miles) to the Cotswolds (2,038 sq km/787 sq miles). AONBs were smaller than national parks, with fewer wild, dramatic landscapes. To an even greater extent, their landscapes have been shaped by human activity. Often they had more limited opportunities for extensive outdoor recreation and restrictions on access, as with the Forest of Bowland in

Lancashire. The aims behind the designation of AONBs were to conserve landscape, with recreation being a much less important objective. Heritage Coasts form another category of landscape designation, accounting for 33 per cent of the English coastline. In addition, many areas ranging from small sites to extensive heather moorlands were classified as Sites of Special Scientific Interest, although the Nature Conservancy, more recently English Nature, had only limited powers to intervene in cases where landowners treated such designations with contempt and managed their land insensitively.

No national parks were established in Scotland, partly because of opposition from vested interests, which included the Forestry Commission, the National Trust for Scotland and private landowners. In addition, in the 1950s and '60s, the Scottish countryside was not felt to be under sufficient pressure, a serious error in retrospect, although efforts to create a Cairngorms national park date from as early as 1927. The only type of designated area currently existing in Scotland is the National Scenic Area. There are 40 of these, covering some 12.7 per cent of Scotland. These form a much weaker structure of landscape protection than in England. A range of insensitive developments, including large-scale forestry and skiing facilities, has affected some of the best of such scenic areas. It is ironic that although national parks now exist in most countries in the world, there is none in Scotland, the birthplace of John Muir, who, more than anyone, started the national parks movement. Plans for Scottish national parks have been revived since the re-establishment of a Scottish parliament. Loch Lomond and the Trossachs was designated in 2002 and the Cairngorms is planned. More tentative plans exist for other areas including Ben Nevis and Glencoe, the north-west Highlands, and maritime national parks covering coastal and island areas of western Scotland. In Scotland, there are also 1,446 SSSIs covering 11.6 per cent of the country, including Arthur's Seat, the Bass Rock and Fingal's Cave. Smaller in extent are 71 National Nature Reserves, covering 1.4 per cent of Scotland, and four regional parks including the Pentland Hills near Edinburgh.

France, like England, has opted for a two-tier structure of landscape protection in its 6 national parks and 32 regional nature parks. The French system of national parks was developed later than in Britain, the first, Vanoise, being created in 1963. Other national parks were established in the mountain regions of the Alps, Pyrenees and Cevennes. The last of these, among lower mountains, has a larger resident population and a landscape that is much more strongly influenced by human activity than previous French national parks. Regional nature parks, like British AONBs, are distributed much more evenly, with a number located within the Paris Basin as well as in more remote, less populated regions. In Spain, a similar two-tier system of National Parks and Natural Areas of National Interest was introduced much earlier, in 1917.

In the second half of the twentieth century, national parks were established throughout the world, often in former colonial areas. The views of landscape held by colonial administrators often had a strong influence on the designation and management of colonial parks. The Serengeti in Tanzania provides a good example. About 14,743 sq km (5,692 sq miles) in extent, it was discovered by Europeans at the end of the nineteenth century. It was designated as a game reserve in 1929 and was upgraded to a national park in 1951. This status was conferred more on account of its wildlife and its distinctive, complex ecosystems than its landscapes, but European landscape images nevertheless affected it profoundly. In particular, the vision of the Serengeti as an Eden in Africa – 'the place on earth where it is still the morning of life and the great herds still run free' – according to one advertisement, strongly influenced the conservationists, who saw a place for Africans in the park only as another wild species requiring protection. Perhaps because of the proximity of Olduvai Gorge, one of the most famous sites for early hominid fossils, the vision of early conservationists was of an area to be kept as empty of humans as possible, as in an English landscape park. Although the Serengeti has developed under the influence of humans over a long time period, it suited the park administrators to believe that the Maasai were merely recent incomers, whose presence could be tolerated only if they kept to what was seen as 'traditional' lifestyles, based on herding with no cultivation and little hunting. Unfortunately, the European idea of traditional African lifestyles was based on inaccurate stereotypes. The Maasai, who had no say in the designation of the park, soon found themselves in trouble, since park administrators objected to practices such as the burning of vegetation and growing crops that were a part of their traditional economy. These restrictions seemed all the more arbitrary to the inhabitants, because cash-cropping commercial agriculture was being encouraged outside the park.[58]

Efforts to designate new national parks have sometimes been thwarted by a lack of resources and pressures for development, as in the Altai Mountains on the borders of the Russian federation, Mongolia and China. Meanwhile, existing parks are experiencing a range of human and environmental pressures, the latter sometimes caused indirectly by human impacts, such as climate change and rising sea levels. In 2000, many US national parks suffered severe forest fires due to lightning strikes, the effects of which were exacerbated by management policies that in previous decades had greatly reduced the impact of fire as a natural agent in modifying forest ecosystems. Wetland areas are particularly vulnerable. In Florida, the Everglades are facing both a rise in sea level and local developments affecting water management. In the Coto Donana national park at the mouth of the Guadalquivir in Spain, there has been conflict between the regional authorities, who have tried to institute tourist, industrial and irrigation developments around the fringes of the park, and the national government, which has tried to prevent them.

At the end of the Second World War, British farmers were seen as the guardians of the countryside, and they were largely exempt from the legislation embodied in the Town and Country Planning Act of 1947. The return of profitability to agriculture after decades of depression, and the opportunities presented by new technology and modern chemical fertilizers, made possible the modernizing of agriculture and the countryside on a huge scale. The creation of almost prairie landscapes in the arable areas of eastern England, with the associated problem of wind erosion of soils, was one result. Another was the ploughing up of large areas of chalk downlands, which had been under permanent grass for much of their history. Extensive landscapes of Iron Age 'Celtic' field systems, recorded before the Second

World War by pioneer aerial archaeologists, were destroyed by deep ploughing.

From being the guardians of the countryside, farmers have received an increasingly bad press since the 1970s as the scale of landscape change associated with agribusiness became clear.[59] The Set Aside scheme, which was designed to take at least some land out of production, had only limited success in reversing landscape change. More recently, initiatives such as the Countryside Stewardship Scheme have encouraged a more environmentally-friendly approach by farmers. From 1991, it offered payments to conserve or restore landscape or features, as well as to improve public access to them with grants that have been discretionary and specifically targeted. There has been a focus on particular endangered landscapes, such as lowland heaths, calcareous grassland, lowland meadows and wet grassland with high landscape and conservation value, along with the preservation of historical and archaeological sites. Maintenance of hedges has also been an important element of the scheme. Due to funding limitations, however, only about 2 per cent of the hedgerows in England have been affected. In the 1950s and '60s, supported by government subsidies, hill farming was comparatively prosperous, but conditions deteriorated in the 1970s and '80s. This led to the overstocking of pastures, and, as labour costs rose and non-family labour almost vanished, the maintenance of stone walls, outbuildings and other landscape features declined. The Environmentally Sensitive Areas scheme, under which upland farmers can enter into contracts to do work such as maintaining stone walls, repairing field barns, managing farm woodlands and wetland sites, restoring flower-rich meadows and reducing stocking levels, has started to make hill farmers part-time countryside stewards. Given the current total lack of profitability of hill farming, this trend is likely to increase in the future, particularly with the probable reduction of grazing densities following the foot-and-mouth outbreak of 2001.

An important influence on recent landscape change in Europe has been the impact of EU legislation, and especially the Common Agricultural Policy (CAP) with its support for overproduction on a massive scale. Despite reforms in 1992, which were designed to cut surpluses and benefit the rural environment, the CAP has failed to prevent the increasing intensification of arable and livestock farming, although there has been a shift in production in both beef and sheep farming from the uplands to the lowlands, which may have started to tackle some of the problems of overgrazing in upland areas. Features of value are still being lost from the landscape as a result of intensive agriculture, although the speed of such changes may be declining. Overall, the quality of the landscape and its local character are still deteriorating, with field sizes increasing and modern farm buildings of standard design proliferating. Between 1983 and 1994, 26,200 km (16,280 miles) of hedges were removed in England, but only 5,190 km (3,225 miles) restored, although the rate of removal is falling. There is recognition that the landscape needs to be managed by farmers with the aid of environmentally-oriented grants, but existing schemes are only tinkering with the problems of landscape change and do not tackle them fundamentally.

Reform of the CAP under Agenda 2000 is currently emphasizing environmental measures that aim to protect Europe's rural landscapes, recognizing the influence of agriculture in shaping them over the centuries. Some 1.35 million contracts, involving one in six of all the farmers in the EU, have been signed relating to more extensive production, organic farming, set-aside schemes and the preservation of landscape features such as hedgerows and woodland.

In post-war Britain, landscape change has generally been piecemeal and uncoordinated. Integrated rural planning on a large scale has been more a feature of France, where mixed-economy companies, financed partly by the state and partly by the private sector, undertook some ambitious schemes between the 1960s and the 1980s. An example was the canalization of the River Rhône to make it navigable for large motorized barges. The raising of the level of the river to accomplish this also provided a head of water for generating hydro-electric power. In addition, it enabled water to be diverted for irrigating farmland in Languedoc, encouraging farmers to switch production from unprofitable vin ordinaire to fruit and vegetables, a local market for which was developing in a string of planned coastal tourist resorts.[60] In Spain, too, landscape transformation on a large scale was associated with the damming of major rivers to provide water for hydro-electric power and irrigation.[61]

The Town and Country Planning Act of 1947 and the National Parks and Access to the Countryside Act of 1949 made landscape evaluation a statutory duty for local and central government in England and Wales. Two styles of study developed. First came attempts to quantify landscape quality by allocating points for the presence/intensity of features.[62] Such schemes have been criticized for the amount of subjectivity they involve. Second, approaches were tried using photographs as substitutes for views of landscapes, and using panels of experts to assess them. Inevitably, there were problems in trying to ensure uniform quality of photography, and also doubts about whether expert and non-expert views coincided. Edward Penning-Rowsell has identified four main objectives associated with landscape evaluation: first, landscape preservation, defining areas for special designation, such AONBs and National Scenic Areas in Scotland; second, landscape protection; third, recreation policy; and finally landscape improvement, removing or modifying existing eyesores.[63] No one technique has been considered appropriate for all four policy areas.

Landscape evaluation involves making comparative assessments between two or more landscapes in terms of their visual quality. Early assessment schemes were purely qualitative, and gave way to quantitative systems such as that developed by David Linton, which involved attempts to rank scenic beauty by giving positive scores to elements such as amplitude of relief, variety of land cover and the presence of water features, with negative scores for flat land or the presence of towns and industry.[64] A lot of research into more refined schemes was carried out in the 1970s as a result of local government reforms, building in various elements of the cultural as well as the physical landscape. Many systems of assessment, however, have tended to focus on the ecological and scenic character of landscape rather than its historical significance.[65] More recently, the Countryside Commission has undertaken a national landscape characterization exercise, which has balanced and integrated topographic and cultural features to produce almost a map of English *pays*, with a stress on recent landscape change and suitable future management policies.[66] English Heritage is currently supporting historical landscape characterization surveys at a county level for the whole of England, in which characteristic field patterns, settlement morphologies and other landscape features are being dated and mapped. On a broader scale, EU initiatives aimed at distinguishing different historic landscapes are also being developed. Historic landscapes are now seen as national assets, which are essential for a sense of national identity and an individual sense of place.

LANDSCAPES OF TOURISM AND LEISURE

If the twentieth century was an age of landscape planning, it was also one in which landscapes were influenced as never before by the growth of tourism and leisure. Improvements in transport in the later nineteenth century, especially the spread of the railway network, widened the tourist market from the small numbers of landowners and professionals of the early part of the century. In Britain, much working-class tourism in the nineteenth and early twentieth centuries was directed at seaside resorts, and was concentrated in its landscape impact to coastal areas close to London and the northern industrial towns. In the eighteenth century, beaches had been seen as hostile, unattractive landscapes, the setting for shipwrecks rather than places for recreation. From the early nineteenth century, however, excursions to the seaside became fashionable, presenting middle-class visitors with opportunities for the study of geology, palaeontology and natural history, as well as sketching, contemplation and physical recreation. In the first half of the twentieth century, in many coastal areas and other tourist venues such as the Norfolk Broads, the construction of plotland landscapes of timber-built chalets, converted railway carriages, caravans and more substantial bungalows, often without proper facilities or road access, was condemned as an especially ugly manifestation of the desire for a weekend retreat.[67] By the end of the nineteenth century, however, other kinds of rural landscapes were starting to become affected by tourism on a significant scale. In mountain areas in the later nineteenth century, the establishment of health resorts such as Bad Gastein, Bad Ischl and St Moritz in the Alps, and Bagnères de Luchon in the Pyrenees, together with the growing popularity of mountaineering, began to influence the economies of hitherto remote valleys.[68] The development of skiing created a new set of resorts. Davos grew from a population of about 1,700 in 1860 to 11,164 by 1930. It was not until after the Second World War, however, with the development of mass tourism linked to package holidays and cheap charter flights, that the landscape impact of tourism in European mountain areas really mushroomed. The skiing boom led to the rapid development of alpine resorts, ending the outward movement of population in many valleys. In the Vorarlberg, Tyrol and Salzburg Alps, the population increased by 10–20 per cent in the 1960s, largely due to tourism. This was accomplished at an environmental price, though. The construction of resorts and their infrastructure, with the clearance of woodland, greatly altered the character of many mountain areas, and led to increased erosion and a higher avalanche risk. A similar sequence of events occurred in parts of the eastern Appalachians.

If the impact of ski developments on alpine valleys was dramatic, the effect of mass tourism around the coasts of the Mediterranean was, in places, traumatic. Uncontrolled and unsightly developments along the Spanish 'costas' and in the Balearic Islands from the 1960s onwards produced blighted coastal strips, with problems of traffic congestion, water supply and waste disposal. Similar developments spread widely round the shores of the Mediterranean, the coasts of Portugal and the Canary Islands. Such developments threatened landscapes and wildlife in coastal wetland areas such as the Coto Donana. In some cases, developments were more controlled and less piecemeal, as along the Languedoc coast between the Rhône delta and the Spanish border, which was transformed from an empty coast of malarial lagoons into a series of carefully planned resort developments and associated marinas, the architecture of which, as at La Grande Motte, was sometimes striking.[69]

In Britain in the later nineteenth century, the railway network turned rambling from a middle-class pursuit into a mass recreation. By the 1860s, excursion trains were bringing workers from industrial Lancashire to the Lake District on day trips, and from Sheffield to the Peak District. Battles over access to the countryside go back to the later nineteenth century, with concerns in northern England and Scotland to preserve access to the uplands, while in the south there were moves to prevent enclosure on the commons around London and to keep them for the recreational use of working-class people: the Commons Preservation Society was founded in 1865. Between 1918 and 1939, outdoor recreation in Britain increased dramatically, affecting people's views of landscape. There was an emphasis on the moral and physical benefits of countryside recreation, promoting good citizenship, and seen especially in the rules, discipline and simple furnishings of youth hostels.[70] The spread of the railways and, later, bus services, as well as rising car ownership among the middle classes, caused outdoor recreation to become increasingly popular by the 1930s, particularly walking and cycling, but also camping, fishing and, to a more limited extent, climbing. Conflicts over access to the countryside were sharpest in the Peak District, where landowners tried to prevent access to their grouse moors by working-class ramblers from cities such as Manchester and Sheffield. The mass trespass on Kinder Scout in 1932 is the most famous of such confrontations, which had a significant influence on the growing campaign for national parks. This period also saw the rise of the Scout and Guide movement, the Youth Hostels Association (1930), and the Ramblers' Association (1935), promoting cheap access to the countryside and a responsible attitude to recreation within it. Nevertheless, the 'right to roam' over uncultivated upland country, which has been the subject of campaigns throughout the twentieth century, only became law in 2000. Debates over access are still as confrontational as they were a century ago, polarized around the same groups: town versus country, landowners versus walkers.

Ordnance Survey maps, made more attractive and colourful, helped to spearhead this rediscovery of the countryside and, through its archaeological division, its history and prehistory. The ability to read and interpret the landscape through maps was seen as a basic skill by organizations such as the Scouts, Guides and the Ramblers' Association. The inter-war period saw a boom in the production of Ordnance Survey maps, especially the one inch to the mile series. Map literacy was seen as an enabling skill that distinguished the urban rambler from the countryfolk, as in J.M.W. Tucker's well-known picture *Hiking* (1936; Laing Art Gallery, Newcastle upon Tyne), showing three girls, suitably dressed for walking, orienting themselves in a Cotswold landscape with the aid of an Ordnance Survey map. As Batsford's *How to See the Country* (1945–6) put it, 'With an inch Ordnance sheet of your selected area you are master of the countryside: it lies symbolically before you'.[71] Ordnance Survey tourist maps, centred on areas such as the Cotswolds, Peak District and Firth of Clyde, or districts with literary associations such as Burns's and Scott's Country, clearly targeted new groups of users.[72] The increasing use of Ordnance Survey maps in schools and growing concern about landscape change, especially worries about the decline of agriculture, led Dudley Stamp to co-ordinate the first British land utilization in the 1930s, the field mapping for which, at a scale of six inches to a mile (1:10,560), was done mainly by schoolchildren.[73]

Since the Second World War, the spread of car ownership and the motorway network has led to a further, massive rise in countryside recreation. The Peak District and Lake District national parks each attract some 12–14 million visitors every year. In the process, the range of recreational activities has greatly expanded, with new activities such as mountain biking, and hang- and para-gliding. Conflicts over the recreational use of the countryside have grown, especially within national parks, where walkers, mountain bikers, motor cyclists and drivers of four-wheel drive vehicles have been in competition for the same routes. Conflicts between water-based recreational activities have been even more contentious. The use of power boats has been banned on most Cumbrian lakes. A recent landmark decision to phase in a speed limit of 10 miles (16 km) an hour on Windermere will effectively end waterskiing there. Changing climates of opinion in favour of access, and the money that can be made from visitors, has led to some marked shifts of attitude among landowners. The Forestry Commission, for instance, although interested in promoting Forest Parks in its early days, moved decisively from the 1960s towards encouraging public access and recreation, so that visitor centres such as Grizedale in the Lake District are now major attractions.

With increasing affluence, free time and mobility for large sections of society, leisure has developed as an important influence on the modern landscape, adding many new and distinctive elements. The distinction between tourism and leisure is not precise, but leisure can be considered as embracing activities reached from home, while tourism involves more extended travel and a temporary change of residence: the same facilities may be used by both groups. A range of sporting activities have had significant effects on the landscape, but perhaps none so extensive and distinctive as golf; the average 18-hole course absorbs around 100 ha (247 a). Golf courses take up substantial areas of land in suburban locations and in the countryside close to large population centres. Theme parks, fewer in number but also covering sizeable areas, have also been important. Shopping is now a major leisure activity, and has increasingly been directed out of crowded town centres to urban fringe locations, where land values are lower, rents cheaper, parking free and access from motorway junctions easier. The French, with higher rates of car ownership than the British in the 1960s and '70s, pioneered the out-of-town shopping centre in Europe, but other countries, including Britain, have started to catch up. The Metro Centre at Gateshead and the Trafford Centre near Manchester represent the translation of the American shopping mall into a British context. Slightly different in character are out-of-town developments that focus on sporting as well as retail facilities, such as the Middlebrook Centre near Bolton.

Another major landscape element associated with leisure, which has not received much attention, is the private garden, ever smaller in size when attached to new housing, but covering large areas in aggregate and supported by a major industry, which, through garden centres, has additional, direct impacts on the landscape, and indirect effects, such as the breaking up of limestone pavements for ornamental rockery stone and the destruction of lowland peat mosses to provide garden compost. Gardens provide ordinary people with one of their main opportunities to modify part of the landscape directly to their personal tastes. While some work has been done on the gardens of large suburban Victorian villas,[74] less attention has been directed to the symbolism of modern gardens and the landscape impact of changing garden fashions, although the undesirable effects of rapidly-growing Leyland cypress hedges have been highlighted by a number of court cases between neighbours. With the transformation of agricultural landscapes mentioned above, private gardens are becoming more and more important as refuges for birds such as song thrushes, which are steadily declining on arable land due to modern farming practices.[75]

Landscapes of leisure have been created from a range of former landscape features. Canals in Britain, long since deprived of any commercial role, have become foci for leisure activities, especially boating and angling, as have many harbours with the decline of coastal shipping and the fishing industry. Redundant railway lines have been converted into footpaths and cycleways. Empty cotton mills have attracted a range of retail outlets, and farms have been turned into craft centres with coffee shops and mini-zoos.

LANDSCAPE AND HERITAGE

Landscape is a marketable commodity, something that can be consumed, visited in package tours, brought home on post-cards, photographs and souvenirs, or represented on calendars. At the same time it is a resource that can be exploited, but which needs to be conserved in a sustainable manner for the benefit of future generations as well as for ourselves. A growing heritage industry is commodifying the past, including landscape, as part of the modern consumption of entertainment. The concern to preserve past landscapes and features in them overlaps the interest in heritage. Landscape is a central element of cultural heritage. It helps, as we have seen, to create a sense of national identity. It enhances our understanding of the past. It highlights regional and local distinctiveness and adds to the quality of life, as well as being of great importance for tourism. David Lowenthal has commented: 'Awareness of the past is essential to the maintenance of purpose in life. Without it we would lack all sense of continuity, all apprehension of causality, all knowledge of our own identity'.[76] He also claims:

> The past is everywhere. All around us lie features which, like ourselves and our thoughts, have more or less recognisable antecedents. Relics, histories, memories suffuse human experience. Each particular trace of the past ultimately perishes, but collectively they are immortal. Whether it is celebrated or rejected, attended to or ignored, the past is omnipresent.[77]

In an 'old country' such as Britain there is a lot of heritage around: Britain has indeed been described as a country with too much past. Currently more than half a million buildings in Britain are listed as being of historic and architectural importance, and more than 8,000 conservation areas have been designated. The extent to which this restricts, or completely freezes, landscape changes, some of which might well be desirable, has become apparent in recent years, and is in future likely to undermine the historic processes that have given us our landscape heritage in the first place, creating instead sterile places, carefully preserved but fossilized. It has been observed that no change can be the most devastating of changes.

'Heritage' is notoriously difficult to define, as is 'landscape' itself. It has recently been described by English Heritage as those features inherited from the past that we consider important enough to want to pass on to future generations. In more practical terms, it has been seen as 'the contemporary use of the past'.[78] Modern societies create the heritage they need and manage it for contemporary purposes. More cynically, it has been considered as anything from the past that can be commercialized and packaged to make a profit.[79] Within the last two decades, for instance, the Irish landscape has been transformed increasingly from one that was predominantly agricultural into a tourist landscape, in which heritage centres, historic trails and visitor attractions figure large. The number of overseas visitors to the Irish Republic rose from 3.5 million in 1991 to 5 million in 1997.[80]

Yet the desire to preserve landscape elements is a relatively recent one. Before Victorian times, the idea of preserving anything from the past just because it was old – if it was no longer useful in its original function or could not be converted to a different purpose – would have struck most people as strange. The pace of change in both townscape and landscape in the middle and late nineteenth century, however, especially the impact of railway construction, which destroyed many historic buildings, gave impetus to a concern for preserving buildings, sites and landscapes. Britain was by no means in the lead with this: Italy and Greece began to consider preservation first. Later nineteenth-century legislation protected sites such as Stonehenge, and a start was made on producing county-by-county inventories of known historical and ancient sites. Gradually, from the 1970s, the English, Welsh and Scottish Royal Commissions on Ancient and Historical Monuments have moved towards looking at a wider range of sites, rather than just the churches, castles and mansions that dominated early inventories, and at landscapes rather than individual sites, notably in marginal areas where large-scale changes in land use, such as afforestation, pose a major threat. For the Scottish Royal Commission, this has included mapping extensive areas of pre-clearance settlements and their landscapes in areas ranging from Perthshire to Sutherland and Skye.[81]

At global as well as local scales, the nature of landscape heritage can be contested and fashions can change over time. This is well seen in the designation of World Heritage Sites by UNESCO. Currently about 630 sites worldwide have received this accolade. Most of them are cultural in character, focusing on historic cities, palaces and cathedrals, but the balance between different parts of the world has varied. In the USA, more than half the designated sites have been national parks, with a focus on dramatic physical landscapes ranging from the Grand Canyon to Carlsbad Caverns. In Australia, almost all the approved sites fall into this category. In Italy, by contrast, the bulk of the sites comprise historic city centres, residences and cathedrals. There has been criticism that the range of sites chosen has been too narrow, concentrating overwhelmingly on the monumental and architectural. The designation of sites such as the Ironbridge Gorge, and the Beemster Polder in the Netherlands, are exceptions. More recently, attempts have been made to widen the choice of sites to highlight, in the case of Britain, industrial and maritime heritage. The recent acceptance of the Blaenavon industrial landscape in South Wales reflects the fact that, directly and indirectly, industrialization has transformed landscape and society throughout the world and that the process started in Britain. Equally, Britain's colonial impact is reflected in the nomination of sites such as the fortifications at St George, Bermuda. Moves have now been made towards nominating important natural habitats, such as the Flow Country of Caithness and the Cairngorms, sites of geological importance, such as the Dorset and east Devon coast, and cultural landscapes of world significance, such as the Lake District and the New Forest.

Heritage has often been an elitist, top-down concept embracing the heritage of the ruling classes: cathedrals and castles, rather than cottages and cowsheds, a conservative force that supports existing patterns of power. Heritage is still largely consumed by the middle classes. While heritage can be imposed in this way, however, it can also be contested, radical and subversive, while attitudes to it may change over time. The identification of country houses and their parks as one of the main popular icons of the English landscape demonstrates the way in which 'their' heritage can become 'our' heritage, although the focus at National Trust properties, such as Erddig on the Welsh border, on the lives of the servants below stairs indicates a more recent wider social concern.

If heritage is situated in particular social and intellectual contexts, it is time-specific and its meanings may alter over time. Equally, the nature of heritage may be viewed in markedly different ways by particular social groups at any period. In either case, heritage is a contested area of knowledge. So heritage sites such as the cathedral of Notre-Dame in Paris that are major tourist attractions may at the same time be other people's places of worship. The contested nature of landscape heritage is well illustrated by Stonehenge. Jacquetta Hawkes once wrote that every generation gets the Stonehenge it deserves and desires. Conflict over the site developed in the late 1980s between on one hand English Heritage, which managed the site 'for the nation', with the National Trust, which owned some of the land around the monument, and 'New Age' travellers on the other, who wanted access to the site at the time of the midsummer solstice. 'Druids' were allowed sole access to Stonehenge for a year or two, although their claim was no stronger than that of the travellers. Then public access was banned entirely. Major police operations to deny access to the travellers and to prevent them from camping in the area made headline news for two or three years. Even at normal times, to prevent the stones from damage and deterioration, visitors to Stonehenge were not allowed to approach the site, although it is in public ownership, supposedly for the people.[82] In June 1999, more than 400 protesters tore down the perimeter fence and occupied the site. In 2000, access to Stonehenge at the summer solstice was restored once more to Druids, New Age travellers and other visitors following a High Court ruling that deemed the exclusion zone around the site illegal. More than 6,000 people, ranging from hippies to yuppies, Druids to witches, gathered for the summer solstice.

Most of the planning and legislative structures that have been developed to manage change in the landscape have focused on individual sites, such as scheduled monuments and listed buildings, or small localities like conservation areas, parks or battlefields, rather than landscapes on a larger scale. There is a danger of preserving only a few important sites without a context for them, while the great diversity and local distinctiveness of the landscapes around them are lost, something clearly evident in the Cotswolds, where conservation has focused on villages and small market towns, while the countryside in between has been dramatically altered by modern agriculture.

In England, the National Trust was founded in 1895 with a remit that included the purchase of land to secure public access and to prevent unsuitable development, notably around some of the larger lakes in Cumbria. In 1907, it was granted the status of a statutory body whose land was inalienable. Today it owns more than 1 per cent of England and Wales, but more than 25 per cent of the land in crucial areas such as the mountain core of the Lake District. The work of the Trust was aided by pioneer conservationists such as Beatrix Potter, who, from the proceeds of her children's stories, bought up a number of hill sheep farms in the Lake District, especially in sensitive locations like valley heads, either donating them outright to the Trust or bequeathing them in her will. It was only gradually from the 1930s, with escalating death duties on country estates, that the Trust began to acquire a growing number of country houses and their parks, leading to its modern popular image as the custodian of stately homes.

Changing fashions in heritage or, more cynically, a wider drive to commercialize it, is evident in the rise of industrial museums and centres such as the Ironbridge Gorge. Not surprisingly, the exploitation of former industrial landscapes as heritage was pioneered in Britain, birthplace of the Industrial Revolution. The Coalbrookdale area was reclaimed from an industrial wasteland in the late 1960s to give the new town of Telford a sense of identity and to contribute to the economic revival of the area through tourism.[83] In the 1960s and early '70s, industrial sites, such as the colliery spoil heaps of the Wigan Alps or the copper-smelting landscapes of the lower Swansea Valley, were seen as eyesores to be demolished, reclaimed and landscaped. Sites that survived this period, when industrial archeology was seen as a minority, slightly cranky interest, have often been reinvented as heritage attractions. The shift in attitudes towards heritage can also be seen in the reopening of railway branch lines, closed in the 1960s under the Beeching axe, as private steam railway lines. The development of industrial landscapes into heritage attractions has spread from Britain to the rest of Europe and the USA.

Robert Hewison has described the heritage industry as using the past to rescue the present.[84] In Britain in the recent past, new heritage sites seem to have been opening every week, but there are signs that something like saturation point has been reached with an over-supply of heritage attractions and less rather than more leisure time among some sections of the population, because some recently-opened sites have struggled to attract sufficient visitors. In Britain, rising petrol prices as well as growing pressure on leisure time may be significant influences behind the levelling off of numbers of visits to heritage attractions. More successful, perhaps, have been lower-key, less capital intensive heritage projects, like the landscape trail laid out at Glenochar in upper Clydesdale, where the remains of a seventeenth-century bastle (fortified farmhouse)

Preserving what kind of folk heritage?: Ballenberg Museum, Swizerland.

The Ukrainian Folk Museum, Kiev.

and associated farming settlement, excavated by the Biggar Museums Trust, form the centrepiece of a self-guided, free trail for visitors.

The heritage industry has even created its own historic landscapes in open-air museums, synthetic ones that may seem realistic to the general public for whom they are designed but which manipulate viewers' perception. Museums such as the Weald and Downland Museum of Rural Life, or the Swiss equivalent at Ballenberg, make a range of cultural landscapes accessible within a single site. They often consist of a series of set-pieces that convey a particular narrative, while playing down any awareness that what is being presented is an authored tale rather than original reality. They frequently focus on a particular developmental theme. For example, the open-air museums in Virginia, especially Jamestown, Colonial Williamsburg, Yorktown and Staunton's Museum of American Frontier Culture, commemorate and explain the American past, but without removing its mythology, with their focus being on 'progress' and 'development'. Specific sets of historical relationships are presented in the landscape through the stated themes of the exhibits.

These deliberately engineered landscapes are simple texts compared to real, historical, multi-authored landscapes. They produce linear narratives that tend to freeze time and frequently present a pastiche of pre-industrial cultural heritage, creating a historical nostalgia for a lost golden age. The representation of buildings and their surroundings does not invite any debate about the past. The landscape is used to sustain a particular view about the past rather than to interrogate it, presenting a past that seems simple, wholesome and community-based. Such museums do not give visitors a realistic picture of the past. The pictures they offer are not only incomplete, they are misleading; such synthetic landscapes cannot easily adapt to changes in scholarship or public taste, so that they are an inflexible way of representing the past. The staff of such museums are very reluctant to admit within their displays that knowledge is historically contingent.[85]

Despite the rapid expansion of the British Empire in the nineteenth century, progress in surveying its overseas territories was slow. Just as it took the Jacobite rebellion of 1745 to highlight the lack of detailed maps of Scotland, leading eventually to the establishment of the Ordnance Survey, so the lack of accurate maps of South Africa during the Boer War emphasized the need for more extensive and better surveys. Mapping and development became synonymous in Africa: mapping was seen both as a form of development in its own right and a means to facilitate further economic change. There were, nevertheless, marked differences in the progress of topographic mapping in twentieth-century British colonial Africa, depending on the political circumstances in the individual colonies. In Swaziland, for instance, early sketch maps were replaced by an official survey at a scale of 1:148,752 in the years 1901–4 and one at 1:59,000 in 1932.[86] But overall achievements were limited until after the Second World War. In 1946, the Directorate of Colonial (later Overseas) Survey was established by the Colonial Office to undertake modern surveys based on aerial photographs, as well as ground survey throughout the colonies. The Directorate's brief in 1946 was to map 2,330,910 sq km (900,000 sq miles) in ten years, beginning with the Gold Coast and moving on to Uganda, Kenya and Tanganyika. The ground control for these surveys was often supplied only with considerable difficulty, but work moved on to even more harsher environments in the British Antarctic territories in the early 1970s.[87]

In terms of mapping, undoubtedly the greatest advance in the twentieth century was the development of remote sensing. The use of aircraft for locating troop positions dates from the early months of the First World War; the most significant development was the fitting of cameras to aircraft, which could generate images that could be brought back and studied in detail by specialists. Some pilots, especially in Palestine, realized that an aerial view provided new perspectives on known ancient sites and also allowed the identification of previously unrecorded ones. After the war, the work of enthusiasts such as O. G. S. Crawford developed aerial archaeology into a distinct specialization. Not only could patterns of features in the land-scape be more clearly appreciated from the air, but aerial photographs, through shadows, soil and crop marks, also revealed sites and indeed entire landscapes that were barely vis-ible, or completely unseen, at ground level, such as patterns of prehistoric 'Celtic' fields over large areas of the chalk down-lands of southern England. After the Second World War, photogrammetry developed rapidly to become the mainstay of new cartographic surveys. The Directorate of Overseas Survey mapping of areas such as the Gambia and Kenya, where much of the terrain was difficult of access, was increasingly under-taken largely by aerial surveys with a minimum of ground control.

From the 1970s, the 'remote' element of remote sensing acquired a new dimension with the development of imaging systems operating from orbiting satellites, like the Landsat series. The ability to view large areas of the world from space, using false colour systems to highlight contrasts in vegetation cover and land use, has brought a new understanding of the fragility of landscapes, such as the destruction of tropical rain forests and the expansion of deserts, and, in the process, has given us a new perspective on the vulnerability of our entire planet.[88] Increasingly sophisticated Landsat imagery in the 1980s led to substantial upwards revisions of estimates of the amount of forest clearance.[89] Computer imaging systems now allow the recreation of past landscapes, such as three-dimen-sional reconstructions of archaeological sites based on excavation data. Possible future landscapes can also be gener-ated; for example, theoretical alternatives based on the application or otherwise of particular management or conserva-tion strategies, such as those relating to Environmentally Sensitive Areas.[90]

FICTIONAL AND FANTASY LANDSCAPES

We have already seen that open-air museums create their own version of the past in the landscape. Sometimes this includes developing a set of existing, genuine sites, as at Ironbridge. But it can also involve the re-erection of buildings and structures from a range of locations on new, purpose-built sites, such as the Weald and Downland Museum and the Beamish open-air museum in Co. Durham. It is only a step from this to the creation of a complete fantasy landscape, as with Disney World, Orlando, Florida (1971), Disneyland, California (1985), and Eurodisney near Paris (1992). Fantasy landscapes are also increasingly familiar from computer games. The quality of the landscape imagery they use has improved dramatically in recent years, so that realistic landscape models of, for example, the battlefield of Gettysburg, or a Sopwith Camel pilot's view of the Western Front, can be presented. Less grounded in reality but equally powerful are images of the landscapes of the Mediterranean or the Nile valley in games such as 'Caesar' or 'Pharoah', in which players build ancient empires and their cities. Such games, and ones like 'Civilization', project particular ideologies of conquest and repression associated with the landscapes they portray, and may reinforce cultural and racial stereotypes in the process.

Throughout this book we have been dealing with imaginary as well as real landscapes, because perceptions of landscape are so individual. But we are also influenced by imaginary landscapes that have been deliberately created by authors. From childhood, the landscapes of Hundred Acre Wood, the Riverbank and the Wild Wood have conditioned our views of the English countryside. Other completely fantasized landscapes, dramatically realized and internally consistent and coherent, have also had a significant impact. The landscapes of Discworld, Gormenghast or Middle Earth are landscapes related to planet earth. The climatic and vegetation patterns of Middle Earth correspond closely with those of Europe, even if the coastline is totally different. In this, J.R.R. Tolkien was following a long-established tradition of creating imaginary, yet completely believable, lands with their own distinctive landscapes and geographies, such as the Costaguana of Conrad's *Nostromo* (1904). Many science fiction novels have taken terrestrial landscapes under extremes sets of conditions – covered once more by ice, or flooded by melted ice caps as a result of global warming, for instance. But landscapes of other worlds can be equally striking. Some, like Frank Herbert's *Dune* (1965), are terrestrial landscapes pushed to an extreme. On the other hand, mysterious and exciting happenings in totally mundane familiar landscapes, like those of J. K. Rowling's Harry Potter novels, can be just as challenging.

CONCLUSION: LANDSCAPES IN A NEW MILLENNIUM

In this book we have explored some of the ways in which landscapes, and perceptions of landscapes, have changed in Britain, Europe and a wider world over the last five centuries. Landscape change has probably been stressed unduly at the expense of continuity. This is because change is often more controversial, more interesting and better recorded than the unobtrusive processes of continuity. Change is an inevitable aspect of landscapes, but in a modern context it needs to be understood, planned and controlled. As we have seen, landscape change does not merely involve physical alterations. The ways in which we look at landscapes have changed in the past and will continue to do so in the future. Some future landscape changes, such as the impacts of creeping suburban development, can be predicted reasonably well for at least two or three decades ahead. Other changes may depend on future trends or government policies, which are harder to second guess. Some landscape changes will be completely unexpected, such as the impact on upland farming landscapes in Britain of the outbreak of foot-and-mouth disease in 2001. More sinister, and much more speculative, are the possible landscape changes resulting, directly and indirectly, from the terrorist attacks on the USA of 11 September 2001.

But none of this should blind us to the importance of continuity in landscapes in providing individuals and societies with a sense of place, a feeling for where they have come from in historical as well as geographical terms. As the last chapter has emphasized, the pace of landscape change worldwide has accelerated dramatically in recent decades. We live in a world where globalization – economic, social, cultural and political linkages at scales greater than those of individual states or even continents – is becoming ever more significant. But at the same time, globalization itself creates a corresponding need for localism, for places and their landscapes that retain their distinctiveness and continuity. To what extent these influences will begin to stabilize or divert the forces encouraging landscape change and the drive towards universal sameness in the twenty-first century is a fascinating topic for speculation.

References

ONE   LANDSCAPE AND HISTORY

1   G. Rose, *Feminism and Geography* (Cambridge, 1993), p. 28.
2   A. R. H. Baker and G. Biger, 'Introduction: An Ideology of Landscape',
     Ideology and Landscape in Historical Perspective, ed. Alan Baker and G.
     Biger (Cambridge, 1992), pp. 1–14.
3   J. Appleton, *The Experience of Landscape* (London, 1975), p. 15.
4   S. Seymour, 'Historical Geographies of Landscape', in *Modern
     Historical Geographies*, ed. B. Graham and C. Nash (London, 2000),
     p. 214.
5   B. Bender, *Landscape: Politics and Responsibility* (Oxford, 1992), p. 21.
6   B. Bender, *Stonehenge: Making Space* (Oxford, 1998), pp. 30–32.
7   *Ibid.*
8   D. W. Meinig, *The Interpretation of Ordinary Landscapes* (Oxford, 1979),
     p. 10.
9   Y.-F. Tuan, *Landscapes of Fear* (Minnesota, 1979), p. 25.
10   D. W. Meinig, 'The Beholding Eye: Ten Versions of the Same Scene',
     Landscape Architecture, LXVI (1976), pp. 47–54.
11   J. W. Watson, 'Geography: A Discipline in Distance', *Scottish
     Geographical Magazine*, LXXI (1955), pp. 1–13.
12   H. Brookfield, 'On the Environment as Perceived', in *Progress in
     Geography*, I, ed. C. Board *et al.* (London, 1969), pp. 51–80.
13   C. Dellheim, 'Imagining England: Victorian Views of the North',
     Northern History, XXIII (1987), pp. 216–30.
14   D. C. D Pocock, 'The Novelist's Image of the North', *Transactions of the
     Institute of British Geographers*, n.s., IV (1979), pp. 62–76.
15   D. Lowenthal and H. Prince, 'The English Landscape', *Geographical
     Review*, LIV (1964), pp. 309–46.
16   P. Howard, *Landscapes: The Artists' Vision* (London, 1991).
17   M. Shoard, 'The Lure of the Moors', in *Valued Environments*, ed. J. R.
     Gold and J. Burgess (London, 1982), pp. 59–73.
18   J. Darvill, 'The Historic Environment, Historic Landscapes, and
     Space–Time–Action Models in Landscape Archaeology', in *The
     Archaeology of Landscape*, ed. P. Ucko and R. Layton (London, 1999),
     pp. 104–18.
19   J. R. Hunn, *Reconstruction and Measurement in Landscape Change: A Study
     of Six Parishes in the St Albans Area*, British Archaeological Reports,

British Series, ccxxxvi (Oxford, 1994).

20 Bender, *Landscape*, p. 15.
21 P. Coones, 'One Landscape or Many? A Geographical Perspective',
    Landscape History, vii (1985), pp. 5–13.
22 H. Morphy, 'Colonialism, History and the Construction of Place: The
    Politics of Land in Northern Australia', in *Landscape: Politics and
    Perspectives*, ed. B. Bender (Oxford, 1992), pp. 205–44.
23 D. Cosgrove, *Social Formation and Symbolic Landscape* (London, 1984),
    p. 12.
24 J. B. Harley, 'Maps, Knowledge and Power', in *The Iconography of
    Landscape*, ed. D. Cosgrove and S. Daniels (Cambridge, 1988),
    pp. 277–312.
25 P. Claval, 'European Rural Societies and Landscapes and the Challenge
    of Urbanization and Industrialization in the Nineteenth Century',
    Geografiska Annaler, lxx/b (1988), pp. 27–38.
26 R. Muir, *Approaches to Landscape* (London, 1999), pp. 2–12.
27 B. K. Roberts, 'Landscape Archaeology', in *Landscape and Culture*,
    ed. J. Wagstaff (Oxford, 1987), pp. 26–37.
28 Muir, *Approaches to Landscape*, pp. 99–114.
29 A. E. Trueman, *Geology and Scenery in England and Wales* (London,
    1949).
30 W. R. Mead, 'The Study of Field Boundaries', *Geographische Zeitschrift*,
    liv (1966), pp. 114–24.
31 Roberts, 'Landscape Archaeology', pp. 26–37.
32 J. Thomas, 'The Politics of Vision and the Archaeology of Landscape',
    in *Landscape: Politics and Perspectives*, ed. B. Bender (Oxford, 1992),
    pp. 19–45.
33 G. Fairclough, 'Protecting Time and Space: Understanding Historic
    Landscape for Conservation in England', in *The Archaeology of
    Landscape*, ed. P. Ucko and R. Layton (London, 1999), pp. 119–34.
34 W. G. Hoskins, *The Making of the English Landscape* (London, 1955).
35 Cosgrove and Daniels, *Iconography*, p. 24.
36 Bender, *Stonehenge*, pp. 28–9.
37 Hoskins, *English Landscape*, p. 298.
38 M. Conzen, *The Making of the American Landscape* (London, 1990).
39 H. C. Darby, *Domesday England* (Cambridge, 1977).
40 R. A. Dodgshon, *The European Past: Social Evolution and Spatial Order*
    (London, 1987), pp. 6–9.
41 J. F. Hart, *The Rural Landscape* (London, 1998), p. 56.
42 A. R. H. Baker, 'Historical Geography and the Study of the European
    Rural Landscape', *Geografiska Annaler*, lxx/b (1988), pp. 5–15.
43 J. Benes and M. Zvelbil, 'A Historical Interactive Landscape in the
    Heart of Europe: The Case of Bohemia', in *The Archaeology of
    Landscape*, ed. P. Ucko and R. Layton (London, 1999), pp. 73–93.
44 M. Williams, *Americans and their Forests: A Historical Geography*
    (Cambridge, 1989).
45 W. J. T. Mitchell, 'Imperial Landscape', in *Landscape and Power*, ed.
    W. J. T. Mitchell (Chicago, 1994), pp. 5–30.

46   J. Darvill, 'The Historic Environment, Historic Landscapes, and
     Space–Time Action Models in Landscape Archaeology', in *The
     Archaeology of Landscape*, ed. P. Ucko and R. Layton (London, 1999),
     pp. 104–18.

47   G. Fairclough, 'Protecting Time and Space: Understanding Historic
     Landscape for Conservation in England', in *The Archaeology of
     Landscape*, ed. P. Ucko and R. Layton (London, 1999), pp. 119–34.

48   T. Ingold, 'The Temporality of Landscape', *World Archaeology*, xxv
     (1993), pp. 152–74.

49   H. C. Darby, 'The Regional Geography of Thomas Hardy's Wessex',
     Geographical Review, xxxviii (1948), pp. 426–43.

50   R. A. Butlin, *Historical Geography: Through the Gates of Space and Time*
     (London, 1993), pp. 132–33.

51   S. Schama, *Landscape and Memory* (London, 1995), p. 16.

52   P. Cloke, P. Milbourne and C. Thomas. 'The English National Forest:
     Local Reactions to Plans for Re-negotiated Nature–Society
     Relationships in the Countryside', *Transactions of the Institute of British
     Geographers*, n.s., xxi (1996), pp. 552–71.

53   J. Appleton, *The Experience of Landscape* (London, 1975).

54   G. H. Orians, 'An Ecological and Evolutionary Approach to Landscape
     Aesthetics', in *Landscape Meaning and Values*, ed. E. C. Penning-Rowsell
     and D. Lowenthal (London, 1986), pp. 3–25.

55   Cosgrove, *Social Formation and Symbolic Landscape*, pp. 10–12.

56   P. Coones, 'One Landscape or Many? A Geographical Perspective',
     Landscape History, vii (1985), pp. 5–13.

57   Mitchell, 'Imperial Landscape', p. 132.

58   Orians, 'Landscape Aesthetics', pp. 3–25.

59   Hart, *Rural Landscape*, p. 18.

60   D. Cosgrove, 'Prospect, Perspective and the Evolution of the
     Landscape Idea', *Transactions of the Institute of British Geographers*, n.s.,
     x (1985), pp. 45–62.

61   Cosgrove, *Social Formation and Symbolic Landscape*, p. 35.

62   D. Cosgrove and S. Daniels, 'Introduction', in *The Iconography of
     Landscape*, ed. D. Cosgrove and S. Daniels (Cambridge, 1988), p. 16.

63   Baker and Biger, 'Ideology of Landscape', pp. 1–14.

64   Rose, *Feminism and Geography*, p. 28.

65   J. Barrell, 'The Public Prospect and the Private View: The Politics of
     Taste in Eighteenth-Century Britain', in *Reading Landscape:
     Country–City–Capital* (Manchester, 1990), pp. 9–40.

66   M. Domosh, 'Towards a Feminist Historiography of Geography',
     Transactions of the Institute of British Geographers, n.s., xviii (1991), pp.
     95–105.

67   M. Andrews, *Landscape and Western Art* (Oxford, 1999), p. 85.

68   *Ibid.*

69   J. Berger, *Ways of Seeing* (London, 1972), p. 120.

70   J. B. Harley, 'Maps, Knowledge and Power', in *The Iconography of
     Landscape*, ed. D. Cosgrove and S. Daniels (Cambridge, 1988),
     pp. 277–312.

71 A. Godlewska, 'Map, Text and Image: The Mentality of Enlightened Conquerors: A New Look at the Description de l'Egypte', *Transactions of the Institute of British Geographers*, n.s., xx (1995), pp. 5–28.
72 Cosgrove, *Social Formation and Symbolic Landscape*, p. 72.
73 Hoskins, *English Landscape*, p. 20.
74 I. G. Simmons, *An Environmental History of Great Britain* (Edinburgh, 2001), pp. 23–50.
75 T. Williamson, 'The Rural Landscape: 1500–1900, the Neglected Centuries', in *Landscape: The Richest Historical Record*, ed. D. Hooke, Society for Landscape Studies Monograph (Birmingham, 2001), pp. 109–17.

TWO   EARLY MODERN LANDSCAPES

1 R. A. Dodgshon, *The European Past: Social Evolution and Spatial Order* (London, 1987), p. 76.
2 P. Atkins, I. Simmons and B. Roberts, *People, Land and Time* (London, 1998), pp. 64–7.
3 M. Williams, 'Dark Ages and Dark Areas: Global Deforestation in the Deep Past', *Journal of Historical Geography*, xxvi (2000), pp. 28–46.
4 F. Braudel, *The Identity of France* (London, 1988), p. 126.
5 J. Thirsk, *England's Agricultural Regions and Agrarian History, 1500–1750* (London, 1987).
6 D. Hooke, 'The Appreciation of Landscape History', in *Landscapes: The Richest Historical Record*, ed. D. Hooke, Society for Landscape Studies Monograph (Birmingham, 2001), pp. 43–55.
7 H. Prince, 'Regional Contrasts in Agrarian Structures', in *Themes in the Historical Geography of France*, ed. H. Clout (London, 1977), pp. 162–5.
8 O. Rackham, *The History of the Countryside* (London, 1986), pp. 4–5.
9 M. Turner, *English Parliamentary Enclosure* (Folkestone, 1980).
10 T. Williamson, 'Exploring Regional Landscapes: Woodland and Champion in Southern and Eastern England', *Landscape History*, x (1988), pp. 5–13.
11 Prince, 'Regional Contrasts', pp. 162–5.
12 B. K. Roberts, 'Rural Settlements in Europe, 500–1500', in *An Historical Geography of Europe*, ed. R. A. Butlin and R. A. Dodgshon (Oxford, 1998), pp. 73–100.
13 J. R. McNeill, *The Mountains of the Mediterranean* (Cambridge, 1992), p. 15.
14 X. de Planhol, *An Historical Geography of France* (Cambridge, 1994), p. 223.
15 A. R. H. Baker and R. A. Butlin, *Studies of Field Systems in the British Isles* (Cambridge, 1973).
16 R. A. Dodgshon, *Land and Society in Early Scotland* (Oxford, 1981), pp. 188–91.
17 I. D. Whyte, 'Rural Europe since 1500: Areas of Retardation and Tradition', in *An Historical Geography of Europe*, ed. R. A. Dodgshon and R. A. Butlin (Oxford, 1998), pp. 243–58.

18 P. D. A. Harvey, *Maps in Tudor England* (London, 1993), p. 99.
19 G. Meirion-Jones, 'Vernacular Architecture and the Peasant House', in *Themes in the Historical Geography of France*, ed. H. D. Clout (Cambridge, 1977), pp. 343–406.
20 G. Meirion-Jones, *The Vernacular Architecture of Brittany: An Essay in Historical Geography* (Edinburgh, 1982), p. 41.
21 M. W. Beresford and J. G. Hurst, *Wharram Percy, Deserted Medieval Village* (London, 1990), pp. 35–41.
22 W. G. Hoskins, *The Making of the English Landscape* (London, 1955), pp. 155–6; S. Denyer, *Traditional Buildings and Life in the Lake District* (London, 1991), pp. 11–18.
23 Roberts, 'Rural Settlements', pp. 73–100.
24 Williams, 'Dark Ages', pp. 28–46.
25 McNeill, *Mountains of the Mediterranean*, p. 154.
26 De Planhol, *Historical Geography*, p. 232.
27 Dodgshon, *European Past*; N. J. G. Pounds, *An Historical Geography of Europe, 1500–1840* (Cambridge, 1979), p. 212.
28 M. L. Parry, *Climatic Change, Agriculture and Settlement* (Folkestone, 1978); J. M. Grove, *The Little Ice Age* (London, 1990).
29 Grove, *Little Ice Age*.
30 M. Widgren, 'Is Landscape History Possible? Or, How Can We Study the Desertion of Farms?', in *The Archaeology of Landscape*, ed. P. Ucko and R. Layton (London, 1999), pp. 96–103.
31 H. Lamb, *Climate, History and the Modern World* (London, 1982), p.207.
32 H. Lamb, *Climate: Past, Present and Future*, 1 (London, 1972), pp. 153–4.
33 Parry, *Climatic Change*, pp. 83–6.
34 E. Le Roy Ladurie, *Times of Feast, Times of Famine: A History of Climate from the Year 1000* (London, 1971), pp. 128–75.
35 Grove, *Little Ice Age*, pp. 64–107.
36 Grove, *Little Ice Age*, p. 232.
37 *Royal Commission on the Ancient and Historical Monuments of Scotland, East Dumfriesshire: Archaeological Landscape* (Edinburgh, 1997), pp. 85–7.
38 Grove, *Little Ice Age*.
39 Roberts, *Rural Settlements*, pp. 94–5.
40 B. H. Slicher van Bath, *The Agrarian History of Western Europe, AD 500–1850* (London, 1963), pp. 132–6.
41 A. B. Appleby, *Famine in Tudor and Stuart England* (Liverpool, 1978).
42 Dodgshon, *Land and Society*, pp. 176–84.
43 J. Yelling, 'Agriculture, 1500–1730', in *An Historical Geography of England*, ed. R. A. Dodgshon and R. A. Butlin (London, 1978), pp. 151–73.
44 R. A. Butlin, *The Transformation of Rural England c. 1580–1800* (Oxford, 1982); J. R. Wordie, 'The Chronology of English Enclosure, 1500–1914', *Economic History Review*, XXXVI (1983), pp. 483–505.
45 I. Wallerstein, *The Modern World System: Capitalist Agriculture and the Origins of the European World Economy in the Sixteenth Century* (London, 1974).
46 A. M. Lambert, *The Making of the Dutch Landscape* (London, 1985).

47 Quoted in R. A. Butlin 'Drainage and Land Use in the Fenlands and Fen-edge of North East Cambridgeshire in the Seventeenth and Eighteenth Centuries', in *Water Engineering and Landscape*, ed. D. Cosgrove and G. Petts (London, 1990), pp. 54–76.

48 Pounds, *Historical Geography*.

49 O. Rackham, *The History of the Countryside* (London, 1986), pp. 109–13.

50 McNeill, *Mountains of the Mediterranean*, p. 223.

51 R. H. Grove, *Green Imperialism: Colonial Expansion, Tropical Island Edens and the Origins of Environmentalism, 1600–1860* (Cambridge, 1995), p. 158.

52 McNeill, *Mountains of the Mediterranean*, p. 69.

53 M. Bowden, *Furness Iron* (London, 2000).

54 McNeill, *Mountains of the Mediterranean*, p. 72.

55 Rackham, *History of the Countryside*, p. 111.

56 I. D. Whyte, *Agriculture and Society in Seventeenth-Century Scotland* (Edinburgh, 1979), pp. 119–22.

57 T. Williamson, *The Norfolk Broads: A Landscape History* (Manchester, 1997).

58 Lambert, *Dutch Landscape*.

59 G. Whittington and J. Jarvis, 'Kilconquhar Loch, Fife: An Historical and Palynological Investigation', *Proceedings of the Society of Antiquaries of Scotland*, cxvi (1986), pp. 413–28.

60 Whyte, *Seventeenth-Century Scotland*, p. 209.

61 M. Airs, *The Buildings of Britain: Tudor and Jacobean* (London, 1982), p. 11.

62 Airs, *Buildings of Britain*, pp. 41–2.

63 Hoskins, *English Landscape*, pp. 157–8.

64 J. G. Dunbar, *The Historic Architecture of Scotland* (London, 1966).

65 Hoskins, *English Landscape*, pp. 138–9.

66 J. R. Short, *Imagined Country: Environment, Culture and Society* (London, 1991), p. 85.

67 A. C. Kitchener, 'Extinctions, Introductions and Colonisations of Scottish Mammals and Birds since the Last Ice Age', in *Species History in Scotland*, ed. R. A. Lambert (Edinburgh, 1998), pp. 63–92.

68 Rackham, *History of the Countryside*, pp. 32–6.

69 E. Weber, *Peasants into Frenchmen: The Modernization of Rural France, 1870–1914* (London, 1977), p. 22.

70 J. Black, *The British Abroad: The Grand Tour in the Eighteenth Century* (London, 1992).

71 F. Braudel, *The Mediterranean and the Mediterranean World in the Age of Philip II* (London, 1975), pp. 178–9.

72 Harvey, *Maps and Tudor England*, p. 37.

73 D. Cosgrove, *Social Formation and Symbolic Landscape* (London, 1984), p. 32.

74 S. Bendall, 'Interpreting Maps of the Rural Landscape: An Example from Late Sixteenth-Century Buckinghamshire', *Rural History*, iv (1993), pp. 107–21.

75 M. Andrews, *Landscape and Western Art* (Oxford, 1999), pp. 79–85.

76 W. Ravenhill, 'Mapping a United Kingdom', *History Today*, xxxv/10 (1985), pp. 27–33.

77 Bendall, 'Interpreting Maps', p. 55.

78 S. Tyacke, *English Map-Making, 1590–1650* (London, 1983), p. 46.

79 D. Buisseret, *Monarchs, Ministers and Maps* (Chicago, 1992).

80 J. C. Stone, 'Timothy Pont and the First Topographical Survey of Scotland, c. 1583–1596', *Scottish Geographical Magazine*, lxxxxix (1983), pp. 161–8.

81 J. Chandler, 'The Discovery of Landscape', in *Landscape: The Richest Historical Record*, ed. D. Hooke, Society for Landscape Studies Monograph (Birmingham, 2001), pp. 33–41.

82 Cosgrove, *Symbolic Landscape*, p. 58.

83 Cosgrove, *Symbolic Landscape*, p. 58.

84 Andrews, *Western Art*, pp. 47–9.

85 D. Cosgrove and S. Daniels, eds, *The Iconography of Landscape* (Cambridge, 1988) p. 19.

86 Cosgrove and Daniels, *Iconography*, p. 19.

87 A. J. Adams, 'Competing Communities in the Great Bog of Europe: Identity and Seventeenth-Century Dutch Landscape Painting', in *Landscape and Power*, ed. W. J. T. Mitchell (Chicago, 1994), pp. 35–76.

88 M. MacCarthy-Morragh, *The Munster Plantation: English Migration to Southern Ireland, 1583–1641* (Oxford, 1986).

89 M. Percival-Maxwell, *The Scottish Migration to Ulster in the Reign of James I* (London, 1973).

90 D. Worster, 'The Vulnerable Earth', in *The Ends of the Earth: Perspectives on Modern Environmental History*, ed. D. Worster (Oxford, 1988), pp. 3–20.

91 J. W. Watson and T. O'Riordan, *The American Environment: Perceptions and Policies* (London, 1976), p. 76.

92 D. Lowenthal, 'The American Scene', *Geographical Review*, lviii (1968), pp. 61–88.

93 L. A. Newson, 'The Population of the Amazon Basin in 1492: A View from the Equadorian Headwaters', *Transactions of the Institute of British Geographers*, n.s., xxi (1996), pp. 5–26.

94 P. Coates, *Nature: Western Attitudes since Ancient Times* (London, 1998), p. 131.

95 Coates, *Nature*.

96 C. M. Cowell, 'Presettlement Piedmont Forests: Patterns of Composition and Disturbance in Central Georgia', *Annals of the Association of American Geographers*, lxxxxv (1995), pp. 65–84.

97 W. Bryson, *A Walk in the Woods* (London, 1997), p. 203.

98 M. Williams, *Americans and their Forests: A Historical Geography* (Cambridge, 1989), p. 47.

99 *Ibid.*

100 M. Conzen, *The Making of the American Landscape* (London, 1990), p. 225.

101 Hart, *Rural Landscape*, p. 89.

102 Conzen, *American Landscape*, p. 232.

103 *Ibid.*

104 Hart, *Rural Landscape*, p. 56.
105 *Ibid.*
106 Grove, *Green Imperialism*, p. 162.
107 T. Musgrave and W. Musgrave, *An Empire of Plants* (London, 2000).
108 L. Pulsipher, 'Seventeenth-Century Montserrat: An Environmental Impact Statement', *Historical Geography Research Group Research Series*, XVII (London, 1986).
109 *Ibid.*

THREE ENLIGHTENMENT, PICTURESQUE AND ROMANTIC
           LANDSCAPES

  1 M. Andrews, *The Search for the Picturesque* (London, 1989), p. 152.
  2 D. Defoe, *A Tour Through the Whole Island of Great Britain*, Penguin Edition (London, 1971), pp. 487–8.
  3 Defoe, *Tour*, p. 550.
  4 Defoe, *Tour*, p. 660.
  5 Defoe, *Tour*, p. 460.
  6 T. C. Smout, *Nature Contested: Environmental History in Scotland and Northern England since 1600* (Edinburgh, 2000), pp. 16–17.
  7 F. Braudel, *The Mediterranean and the Mediterranean World in the Age of Philip II* (London, 1975), I, pp. 25–47.
  8 A. J. L. Winchester, *The Harvest of the Hills: Rural Life in Northern England and the Scottish Borders, 1400–1700* (Edinburgh, 2000), pp. 3–4.
  9 M. E. Burkett, *Read's Point of View: Paintings of the Cumbrian Countryside: Matthias Read, 1669–1747* (Kendal, 1995).
 10 Andrews, *Picturesque*, pp. 132–4.
 11 H. Prince, 'Art and Agrarian Change, 1710–1815', in *The Iconography of Landscape*, ed. D. Cosgrove and S. Daniels (Cambridge, 1988), pp. 98–119.
 12 J. Barrell, *The Dark Side of the Landscape: The Rural Poor in English Painting, 1730–1840* (Cambridge, 1980).
 13 Prince, 'Art and Agrarian Change'.
 14 A. Bermingham, *Landscape and Ideology: The English Rustic Tradition, 1740–1860* (Berkeley, 1987), p. 56.
 15 G. Rose, *Feminism and Geography* (Cambridge, 1993), p. 72.
 16 Smout, *Nature Contested*, p. 20.
 17 M. Turner, *English Parliamentary Enclosure* (Folkestone, 1980), p. 5.
 18 M. Overton, *Agricultural Revolution in England: The Transformation of the Agrarian Economy, 1500–1850* (Cambridge, 1996), p. 190.
 19 J. Chapman, 'Enclosure Commissioners as Landscape Planners', *Landscape History*, XV (1993), pp. 51–5.
 20 Quoted in R. Williams, *The Country and the City* (London, 1973), p. 136.
 21 O. Rackham, *The History of the Countryside* (London, 1986), p. 190.
 22 Bermingham, *Landscape and Ideology*, p. 121.
 23 I. H. Adams, 'The Agents of Agricultural Change', in *The Making of the Scottish Countryside*, ed. M. L. Parry and T. R. Slater (London, 1981),

pp. 155–76.

24 I. D. Whyte and K. A. Whyte, *The Changing Scottish Landscape, 1500–1800* (London, 1991), pp. 126–50.

25 T. C. Smout, *A History of the Scottish People, 1560–1830* (London, 1972), pp. 287–94.

26 D. G. Lockhart, 'The Planned Villages', in *The Making of the Scottish Countryside*, ed. M. L. Parry and T. R. Slater (London, 1981), pp. 249–70.

27 I. H. Adams, *The Making of Urban Scotland* (London, 1978), p. 46.

28 L. Proudfoot, 'Property Ownership and Urban and Village Improvement in Provincial Ireland ca.1700–1845', *Institute of British Geographers Historical Geography Research Series*, XXXIII (1997).

29 F. H. A. Aalen, K. Whelan and M. Stout, eds, *Atlas of the Irish Rural Landscape* (Cork, 1997), p. 54.

30 A. D. M. Phillips, *The Underdraining of Farmland in England during the Nineteenth Century* (Cambridge, 1989).

31 Rackham, *History of the Countryside*, pp. 91–106.

32 S. Seymour, 'Landed Estates, the "Spirit of Planning" and Woodland Management in Later Georgian Britain: A Case Study from the Dukeries, Nottinghamshire', in *European Woods and Forests: Studies in Cultural History*, ed. C. Watkins (London, 1998), pp. 115–34.

33 D. Worster, 'The Vulnerable Earth', in *The Ends of the Earth: Perspectives on Modern Environmental History*, ed. D. Worster (Cambridge, 1988), pp. 3–20.

34 M. Reed, *The Georgian Triumph, 1700–1830* (London, 1984), pp. 247–54.

35 N. Everett, *The Tory View of Landscape* (New York, 1994).

36 T. Williamson, *Polite Landscape: Gardens and Society in Eighteenth-Century England* (Stroud, 1998).

37 Reed, *Georgian Triumph*, pp. 247–9.

38 T. Williamson, 'The Archaeology of the Landscape Park', *British Archaeological Reports*, British Series, CCLXVIII (1998).

39 I. G. Lindsay and M. Cosh, *Inveraray and the Dukes of Argyll* (Edinburgh, 1972).

40 Reed, *Georgian Triumph*, p. 248.

41 Everett, *Tory View*.

42 Williamson, *Archaeology of the Landscape Park*, p. 10.

43 Williamson, *Archaeology of the Landscape Park*, p. 32.

44 Williamson, *Polite Landscape*, p. 55.

45 Bermingham, *Landscape and Ideology*, p. 142.

46 Seymour, 'Landed Estates', pp. 115–34.

47 R. Muir, *The Lost Villages of Britain* (London, 1982), pp. 215–18.

48 Williamson, *Polite Landscape*, p. 96.

49 S. Daniels, 'The Political Iconography of Woodland in Later Georgian England', in *The Iconography of Landscape*, ed. D. Cosgrove and S. Daniels (Cambridge, 1988), pp. 43–82.

50 Whyte and Whyte, *Changing Scottish Landscape*, p. 163.

51 Aalen, Whelan and Stout, *Irish Rural Landscape*, p. 87.

52 L. A. Clarkson, *Proto-Industrialization: The First Phase of*

Industrialization? (London, 1985).

53   B. Trinder, *The Making of the Industrial Landscape* (London, 1982), p. 76.
54   Whyte and Whyte, *Changing Scottish Landscape*, p. 221.
55   J. M. Lindsay, 'The Iron Industry in the Highlands: Charcoal Blast
      Furnaces', *Scottish Historical Review*, LVI (1977), pp. 49–63.
56   B. Bailey, *The Industrial Heritage of Britain* (London, 1982), p. 177.
57   P. J. C. Ransom, *The Archaeology of the Transport Revolution, 1750–1850*
      (Tadworth, 1984), pp. 21–3.
58   J. Langton, *Geographical Change and Industrial Revolution: Coalmining in
      South West Lancashire, 1590–1799* (Cambridge, 1979).
59   Ransom, *Transport Revolution*, pp. 36–72.
60   J. Black, *The British Abroad: The Grand Tour in the Eighteenth Century*
      (London, 1992).
61   Burkett, *Read's Point of View*.
62   Barrell, *Dark Side of the Landscape*, p. 48.
63   Bermingham, *Landscape and Ideology*, p. 110.
64   Turner, *Parliamentary Enclosure*, p. 124.
65   Overton, *Agricultural Revolution*.
66   Bermingham, *Landscape and Ideology*, p. 105.
67   S. Schama, *Landscape and Memory* (London, 1995), pp. 466–71.
68   G. Whittington and A. Gibson, 'The Military Survey of Scotland,
      1747–1755: A Critique', *Institute of British Geographers Historical
      Geography Research Series*, XVIII (1986).
69   R. J. Dabundo, *Encyclopaedia of Romanticism: Culture in Britain,
      1780s–1830s* (London, 1994).
70   Whyte and Whyte, Changing Sco*ttish Landscape*, pp. 189–95.
71   P. Hindle, *Maps for Historians* (London, 1998), p. 62.
72   Adams, 'Agents of Agricultural Change', p. 167.
73   J. W. Konvitz, *Cartography in France, 1660–1848: Science, Engineering
      and Statecraft* (Chicago, 1987); J. W. Konvitz, 'The Nation State, Paris
      and Cartography in Eighteenth- and Nineteenth-century France',
      Journal of Historical Geography, XVI (1990), pp. 3–16.
74   J. F. Hart, *The Rural Landscape* (London, 1998), p. 232.
75   R. H. Grove, *Green Imperialism: Colonial Expansion, Tropical Island Edens
      and the Origins of Environmentalism 1600–1860* (Cambridge, 1995), p. 253.
76   S. Copley, 'Gilpin on the Wye: Tourists, Tintern Abbey and the
      Picturesque', in *Prospects for the Nation: Recent Essays in British Landscape,
      1750–1880*, ed. M. Rosenthal, C. Payne and S. Wilcox (New York,
      1997), pp. 133–56.
77   C. P. Barbier, *Samuel Rogers and William Gilpin: Their Friendship and
      Correspondence* (Oxford, 1959), p. 10.
78   M. Andrews, *The Search for the Picturesque* (London, 1989), p. 173.
79   Bermingham, *Landscape and Ideology*, p. 94.
80   Andrews, *Picturesque*, p. 64.
81   A. Howkins, 'Land, Locality, People, Landscape: The Nineteenth-
      Century Countryside', in *Prospects for the Nation: Recent Essays in British
      Landscape, 1750–1880*, ed. M. Rosenthal, C. Payne and S. Wilcox (New
      York, 1997), pp. 97–114.

82   N. Nicholson, *The Lakers: The Adventures of the First Tourists* (London, 1955), p. 45.
83   Bermingham, *Landscape and Ideology*, p. 7.
84   M. Bunce, *The Countryside Ideal: Anglo-American Images of Landscape* (London, 1994).
85   Schama, *Landscape and Memory*, pp. 411–14.
86   C. E. Searle, 'Customary Tenants and the Economy of the Cumbrian Commons', *Northern History*, XXIX (1993), pp. 126–53.
87   I. D. Whyte, 'William Wordsworth's Guide to the Lakes and the Geographical Tradition', *Area*, XXXII (2000), pp. 101–6.
88   A. I. Macinnes, Clanship, *Commerce and the House of Stuart, 1603–1788* (East Linton, 1996).
89   P. Womack, *Improvement and Romance: Constructing the Myths of the Highlands* (London, 1989), p.95.
90   *Ibid.*
91   Smout, *Nature Contested*, pp. 37–46.
92   J. Vernon, 'Border Crossing: Cornwall and the English (Imagi)nation', in *Imagining Nations*, ed. ed. G. Cubitt (Manchester, 1998), pp. 153–72.
93   R. J. Chorley, A. J. Dunn and R. P. Beckinsale, *The History of the Study of Landforms; or, the Development of Geomorphology, I* (London, 1964), pp. 193–205.
94   Whyte, 'Wordsworth's Guide'.
95   R. J. Evans. 'An Autumn of German Romanticism', *History Today*, XLIV/10 (1994), pp. 9–12.
96   Daniels, 'Iconography of Woodland'.
97   C. Whatley, 'How Tame Were the Scottish Lowlanders during the Eighteenth Century?', in *Conflict and Stability in Scottish Society, 1700–1850*, ed. T. M. Devine (Edinburgh, 1990), pp. 22–3.
98   Schama, *Landscape and Memory*, pp. 170–74.
99   Daniels, 'Iconography of Woodland'.

FOUR   INDUSTRIAL AND IMPERIAL LANDSCAPES

 1   B. Trinder, *The Making of the Industrial Landscape* (London, 1982), pp. 87–92.
 2   M. Jones, 'The Rise, Decline and Extinction of Coppice Wood Management in South-West Yorkshire', in *European Woods and Forests: Studies in Cultural History*, ed. C. Watkins (London, 1998), pp. 55–71; J. Tsouvalis-Gerber, 'Making the Invisible Visible: Ancient Woodlands, British Forest Policy and the Social Construction of Reality', in *ibid.*, pp. 215–29.
 3   S. Pollard, *Peaceful Conquest: The Industrialization of Europe, 1760–1970* (Oxford, 1981).
 4   R. Hardington, 'The Neuroses of the Railway', *History Today*, XLIV/7 (1994), pp. 15–21.
 5   R. A. Dodgshon, 'Strategies of Farming in the Western Highlands and Islands of Scotland prior to Crofting and the Clearances', *Economic History Review*, XLVI (1993), pp. 679–701.

6   A. J. Youngson, *After the Forty-Five* (Edinburgh, 1973), p. 152.
7   *Ibid.*
8   R. Hingley, *Medieval or Later Rural Settlement in Scotland* (Edinburgh, 1993).
9   E. Richards, *A History of the Highland Clearances, I* (London, 1982), pp. 316–58.
10 W. Orr, Deer Forests, *Landlords and Crofters: The Western Highlands in Victorian and Edwardian Times* (Edinburgh, 1982); D Turnock, *Patterns of Highland Development* (London, 1970).
11 F. H. A. Aalen, K. Whelan and M. Stout, eds, *Atlas of the Irish Rural Landscape* (Cork, 1997), p. 104.
12 J. R. McNeill, *The Mountains of the Mediterranean* (Cambridge, 1992).
13 E. Lichtenberger, *The Eastern Alps* (Oxford, 1975).
14 S. Schama, *Landscape and Memory* (London, 1995), pp. 24–31.
15 W. R. Mead, *An Historical Geography of Scandinavia* (London, 1981).
16 D. Turnock, *Patterns of Highland Development* (London, 1970).
17 McNeill, *Mountains of the Mediterranean.*
18 R. Price, *An Economic History of Modern France, 1739–1914* (London, 1981).
19 H. D. Clout, 'Retreat of Settlement', in *Themes in the Historical Geography of France*, ed. H. D. Clout (London, 1977), pp. 107–28.
20 R. Millward, *Scandinavian Lands* (London, 1964), p. 63.
21 M. Berg, 'Representations of Early Industrial Towns: Turner and his Contemporaries', in *Prospects For the Nation: Recent Essays in British Landscape, 1750–1880*, ed. M. Rosenthal, C Payne and S. Wilcox (New Haven, 1997), pp. 115–37.
22 D. Fraser, '"Fields of radiance": The Scientific and Industrial Scenes of Joseph Wright', in *The Iconography of Landscape*, ed. D. Cosgrove and S. Daniels (Cambridge, 1988), pp. 119–41.
23 E. K. Helsinger. 'Land and National Representation in Britain', in *Prospects for the Nation: Recent Essays in British Landscape, 1750–1850*, ed. M. Rosenthal, C. Payne and S. Wilcox (London, 1994), pp. 13–26.
24 D. Cosgrove and S. Daniels, eds, *The Iconography of Landscape* (Cambridge, 1988), p. 45.
25 M. Bunce, *The Countryside Ideal: Anglo-American Images of Landscape* (London, 1994), p. 85.
26 T. R. Pringle, 'The Privation of History" Landseer, Victoria and the Highland Myth', in *The Iconography of Landscape*, ed. D. Cosgrove and S. Daniels (Cambridge, 1988), pp. 142–61.
27 *Ibid.*
28 S. Adams, *The World of the Impressionists* (London, 2000); W. Gaunt, *The Impressionists* (London, 1985).
29 Bunce, *Countryside Ideal*, p. 182.
30 J. R. Ryan, 'Imperial Landscapes: Photography, Geography and British Overseas Exploration, 1858–1872', in *Geography and Imperialism, 1820–1940*, ed. M. Bell, R. Butlin and M. Heffernan (Manchester, 1995), pp. 53–79.
31 D. C. D. Pocock, 'Place and the Novelist', *Transactions of the Institute of*

British Geographers, n.s., VI (1981), pp. 337–47.

32 Pocock, 'Place and the Novelist', pp. 337–47.

33 J. Barrell, *The Dark Side of the Landscape: The Rural Poor in English Painting, 1730–1840* (Cambridge, 1982), pp. 352–3.

34 Pocock, 'Place and the Novelist', pp. 337–47.

35 G. Whittington, 'The Regionalisation of Lewis Grassic Gibbon', *Scottish Geographical Magazine*, LXXXX (1974), pp. 74–85; G. Whittington, 'Agriculture and Society in Lowland Scotland, 1750–1870', in *An Historical Geography of Scotland*, ed. G. Whittington and I. D. Whyte (London, 1983), pp. 148–52.

36 A. W. Crosby, *Ecological Imperialism: The Biological Expansion of Europe, 900–1900* (Cambridge, 1986), p. 38.

37 R.H. Grove, *Green Imperialism: Colonial Expansion, Tropical Island Edens and the Origins of Environmentalism, 1600–1860* (Cambridge, 1995), pp. 70–79.

38 E. Said, *Orientalism* (London, 1978).

39 A. Godlewska, 'Map, Text and Image: The Mentality of Enlightened Conquerors. A New Look at the Description de l'Egypte', *Transactions of the Institute of British Geographers*, n.s., XX (1995), pp. 5–28.

40 D. Gregory, 'Between the Book and the Lamp: Imaginative Geographies of Egypt, 1849–1850', *Transactions of the Institute of British Geographers*, n.s., XX (1995), pp. 29–57.

41 E. Grant, 'The Sphinx in the North: Egyptian Influences on Landscape Architecture and Interior Design in Eighteenth- and Nineteenth-Century Scotland', in *The Iconography of Landscape*, ed. D. Cosgrove and S. Daniels (Cambridge, 1988), pp. 236–53.

42 J. M. Mackenzie, *Imperialism and Popular Culture* (Manchester, 1986).

43 A. Godlewska, 'Napoleon's Geographers (1797–1815): Imperialists and Soldiers of Modernity', in *Geography and Empire*, ed. A. Godlewska and N. Smith (Oxford, 1994), pp. 31–54.

44 R. Oliver, *Ordnance Survey Maps: A Concise Guide for Historians* (London, 1993), p. 10.

45 J. H. Andrews, *A Paper Landscape: The Ordnance Survey in Nineteenth-Century Ireland* (Oxford, 1975).

46 C. W. J. Withers, 'Authorizing Landscape: "Authority", Naming and the Ordnance Survey's Mapping of the Scottish Highlands in the Nineteenth Century', *Journal of Historical Geography*, XXVI (2000), pp. 532–54.

47 F. Spufford, *I May Be Some Time* (London, 1996).

48 M. Heffernan, 'Bringing the Desert to Bloom: French Ambitions in the Sahara Desert during the Late Nineteenth Century – The Strange Case of "La Mer Interieure"', in *Water, Engineering and Landscape: Water Control and Landscape Formation in the Modern World*, ed. D. Cosgrove and G. Petts (London, 1990), pp. 94–114.

49 T. E. Saarinen, *Perception of the Drought Hazard on the Great Plains* (Chicago, 1966).

50 D. Worster, 'The Vulnerable Earth', in *The Ends of the Earth: Perspectives on Modern Environmental History*, ed. D. Worster (Oxford,

1988), pp. 3–20.

51 A. Chadha, 'The Anatomy of Dispossession: A Study in the Displacement of the Tribals from their Traditional Landscape in the Marmada Valley due to the Sardar Sarovar Project', in *The Archaeology of Landscape*, ed. P. Ucko and R. Layton (London, 1999), pp. 146–58.

52 R. P. Tucker, 'The Depletion of India's Forests under British Imperialism: Planters, Forests and Peasants in Assam and Kerala', in *The Ends of the Earth: Perspectives on Modern Environmental History*, ed. D. Worster (Cambridge, 1988), pp. 118–40.

53 T. Musgrave and W. Musgrave, *An Empire of Plants* (London, 2000), p. 65.

54 J. T. Kenny, 'Climate, Race and Imperial Authority – The Symbolic Landscape of the British Hill Station in India', *Annals of the Association of American Geographers*, LXXXV (1995), pp. 694–714.

55 C. Gordon and C. Gordon, 'Gardens of the Raj', *History Today*, XLVI/7 (1996), pp. 22–9.

56 G. Wynn, 'Re-mapping Tutira: Contours in the Environmental History of New Zealand', *Journal of Historical Geography*, XXIII (1997), pp. 418–46.

57 M. Roche, 'The Land We Have, We Must Hold: Soil Erosion and Soil Conservation in Late Nineteenth-Century and Early Twentieth-Century New Zealand', *Journal of Historical Geography*, XXIII (1997), pp. 442–58.

58 M. Williams, *The Making of the South Australian Landscape* (London, 1974).

59 W. Bryson, *Down Under* (London, 2000), p. 103.

60 G. McEwan, 'Paradise or Pandemonium? West African Landscapes in the Travel Accounts of Victorian Women', *Journal of Historical Geography*, XXII (1996), pp. 68–83.

61 R. G. David, *The Arctic in British Imagination, 1818–1914* (Manchester, 2000).

62 Spufford, *I May Be Some Time*.

63 R. L. Gerlach, 'A Contrast in Old World Ideology: German and Scotch-Irish in the Ozarks', in *Ideology and Landscape in Historical Perspective*, ed. A. Baker and G. Biger (Cambridge, 1992), pp. 289–302.

64 J. F. Hart, *The Rural Landscape* (London, 1998).

65 *Ibid.*

66 D. Lowenthal, 'The Place of the Past in the American Landscape', in *Geographies of the Mind*, ed. D. Lowenthal and M. J. Bowden (New York, 1976), pp. 89–117.

67 P. Coates, *Nature: Western Attitudes since Ancient Times* (London, 1998).

68 J. Appleton, *The Experience of Landscape* (London, 1975).

69 S. Daniels, *Fields of Vision: Landscape and Identity in Europe and the United States* (Princeton, 1993).

70 D. Lowenthal, 'The American Scene', *Geographical Review*, LVIII (1968), pp. 61–8.

71 J. L. Allen, 'Geographical Knowledge and American Images of the Louisiana Territory', *Western Historical Quarterly*, II (1971), pp. 151–70.

72 M. J. Bowden, 'The Great American Desert in the American Mind: The Historiography of a Geographical Notion', in *Geographies of the Mind*, ed. D. Lowenthal and M. J. Bowden (New York, 1976), pp. 119–47.

73 D. W. Meinig, *The Interpretation of Ordinary Landscapes* (Oxford, 1979), p. 62.

74 J. R. Shortridge, 'The Vernacular Middle West', *Annals of the Association of American Geographers*, LXXV (1985), pp. 48–57.

75 G. Rose, 'Place and Identity: A Sense of Place', in *A Place in the World?*, ed. D. Massey and P. Jess (London, 1995), pp. 87–132.

76 Worster, *Ends of the Earth*, p. 10.

77 H. W. Prince, 'A Marshland Chronicle, 1830–1960: From Artificial Drainage to Outdoor Recreation in Central Wisconsin', *Journal of Historical Geography*, XXI (1995), pp. 3–22.

78 Allen, 'Louisiana Territory', pp. 151–70.

FIVE   MODERN AND POST-MODERN LANDSCAPES

1 A. Chadha, 'The Anatomy of Dispossession: A Study in the Displacement of the Tribals from their Traditional Landscape in the Marmada Valley due to the Sardar Sarovar Project', in *The Archaeology of Landscape*, ed. P. Ucko and R. Layton (London, 1999), pp. 146–58.

2 D. Worster, 'The Vulnerable Earth', in *The Ends of the Earth: Perspectives on Modern Environmental History*, ed. D. Worster (Oxford, 1988), pp. 3–20.

3 C. Park, *Tropical Rainforests* (London, 1992), pp. 33–6.

4 J. F. Hart, *The Rural Landscape* (London, 1998), p. 232.

5 M. Williams, 'Dark Ages and Dark Areas: Global Deforestation in the Deep Past', *Journal of Historical Geography*, XXVI (2000), pp. 28–46.

6 M. Shoard, *The Theft of the Countryside* (London, 1980), pp. 34–97.

7 P. Gruffudd, '"Uncivil Engineering": Nature, Nationalism and Hydro-electrics in North Wales', in *Water, Engineering and Landscape*, ed. D. Cosgrove and G. Petts (London, 1990), pp. 159–73.

8 N. Fairbrother, *New Lives, New Landscapes* (London, 1970).

9 D. Cosgrove, B. Roscoe and S. Ryorof, 'Landscape and Identity at Ladybower Reservoir and Rutland Water', *Transactions of the Institute of British Geographers*, n.s., XXVI (1996), pp. 534–51.

10 T. C. Smout, *Nature Contested: Environmental History in Scotland and Northern England since 1600* (Edinburgh, 2000), pp. 90–115.

11 T. C. Smout, *Scottish Woodland History* (Edinburgh, 1997), p. 52.

12 D. Cannadine, *G. M. Trevelyan: A Life in History* (London, 1992), p. 256.

13 Smout, *Nature Contested*, pp. 59–60.

14 M. Atherden, *Upland Britain: A Natural History* (Manchester, 1992), pp. 124–35.

15 P. Cloke, P. Milbourne and C. Thomas, 'The English National Forest: Local Reactions to Plans for Renegotiated Nature–Society Relationships in the Countryside', *Transactions of the Institute of British Geographers*, n.s., XXI (1996), pp. 552–71.

16 E. R. Boquete, 'The Expansion of the Forest and the Defence of Nature: The Work of Forest Engineers in Spain, 1900–36', in *European Woods and Forests: Studies in Cultural History*, ed. C. Watkins (London, 1998), pp. 181–90.

17 F. H. A. Aalen, K. Whelan and M. Stout, *Atlas of the Irish Rural Landscape* (Cork, 1997), p. 89.

18 J. Ardagh, *France in the New Century* (London, 1999), p. 344.

19 E. Hobsbawm, *Nations and Nationalism since 1780: Programme, Myth, Reality* (Cambridge, 1990); L. Colley, *Britons: Forging the Nation* (London, 1992).

20 B. Graham, 'The Past in Europe's Present: Diversity, Identity and the Construction of Place', in *Modern Europe: Place Culture and Identity*, ed. B. Graham (London, 1998), pp. 19–52.

21 S. Daniels, 'Mapping National Identities: The Culture of Cartography with Particular Reference to Ordnance Survey', in *Imagining Nations*, ed. G. Cubitt (Manchester, 1998), pp. 112–31.

22 G. Cubitt, 'Introduction', in *Imagining Nations*, ed. G. Cubitt (Manchester, 1998), pp. 1–20.

23 J. Agnew, 'European Landscape and Identity', in *Modern Europe: Place, Culture and Identity*, ed. B. Graham (London, 1998), pp. 213–35.

24 A. Leyshon, D. Matless and G. Revill. 'The Place of Music', *Transactions of the Institute of British Geographers*, n.s., xx (1995), pp. 423–33; S. J. Smith, 'Soundscape', *Area*, xxvi (1994), pp. 232–40.

25 S. Schama, *Landscape and Memory* (London, 1995), pp. 3–22.

26 D. Matless, *Landscape and Englishness* (London, 1998), p. 48.

27 J. R. Short, *Imagined Countryside: Environment, Culture and Society* (London, 1991).

28 S. Daniels, *Fields of Vision: Landscape and Identity in Europe and the United States* (Princeton, 1993), p. 132.

29 G. Rose, 'Place and Identity: A Sense of Place', in *A Place in the World?*, ed. D. Massey and P. Jess (London, 1995), pp. 87–132.

30 D. Cosgrove, 'Landscape and Myths: Gods and Humans', in *Landscape: Politics and Perspectives*, ed. B. Bender (Oxford, 1993), pp. 281–305.

31 D. W. Meinig, *The Interpretation of Ordinary Landscapes* (Oxford, 1979), p. 143.

32 S. Daniels, 'The Making of Constable Country, 1880–1940', *Landscape Research*, xii (1991), pp. 9–17.

33 G. L. Mosse, *Fallen Soldiers: Reshaping the Memory of the World Wars* (London, 1990).

34 D. Lowenthal, 'British National Identity and the English Landscape', *Rural History*, ii (1991), pp. 205–30.

35 P. Gruffudd, 'The Countryside as Educator: Schools, Rurality and Citizenship in Inter-War Wales', *Journal of Historical Geography*, xxii (1996), pp. 412–33.

36 P. Gruffudd, D. T. Herbert and A. Piccini, 'In Search of Wales: Travel Writings and Narratives of Difference, 1918–50', *Journal of Historical Geography*, xxvi (2000), pp. 589–604.

37 B. Graham, 'Heritage Conservation and Revisionist Nationalism in

Ireland', in *Building a New Heritage: Tourism, Culture and Identity in the New Europe*, ed. G. J. Ashworth and P. J. Larkham (London, 1994), pp. 135–58.

38 J. Agnew, 'European Landscape and Identity', in *Modern Europe: Place, Culture and Identity*, ed. B. Graham (London, 1998), pp. 213–35.

39 P. Coates, *Nature: Western Attitudes since Ancient Times* (London, 1998).

40 *Ibid.*

41 Schama, *Landscape and Memory*, pp. 67–70.

42 G. Groening, 'The Feeling for Landscape: A German Example', *Landscape Research*, XVII (1992), pp. 108–15; Schama, *Landscape and Memory*, pp. 68–74.

43 W. H. Rollins, 'Whose Landscape? Technology, Fascism and Environmentalism on the National Socialist Autobahn', *Annals of the Association of American Geographers*, LXXXV (1995), pp. 494–520.

44 N. C. Johnson, 'Sculpting Heroic Histories: Celebrating the Centenary of the 1798 Rebellion in Ireland', *Transactions of the Institute of British Geographers*, n.s., XIX (1994), pp. 78–93.

45 M. Heffernan, 'Forever England: The Western Front and the Politics of Remembrance in Britain', *Ecumene*, II (1995), pp. 293–325.

46 C. W. J. Withers 'Place, Meaning, Monument: Memoralising the Past in Contemporary Highland Society', *Ecumene*, III (1996), pp. 325–44.

47 P. Basu, 'Sites of Memory – Sources of Identity: Landscape Narratives of the Sutherland Clearances', in *Townships to Farmsteads: Rural Settlement Studies in Scotland, England and Wales*, ed. J. Atkinson, A. Banks and G. MacGregor, *British Archaeological Reports*, British Series, CCLXXXIII (2000), pp. 225–36.

48 N. Cameron, 'Rustic Folly to Romantic Folly: The Glenfinnan Monument Re-assessed', *Proceedings of the Society of Antiquaries of Scotland*, CXXIX (1999), pp. 882–907.

49 H. Clout, 'War and Recovery in the Countryside of North Eastern France: The Example of Meurthe-et-Moselle', *Journal of Historical Geography*, XXXIII (1997), pp. 164–86.

50 D. de Olivier, 'Historical Presentation and Identity: The Alamo and the Production of a Consumer Landscape', *Antopode*, XXVIII (1996), pp. 1–23.

51 Matless, *Landscape and Englishness*, p. 98.

52 I. B. Thompson, *The Paris Basin* (Oxford, 1973), p. 25.

53 Matless, *Landscape and Englishness*, p. 142.

54 B. Graham, G. J. Ashworth and J. E. Tunbridge, *A Geography of Heritage* (London, 2000), p. 13.

55 Coates, *Nature*, p. 336.

56 Smout, *Nature Contested*, pp. 26–7.

57 J. Tsouvalis-Gerber, 'Making the Invisible Visible: Ancient Woodlands, British Forest Policy and the Social Construction of Reality', in *European Woods and Forests: Studies in Cultural History*, ed. C. Watkins (London, 1998), pp. 215–29.

58 R. P. Neuman, 'Ways of Seeing Africa: Colonial Recasting of African Society and Landscape in the Serengeti National Park', *Ecumene*, II (1995), pp. 149–69.

59 Shoard, *Theft of the Countryside*.
60 I. B. Thompson, *The Lower Rhône and Marseilles* (Oxford, 1975), p. 26.
61 J. Naylon, *Andalusia* (Oxford, 1975), pp. 24–7.
62 D. L. Linton, 'The Assessment of Scenery as a Natural Resource', *Scottish Geographical Magazine*, LXXXIV (1968), pp. 219–38.
63 E. Penning-Rowsell, *Alternative Approaches to Landscape Evaluation* (Enfield, 1973).
64 Linton, 'Assessment of Scenery'.
65 G. Fairclough, 'Protecting Time and Space: Understanding Historic Landscape for Conservation in England', in *The Archaeology of Landscape*, ed. P. Ucko and R. Layton (London, 1999), pp. 119–34.
66 Countryside Commission, *Countryside Character: The Character of England's Natural and Man-made Landscape, II: The North West* (Cheltenham, 1998).
67 Matless, *Landscape and Englishness*, p. 92.
68 P. Viazzo, *Upland Communities: Environment, Population and Social Changes in the Alps since the Sixteenth Century* (Cambridge, 1989).
69 Thompson, *Lower Rhône*, pp. 32–3.
70 D. Matless, '"The Art of Right Living": Landscape and Citizenship, 1918–39', in *Mapping the Subject: Geographies of Cultural Transformation*, ed. S. Pile and N. Thrift (London, 1995), pp. 93–122.
71 Daniels, 'Mapping National Identities'.
72 J. P. Browne, *Map Cover Art: A Pictorial History of Ordnance Survey Cover Illustrations* (London, 1990); Daniels, 'Mapping National Identities'.
73 R. Preston, '"The Scenery of the Torrid Zone": Imagined Travels and the Culture of Exotics in Nineteenth Century British Gardens', in *Imperial Cities: Landscape, Display and Identity*, ed. F. Driver and D. Gilbert (Manchester, 1999), pp. 194–214.
74 C. Taylor, 'The Plus Fours in the Wardrobe: A Personal View of Landscape History', in *Landscape: The Richest Historical Record*, ed. D. Hooke, Society for Landscape Studies Monograph (Birmingham, 2001), pp. 157–62.
76 D. Lowenthal, 'Past Time, Present Place', *Geographical Review*, LXV (1975), p. 136.
77 *Ibid.*
78 Graham, *Modern Europe*, p. 2.
79 R. Hewison, *The Heritage Industry: Britain in a Climate of Decline* (London, 1987).
80 N. O. Johnson, 'Historical Geographies of the Present', in *Modern Historical Geographies*, ed. B. Graham and C. Nash (London, 2000), pp. 251–72.
81 Royal Commission on the Ancient and Historical Monuments of Scotland, *Strath of Kildonan: An Archaeological Survey* (Edinburgh, 1993); *East Dumfriesshire: An Archaeological Landscape* (Edinburgh, 1997).
82 C. Chippendale, P. Devereux, P. Fowler and T. Sebastian, eds, *Who Owns Stonehenge?* (London, 1990).
83 S. Daniels, *Fields of Vision: Landscape and Identity in Europe and the*

United States (Princeton, 1993), p. 145.
84 Hewison, *Heritage Industry*.
85 S. F. Mills, 'Landscape Simulation and the Open-Air Museum',
    Landscapes, 1 (2000), pp. 80–95.
86 J. C. Stone, 'The Cartography of Colonialism and Decolonisation:
    The Case of Swaziland', in *Geography and Imperialism*, ed. M. Bell, R.
    Butlin and M. Heffernan (Manchester, 1995), pp. 298–324.
87 A. Macdonald, *Mapping the World: A History of the Directorate of Overseas
    Surveys, 1946–1985* (London, 1996).
88 Worster, *Ends of the Earth*.
89 Park, *Tropical Rainforests*, p. 37.
90 I. A. Simpson, D. Parsisson, N. Hancey and C. U. Bullock,
    'Envisioning Future Landscapes in the Environmentally Sensitive
    Areas of Scotland', *Transactions of the Institute of British Geographers*, n.s.,
    XXII (1997), pp. 307–20.

Bibliography

Aalen, F. H. A., Whelan, K., and Stout, M., eds, *Atlas of the Irish Rural Landscape* (Cork, 1997)

Adams, A. J., 'Competing Communities in the Great Bog of Europe: Identity and Seventeenth-Century Dutch Landscape Painting', in *Landscape and Power*, ed. W. J. T. Mitchell (Chicago, 1994), pp. 35–76

Adams, Ian. H., *The Making of Urban Scotland* (London, 1978)

—, 'The Agents of Agricultural Change', in *The Making of the Scottish Countryside*, ed. Martin L. Parry and Terry R. Slater (London, 1981), pp. 155–76

Adams, S., *The World of the Impressionists* (London, 2000)

Agnew, J., 'European Landscape and Identity', in *Modern Europe Place, Culture and Identity*, ed. B. Graham (London, 1998), pp. 213–35

Airs, M., *The Buildings of Britain: Tudor and Jacobean* (London, 1982)

Allen, J. L., 'Geographical Knowledge and American Images of the Louisiana Territory', *Western Historical Quarterly*, II (1971), pp. 151–70

Andrews, J. H., *A Paper Landscape: The Ordnance Survey in Nineteenth-Century Ireland* (Oxford, 1975)

Andrews, Malcolm, *The Search for the Picturesque* (London, 1989)

—, *Landscape and Western Art* (Oxford, 1999)

Appleby, Andrew B., *Famine in Tudor and Stuart England* (Liverpool, 1978)

Appleton, Jay, *The Experience of Landscape* (London, 1975)

Ardagh, John, *France in the New Century* (London, 1999)

Atherden, Margaret, *Upland Britain: A Natural History* (Manchester, 1992)

Atkins, P., Simmons, Ian, and Roberts, Brian, *People, Land and Time* (London, 1998)

Bailey, B., *The Industrial Heritage of Britain* (London, 1982)

Baker, Alan, and Biger, G., 'Introduction: An Ideology of Landscape', in *Ideology and Landscape in Historical Perspective*, ed. Alan Baker and G. Biger (Cambridge, 1992), pp. 1–14

Baker, Alan R. H., 'Historical Geography and the Study of the European Rural Landscape', *Geografiska Annaler*, LXX/B (1988), pp. 5–15

—, and Butlin, Robin A., *Studies of Field Systems in the British Isles* (Cambridge, 1973)

Barbier, C. P., *Samuel Rogers and William Gilpin: Their Friendship and Correspondence* (Oxford, 1959)

Barrell, J., 'Geographies of Hardy's Wessex', *Journal of Historical Geography*, VIII (1982), pp. 347–61

—, *The Dark Side of the Landscape: The Rural Poor in English Painting,*

1730–1840 (Cambridge, 1980)

—, 'The Public Prospect and the Private View: The Politics of Taste in Eighteenth-Century Britain', in *Reading Landscape: Country–City–Capital*, ed. S. Pugh (Manchester, 1990), pp. 9–40

Basu, P., 'Sites of Memory – Sources of Identity: Landscape Narratives of the Sutherland Clearances', in *Townships to Farmsteads. Rural Settlement Studies in Scotland, England and Wales*, ed. John A. Atkinson, Ian Banks and G. Macgregor, *British Archaeological Reports*, British Series, CCXCIII (Oxford, 2000), pp. 225–36

Bendall, S., 'Interpreting Maps of the Rural Landscape: An Example from Late Sixteenth-Century Buckinghamshire', *Rural History*, IV (1993), pp. 107–21

Bender, Barbara, *Landscape: Politics and Responsibility* (Oxford, 1992)
—, *Stonehenge: Making Space* (Oxford, 1998)

Benes, J., and Zvelebil, M., 'A Historical interactive Landscape in the Heart of Europe: The Case of Bohemia', in *The Archaeology of Landscape*, ed. P. Ucko and R. Layton (London, 1999), pp. 73–93

Beresford, Maurice W., and Hurst, John G., *Wharram Percy, Deserted Medieval Village* (London, 1990)

Berg, M., 'Representations of Early industrial Towns: Turner and his Contemporaries', in *Prospects for the Nation: Recent Essays in British Landscape, 1750–1880*, ed. Michael Rosenthal, Christiana Payne and Scott Wilcox (New Haven, 1997), pp. 115–37

Berger, J., *Ways of Seeing* (London, 1972)

Bermingham, A., *Landscape and Ideology: The English Rustic Tradition, 1740–1860* (Berkeley, 1987)

Berglund, B. E., ed., *The Cultural Landscape During 6,000 Years in Southern Sweden: The Ystad Project*, Ecological Bulletins, XLI (1991)

Black, Jeremy, *The British Abroad: The Grand Tour in the Eighteenth Century* (London, 1992)

Boquete, E. R., 'The Expansion of the Forest and the Defence of Nature: The Work of Forest Engineers in Spain, 1900–36', in *European Woods and Forests: Studies in Cultural History*, ed. Charles Watkins (London, 1998), pp. 181–90

Bowden, M. J., 'The Great American Desert in the American Mind: The Historiography of a Geographical Notion', in *Geographies of the Mind*, ed. David Lowenthal and M. J. Bowden (New York, 1976), pp. 119–47
—, 'The Invention of American Tradition', *Journal of Historical Geography*, XVIII (1992), pp. 3–26

Bowden, Mark, *Furness Iron* (London, 2000)

Braudel, Fernand, *The Mediterranean and the Mediterranean World in the Age of Philip II* (London, 1975)
—, *The Identity of France* (London, 1988)

Brookfield, Harold, 'On the Environment as Perceived', in *Progress in Geography, I*, ed. C. Board *et al.* (London, 1969), pp. 51–80

Browne, J. P., *Map Cover Art: A Pictorial History of Ordnance Survey Cover Illustrations* (London, 1990)

Bryson, William, *A Walk in the Woods* (London, 1997)

—, *Down Under* (London, 2000)

Buisseret, D., *Monarchs, Ministers and Maps* (Chicago, 1992)

Bunce, M., *The Countryside Ideal: Anglo-American Images of Landscape* (London, 1994)

Burkett, M. E., *Read's Point of View: Paintings of the Cumbrian Countryside: Mathias Read, 1669–1747* (Kendal, 1995)

Butlin, Robin A., *The Transformation of Rural England c. 1580–1800* (Oxford, 1982)

—, 'Drainage and Land Use in the Fenlands and Fen-Edge of North East Cambridgeshire in the Seventeenth and Eighteenth Centuries', in *Water, Engineering and Landscape: Water Control and Landscape Formation in the Modern World*, ed. Denis Cosgrove and Geoffrey Petts (London, 1990), pp. 54–76

—, *Historical Geography: Through the Gates of Space and Time* (London, 1993)

Cameron, N., 'Rustic Folly to Romantic Folly: The Glenfinnan Monument Re-Assessed', *Proceedings of the Society of Antiquaries of Scotland*, CXXIX (1999), pp. 882–907

Cannadine, D., *G. M. Trevelyan: A Life in History* (London, 1992)

Chadha, A., 'The Anatomy of Dispossession: A Study in the Displacement of the Tribals from their Traditional Landscape in the Marmada Valley due to the Sardar Sarovar Project', in *The Archaeology of Landscape*, ed. P. Ucko and R. Layton (London, 1999), pp. 146–58

Chandler, John, 'The Discovery of Landscape', in *Landscape: The Richest Historical Record*, ed. D. Hooke, Society for Landscape Studies Monograph (Birmingham, 2001), pp. 133–41

Chapman, John, 'Enclosure Commissioners as Landscape Planners', *Landscape History*, XV (1993), pp. 51–5

Chippendale, C., Devereux, P., Fowler, P., Jones, R., and Sebastian, T., eds, *Who Owns Stonehenge?* (London, 1990)

Chorley, Richard J., Dunn, A. J., and Beckinsale, R. P., *The History of the Study of Landforms; or, the Development of Geomorphology* (London, 1964)

Clark, Kenneth, *Landscape into Art* (London, 1949)

Clarkson, Leslie A., *Proto-Industrialization: The First Phase of Industrialization?* (London, 1985)

Claval, Paul, 'European Rural Societies and Landscapes and the Challenge of Urbanization and Industrialization in the Nineteenth Century', *Geografiska Annaler*, LXX/B (1988), pp. 27–38

Cloke, Paul, Milbourne, P., and Thomas, C., 'The English National Forest: Local Reactions to Plans for Renegotiated Nature–Society Relationships in the Countryside', *Transactions of the Institute of British Geographers*, n.s., XXI (1996), pp. 552–71

Clout, Hugh D., *The Franco-Belgian Border Region* (Oxford, 1975)

—, 'Retreat of Rural Settlement', in *Themes in the Historical Geography of France*, ed. Hugh D. Clout (London, 1977), pp. 107–28

—, 'War and Recovery in the Countryside of North Eastern France: The Example of Meurthe-Et-Moselle', *Journal of Historical Geography*, XXXIII (1997), pp. 164–86

Coates, P., *Nature: Western Attitudes since Ancient Times* (London, 1998)

Colley, Linda, *Britons: Forging the Nation* (London, 1992)

Conzen, Michael, *The Making of the American Landscape* (London, 1990)

Coones, Paul, 'One Landscape or Many? A Geographical Perspective', *Landscape History*, VII (1985), pp. 5–13

Copley, S., 'Gilpin on the Wye: Tourists, Tintern Abbey and the Picturesque', in *Prospects for the Nation: Recent Essays in British Landscape, 1750–1880*, ed. Michael Rosenthal, Christiana Payne and Scott Wilcox (New Haven, 1997), pp. 133–56

Cosgrove, Denis, *Social Formation and Symbolic Landscape* (London, 1984)

—, 'Prospect, Perspective and the Evolution of the Landscape Idea', *Transactions of the institute of British Geographers*, n.s., X (1985), pp. 45–62

—, 'The Geometry of Landscape: Practical and Speculative Arts in the Sixteenth-Century Venetian Land Territories', in *The Iconography of Landscape*, ed. Denis Cosgrove and Stephen Daniels (Cambridge, 1988), pp. 254–76

—, 'Landscape and Myths: Gods and Humans', in *Landscape: Politics and Perspective*, ed. B. Bender (Oxford, 1993), pp. 281–305

Cosgrove, Denis, and Daniels, Stephen, eds, *The Iconography of Landscape* (Cambridge, 1988)

Cosgrove, Denis, and Petts, Geoffrey, eds, *Water, Engineering and Landscape: Water Control and Landscape Formation in the Modern World* (London, 1990)

Cosgrove, Denis, Roscoe, B., and Ryorof, S., 'Landscape and Identity at Ladybower Reservoir and Rutland Water', *Transactions of the Institute of British Geographers*, n.s., XXVI (1996), pp. 534–51

Countryside Commission, *Countryside Character: The Character of England's Natural and Man-Made Landscape, II: The North West* (Cheltenham, 1998)

Cowell, C. M., 'Presettlement Piedmont Forests: Patterns of Composition and Disturbance in Central Georgia', *Annals of the Association of American Geographers*, LXXXV (1995), pp. 65–84

Crosby, A. W., *Ecological Imperialism: The Biological Expansion of Europe, 900–1900* (Cambridge, 1986)

Cubitt, Geoffrey, ed., *Imagining Nations* (Manchester, 1998)

Dabundo, R. J., *Encyclopaedia of Romanticism: Culture in Britain, 1780s–1830s* (London, 1994)

Daiches, David, and Flower, J., *Literary Landscapes of the British Isles: A Narrative Atlas* (London, 1979)

Daniels, Stephen, 'The Political Iconography of Woodland in Later Georgian England', in *The Iconography of Landscape*, ed. Denis Cosgrove and Stephen Daniels (Cambridge, 1988), pp. 43–82

—, 'The Implications of Industry: Turner and Leeds, 1816', in *Reading Landscape: Country–City–Capital*, ed. S. Pugh (Manchester, 1990), pp. 66–80

—, 'The Making of Constable Country, 1880–1940', *Landscape Research*, XII (1991), pp. 9–17

—, *Fields of Vision: Landscape and Identity in Europe and the United States* (Princeton, 1993)

—, 'Mapping National Identities: The Culture of Cartography with

Particular Reference to the Ordnance Survey', in *Imagining Nations*, ed. G. Cubitt (Manchester, 1998), pp. 112–31

—, Seymour, Susanne, and Watkins, Charles, 'Border Country: The Politics of the Picturesque in the Middle Wye Valley', in *Prospects for the Nation: Recent Essays in British Landscape, 1750–1880*, ed. Michael Rosenthal, Christiana Payne and Scott Wilcox (New Haven, 1997), pp. 157–82

Darby, H. C., 'The Regional Geography of Thomas Hardy's Wessex', *Geographical Review*, XXXVIII (1948), pp. 426–43

—, *Domesday England* (Cambridge, 1977)

Darvill, J., 'The Historic Environment, Historic Landscapes, and Space–Time–Action Models in Landscape Archaeology', in *The Archaeology of Landscape*, ed. P. Ucko and R. Layton (London, 1999), pp. 104–18

David, Robert G., *The Arctic in British Imagination, 1818–1914* (Manchester, 2000)

Delheim C., 'Imagining England: Victorian Views of the North', *Northern History*, XXIII (1987), pp. 216–30

Denyer, S., *Traditional Buildings and Life in the Lake District* (London, 1991)

De Olivier, D., 'Historical Presentation and Identity: The Alamo and the Production of a Consumer Landscape', *Antipode*, XXVIII (1996), pp. 1–23

De Planhol, Xavier, *An Historical Geography of France* (Cambridge, 1994)

Dodgshon, Robert A., *Land and Society in Early Scotland* (Oxford, 1981)

Dodgshon, Robert A., *The European Past: Social Evolution and Spatial Order* (London, 1987)

—, 'Strategies of Farming in the Western Highlands and Islands of Scotland prior to Crofting and the Clearances', *Economic History Review*, XLVI (1993), pp. 679–701

Domosh, Mona, 'Towards a Feminist Historiography of Geography', *Transactions of the Institute of British Geographers*, n.s., XVIII (1991), pp. 95–105

Dunbar, John G., *The Historic Architecture of Scotland* (London, 1966)

Evans, R. J., 'An Autumn of German Romanticism', *History Today*, XLIV/10 (1994), pp. 9–12

Everett, N., *The Tory View of Landscape* (New York, 1994)

Fairbrother, Nan, *New Lives, New Landscapes* (London, 1970)

Fairclough, G., 'Protecting Time and Space: Understanding Historic Landscape for Conservation in England', in *The Archaeology of Landscape*, ed. P. Ucko and R. Layton (London, 1999), pp. 119–34

Fraser, D., '"Fields of Radience": The Scientific and Industrial Scenes of Joseph Wright', in *The Iconography of Landscape*, ed. Denis Cosgrove and Stephen Daniels (Cambridge, 1988), pp. 119–41

Gaunt, W., *The Impressionists* (London, 1985)

Gerlach, R. L., 'A Contrast in Old World Ideology: German and Scotch-Irish in the Ozarks', in *Ideology and Landscape in Historical Perspective*, ed. Alan Baker and G. Biger (Cambridge, 1992), pp. 289–302

Godlewska, Anne, 'Napoleon's Geographers (1797–1815): Imperialists and Soldiers of Modernity', in *Geography and Empire*, ed. Anne Godlewska and N. Smith (Oxford, 1994), pp. 31–54

—, 'Map, Text and Image. The Mentality of Enlightened Conquerors:

A New Look at the Description de L'Egypte', *Transactions of the Institute of British Geographers*, n.s., xx (1995), pp. 5–28

Gordon, C., and Gordon, C., 'Gardens of the Raj', *History Today*, XLVI/7 (1996), pp. 22–9

Graham, Brian, 'Heritage Conservation and Revisionist Nationalism in Ireland', in *Building a New Heritage: Tourism, Culture and Identity in the New Europe*, ed. G. J. Ashworth and P. J. Larkham (London, 1994), pp. 135–58

—, 'The Past in Europe's Present: Diversity, Identity and the Construction of Place', in *Modern Europe: Place, Culture and Identity*, ed. B. Graham (London, 1998), pp. 19–52

—, Ashworth, G. J., and Tunbridge, J. E., *A Geography of Heritage* (London, 2000)

Grant, E., 'The Sphinx in the North: Egyptian influences on Landscape Architecture and Interior Design in Eighteenth- and Nineteenth-Century Scotland', in *The Iconography of Landscape*, ed. Denis Cosgrove and Stephen Daniels (Cambridge, 1988), pp. 236–53

Gregory, Derek. 'Between the Book and the Lamp: Imaginative Geographies of Egypt, 1849–1850', *Transactions of the Institute of British Geographers*, n.s., xx (1995), pp. 29–57

Groening, G., 'The Feeling for Landscape: A German Example', *Landscape Research*, XVII (1992), pp. 108–15

Grove, Jean M., *The Little Ice Age* (London, 1990)

Grove, R. H., *Green Imperialism: Colonial Expansion, Tropical Island Edens and The Origins of Environmentalism, 1600–1860* (Cambridge, 1995)

Gruffudd, Piers, '"Uncivil Engineering": Nature, Nationalism and Hydro Electrics in North Wales', in *Water, Engineering and Landscape: Water Control and Landscape Formation in the Modern World*, ed. Denis Cosgrove and Geoffrey Petts (London, 1990), pp. 159–73

—, 'The Countryside as Educator: Schools, Rurality and Citizenship in Inter-War Wales', *Journal of Historical Geography*, XXII (1996), pp. 412–33

—, Herbert, David T., and Piccini, A., 'In Search of Wales: Travel Writings and Narratives of Difference, 1918–50', *Journal of Historical Geography*, XXVI (2000), pp. 589–604

Hardington, R., 'The Neuroses of the Railway', *History Today*, XLIV/7 (1994), pp. 15–21

Harley, J. Brian, 'Maps, Knowledge and Power', in *The Iconography of Landscape*, ed. Denis Cosgrove and Stephen Daniels (Cambridge, 1988), pp. 277–312

Hart, John Fraser, *The Rural Landscape* (London, 1998)

Harvey, P. D. A., *The History of Topographic Maps* (London, 1980)

—, *Maps in Tudor England* (London, 1993)

Heffernan, Michael, 'The Parisian Poor and the Colonisation of Algeria during the Second Republic', *French History*, III (1989), pp. 377–403

—, 'Bringing the Desert to Bloom: French Ambitions in the Sahara Desert during the Late Nineteenth Century – The Strange Case of "La Mer Interieure"', in *Water, Engineering and Landscape: Water Control and Landscape Formation in the Modern World*, ed. Denis Cosgrove and

Geoffrey Petts (London, 1990), pp. 94–114

—, 'Forever England: The Western Front and the Politics of Remembrance in Britain', *Ecumene*, II (1995), pp. 293–325

Helsinger, E. K., 'Land and National Representation in Britain', in *Prospects for the Nation: Recent Essays in British Landscape, 1750–1880*, ed. Michael Rosenthal, Christiana Payne and Scott Wilcox (London, 1997), pp. 13–26

Hewison, Robert, *The Heritage Industry: Britain in a Climate of Decline* (London, 1987)

Hindle, Paul, *Maps for Historians* (London, 1988)

Hingley, Richard, ed., *Medieval or Later Rural Settlement in Scotland* (Edinburgh, 1993)

Hobsbawm, Eric, *Nations and Nationalism since 1780: Programme, Myth, Reality* (Cambridge, 1990)

Hooke, Della, 'The Appreciation of Landscape History', in *Landscape: The Richest Historical Record*, ed. D. Hooke, Society For Landscape Studies Monograph (Birmingham, 2001), pp. 43–55

Hoskins, William G., *The Making of the English Landscape* (London, 1955)

Houston, J. M., *The West Mediterranean World* (London, 1964)

Howard, Peter, *Landscapes: The Artists' Vision* (London, 1991)

Howkins, Alun, 'Land, Locality, People, Landscape: The Nineteenth-Century Countryside', in *Prospects for the Nation: Recent Essays in British Landscape, 1750–1880*, ed. Michael Rosenthal, Christiana Payne and Scott Wilcox (New Haven, 1997), pp. 97–114

Hunn, J. R., Reconstruction and Measurement in *Landscape Change: A Study of Six Parishes in the St Albans Area*, British Archaeological Reports, British Series, CCXXXVI (Oxford, 1994)

Ingold, T., 'The Temporality of Landscape', *World Archaeology*, XXV (1993), pp. 152–74

Jeffrey, I., *The British Landscape, 1920–1950* (London, 1984)

Johnson, N. C., 'Sculpting Heroic Histories: Celebrating the Centenary of the 1798 Rebellion in Ireland', *Transactions of the Institute of British Geographers*, n.s., XIX (1994), pp. 78–93

Johnson, N. O., 'Historical Geographies of the Present', in *Modern Historical Geographies*, ed. B. Graham and C. Nash (London, 2000), pp. 251–72

Jones, M., 'The Rise, Decline and Extinction of Coppice Wood Management in South-West Yorkshire', in *European Woods and Forests: Studies in Cultural History*, ed. Charles Watkins (London, 1998), pp. 55–71

Kenny, J. T., 'Climate, Race and Imperial Authority: The Symbolic Landscape of the British Hill Station in India', *Annals of the Association of American Geographers*, LXXXV (1995), pp. 694–714

Kitchener, A. C., 'Extinctions, Introductions and Colonisations of Scottish Mammals and Birds since the Last Ice Age', in *Species History in Scotland*, ed. R. A. Lambert (Edinburgh, 1998), pp. 63–92

Konvitz, J. W., *Cartography in France, 1660–1848: Science, Engineering and Statecraft* (Chicago, 1987)

—, 'The Nation-State, Paris and Cartography in Eighteenth- and Nineteenth-Century France', *Journal of Historical Geography*, XVI (1990), pp. 3–16

Lamb, Hubert, *Climate: Present, Past and Future* (London, 1972)
—, *Climate, History and the Modern World* (London, 1982)
Lambert, Audrey M., *The Making of the Dutch Landscape* (London, 1985)
Langton, John, *Geographical Change and Industrial Revolution: Coalmining in South West Lancashire, 1590–1799* (Cambridge, 1979)
Le Roy Ladurie, Emmanuel, *Times of Feast, Times of Famine: A History of Climate from the Year 1000* (London, 1971)
Leyshon, A., Matless, David, and Revill, G., 'The Place of Music', *Transactions of the Institute of British Geographers*, n.s., xx (1995), pp. 432–33
Lichtenberger, E., *The Eastern Alps* (Oxford, 1975)
Lindsay , I. G., and Cosh, M., *Inveraray and the Dukes of Argyll* (Edinburgh, 1972)
Lindsay, James M., 'The Iron Industry in the Highlands: Charcoal Blast Furnaces', *Scottish Historical Review*, LVI (1977), pp. 49–63
Linton, David L., 'The Assessment of Scenery as a Natural Resource', *Scottish Geographical Magazine*, LXXXIV (1968), pp. 219–38
Lockhart, Douglas G., 'The Planned Villages', in *The Making of the Scottish Countryside*, ed. Martin L. Parry and Terry R. Slater (London, 1981), pp. 249–70
Lowenthal, David, and Prince, Hugh, 'The English Landscape', *Geographical Review*, LIV (1964), pp. 309–46
—, 'The American Scene', *Geographical Review*, LVIII (1968), pp. 61–8
—, 'Past Time, Present Place', *Geographical Review*, LXV (1975), pp. 124–36
—, 'The Place of the Past in the American Landscape', in *Geographies of the Mind*, ed. David Lowenthal and M. J. Bowden (New York, 1976), pp. 89–117
—, 'British National Identity and The English Landscape', *Rural History*, II (1991), pp. 205–30
MacCarthy-Morrogh, M., *The Munster Plantation: English Migration to Southern Ireland, 1583–1641* (Oxford, 1986)
Macdonald, A., *Mapping The World: A History of the Directorate of Overseas Surveys, 1946–1985* (London, 1996)
McEwan, G., 'Paradise or Pandemonium? West African Landscapes in the Travel Accounts of Victorian Women', *Journal of Historical Geography*, XXII (1996), pp. 68–83
Macinnes, Allan I., *Clanship, Commerce and the House of Stuart, 1603–1788* (East Linton, 1966)
Mackenzie, John M., *Imperialism and Popular Culture* (Manchester, 1986)
McNeill, J. R., *The Mountains of the Mediterranean* (Cambridge, 1992)
Matless, David, '"The Art of Right Living": Landscape and Citizenship, 1918–39', in *Mapping The Subject: Geographies of Cultural Transformation*, ed. S. Pile and N. Thrift (London, 1995), pp. 93–122
—, *Landscape and Englishness* (London, 1998)
Mead, William R., 'The Study of Field Boundaries', *Geographische Zeitschrift*, LIV (1966), pp. 114–24
—, *An Historical Geography of Scandinavia* (London, 1981)
Meinig, D. W., 'The Beholding Eye: Ten Versions of the Same Scene', *Landscape Architecture*, LVI (1976), pp. 47–54
—, *The Interpretation of Ordinary Landscapes* (Oxford, 1979)

Meirion-Jones, G. I., 'Vernacular Architecture and the Peasant House', in
  Themes in the Historical Geography of France, ed. H. D. Clout (Cambridge,
  1977), pp. 343–406
—, *The Vernacular Architecture of Brittany: An Essay in Historical Geography*
  (Edinburgh, 1982)
Mills, S. F., 'Landscape Simulation and the Open-Air Museum', *Landscapes*, 1
  (2000), pp. 80–95
Millward, R., *Scandinavian Lands* (London, 1964)
Mitchell, W. J. T., 'Imperial Landscape', in *Landscape and Power*, ed. W. J. T.
  Mitchell (Chicago, 1994), pp. 5–30
Morphy, H., 'Colonialism, History and the Construction of Place: The
  Politics of Land in Northern Australia', in *Landscape: Politics and
  Perspective*, ed. B. Bender (Oxford, 1993), pp. 205–44
Mosse, G. L., *Fallen Soldiers: Reshaping the Memory of the World Wars*
  (London, 1990)
Muir, Richard, *The Lost Villages of Britain* (London, 1982)
—, *Approaches to Landscape* (London, 1999)
Musgrave T., and Musgrave, W., *An Empire of Plants* (London, 2000)
Naylon, J., *Andalusia* (Oxford, 1975)
Neuman, R. P., 'Ways of Seeing Africa: Colonial Recasting of African
  Society and Landscape in the Serengeti National Park', *Ecumene*, (1995),
  pp. 149–69
Newson, L. A., 'The Population of the Amazon Basin in 1492: A View from
  the Equadorian Headwaters', *Transactions of the Institute of British
  Geographers*, n.s., XXI (1996), pp. 5–26
Nicholson, Norman, *The Lakers: The Adventures of the First Tourists* (London,
  1955)
Oliver, R., *Ordnance Survey Maps: A Concise Guide for Historians* (London,
  1993)
Orians, G. H., 'An Ecological and Evolutionary Approach to Landscape
  Aesthetics', in *Landscape Meaning and Values*, ed. Edward C. Penning
  Rowsell and David Lowenthal (London, 1986), pp. 3–25
Orr, William, Deer Forests, *Landlords and Crofters: The Western Highlands in
  Victorian and Edwardian Times* (Edinburgh, 1982)
Overton, Mark, *Agricultural Revolution in England: The Transformation of the
  Agrarian Economy, 1500–1850* (Cambridge, 1996)
Park, Christopher, *Tropical Rainforests* (London, 1992)
Parry, Martin L., *Climatic Change, Agriculture and Settlement* (Folkestone,
  1978)
—, and Slater, Terry R., eds., *The Making of the Scottish Countryside* (London,
  1981)
Penning-Rowsell, Edward, *Alternative Approaches to Landscape Evaluation*
  (Enfield, 1973)
—, and Lowenthal, David, *Landscape Meaning and Values* (London, 1986)
Percival-Maxwell, M., *The Scottish Migration to Ulster in the Reign of James I*
  (London, 1973)
Phillips, A. D. M., *The Underdraining of Farmland in England during the
  Nineteenth Century* (Cambridge, 1989)

Pocock, D. C. D., 'The Novelist's Image of the North', *Transactions of the Institute of British Geographers*, n.s., IV (1979), pp. 62–76

—, 'Place and the Novelist', *Transactions of the Institute of British Geographers*, n.s., VI (1981), pp. 337–47

Pollard, S., *Peaceful Conquest: The Industrialization of Europe, 1760–1970* (Oxford, 1981)

Pounds, Norman J. G., *An Historical Geography of Europe, 1500–1840* (Cambridge, 1979)

Preston, R., '"The Scenery of the Torrid Zone": Imagined Travels and the Culture of Exotics in Nineteenth-Century British Gardens', in *Imperial Cities: Landscape, Display and Identity*, ed. F. Driver and D. Gilbert (Manchester, 1999), pp, 194–214

Price, R., *An Economic History of Modern France, 1739–1914* (London, 1981)

Prince, Hugh, 'Regional Contrasts in Agrarian Structures' in *Themes in the Historical Geography of France*, ed. H. D. Clout (London, 1977), pp. 43–55

—, 'Art and Agrarian Change, 1710–1815', in *The Iconography of Landscape*, ed. Denis Cosgrove and Stephen Daniels (Cambridge, 1988), pp. 98–119

Prince, Hugh W., 'A Marshland Chronicle, 1830–1960; from Artificial Drainage to Outdoor Recreation in Central Wisconsin', *Journal of Historical Geography*, XXI (1995), pp. 3–22

Pringle, T. R., 'The Privation of History: Landseer, Victoria and the Highland Myth', in *The Iconography of Landscape*, ed. D. Cosgrove and S. Daniels (Cambridge, 1988), pp. 142–61

Proudfoot, Lindsay, 'Property Ownership and Urban and Village Improvement in Provincial Ireland ca. 1700–1845', *Institute of British Geographers*, Historical Geography Research Series, XXXIII (1997)

Pulsipher, Lydia, 'Seventeenth-Century Montserrat: An Environmental Impact Statement', *Historical Geography Research Group Research Series*, XVII (1986)

Rackham, Oliver, *The History of the Countryside* (London, 1986)

—, *Trees and Woodland in the British Landscape* (London, 1996)

Ransom, P. J. C., *The Archaeology of the Transport Revolution, 1750–1850* (Tadworth, 1984)

Ravenhill, William, 'Mapping a United Kingdom', *History Today*, XXXV/10 (1985), pp. 27–33

Reed, Michael, *The Georgian Triumph, 1700–1830* (London, 1984)

Richards, E., *A History of the Highland Clearances, I* (London, 1982)

Roberts, Brian K., 'Landscape Archaeology', in *Landscape and Culture*, ed. John M. Wagstaff (Oxford, 1987), pp. 26–37

—, 'Rural Settlement in Europe, 500–1500', in *An Historical Geography of Europe*, ed. Robin A. Butlin and Robert A. Dodgshon (Oxford, 1998), pp. 73–100

Roche, M., 'The Land We Have, We Must Hold: Soil Erosion and Soil Conservation in Late Nineteenth Century and Early Twentieth Century New Zealand', *Journal of Historical Geography*, XXIII (1997), pp. 442–58

Rollins, W. H., 'Whose Landscape? Technology, Fascism and Environmentalism on the National Socialist Autobahn', *Annals of the Association of American Geographers*, LXXXV (1995), pp. 494–520

Rose, Gillian, *Feminism and Geography* (Cambridge, 1993)
—, 'Place and Identity: A Sense of Place', in *A Place in the World?*, ed. Doreen
    Massey and P. Jess (London, 1995), pp. 87–132
Rosenthal, Michael, Payne, Christiana, and Wilcox, Scott, eds, *Prospects for
    the Nation: Recent Essays in British Landscape, 1750–1880* (New Haven,
    1997)
Royal Commission on the Ancient and Historical Monuments of Scotland,
    North-East Perthshire: An Archaeological Landscape (Edinburgh, 1990)
Royal Commission on the Ancient and Historical Monuments of Scotland,
    Strath of Kildonan: An Archaeological Survey (Edinburgh, 1993)
Royal Commission on the Ancient and Historical Monuments of Scotland,
    East Dumfriesshire: An Archaeological Landscape (Edinburgh, 1997)
Ryan, J. R., 'Imperial Landscapes: Photography, Geography and British
    Overseas Exploration, 1858–1872', in *Geography and Imperialism,
    1820–1940*, ed. M. Bell, Robin A. Butlin and Michael Heffernan
    (Manchester, 1995), pp. 53–79
Saarinen, T. E., *Perception of the Drought Hazard on the Great Plains* (Chicago,
    1966)
Said, E., *Orientalism* (London, 1978)
Schama, Simon, *Landscape and Memory* (London, 1995)
Schwartz, J. M., '"The Geography Lesson": Photographs and the
    Construction of Imaginative Geographies', *Journal of Historical
    Geography*, XXII (1996), pp. 16–45
Searle, C. E., 'Customary Tenants and the Economy of the Cumbrian
    Commons', *Northern History*, XXIX (1993), pp. 126–53
Seymour, S., 'Landed Estates, the "Spirit of Planting" and Woodland
    Management in Later Georgian Britain: A Case Study from the
    Dukeries, Nottinghamshire', in *European Woods and Forests: Studies in
    Cultural History*, ed. Charles Watkins (London, 1998), pp. 115–34
—, 'Historical Geographies of Landscape', in *Modern Historical Geographies*,
    ed. Brian Graham and C. Nash (London, 2000)
Shoard, Marion, *The Theft of the Countryside* (London, 1980)
—, 'The Lure of the Moors', in *Valued Environments*, ed. J. R. Gold and J.
    Burgess (London, 1982), pp. 59–73
Short, J. R., *Imagined Country: Environment, Culture and Society* (London,
    1991)
Shortridge, J. R., 'The Vernacular Middle West', *Annals of the Association of
    American Geographers*, LXXV (1985), pp. 48–57
Simmons, Ian G., *An Environmental History of Great Britain* (Edinburgh,
    2001)
Simpson, I. A., Parsisson, D., Hancey, N., and Bullock, C. U., 'Envisioning
    Future Landscapes in the Environmentally Sensitive Areas of Scotland',
    Transactions of the Institute of British Geographers, n.s., XXII (1997), pp.
    307–20
Slicher van Bath, B. H., *The Agrarian History of Western Europe, AD
    500–1850* (London, 1963)
Smith, Susan J., 'Soundscape', *Area*, XXVI (1994), pp. 232–40
Smout, T. Christopher, *A History of the Scottish People, 1560–1830* (London,

1972)

—, *Scottish Woodland History* (Edinburgh, 1997)

—, *Nature Contested: Environmental History in Scotland and Northern England since 1600* (Edinburgh, 2000)

Spufford, F., *I May Be Some Time* (London, 1996)

Stone, Jeffrey C., 'Timothy Pont and the First Topographical Survey of Scotland c. 1583–1596', *Scottish Geographical Magazine*, XCIX (1983), pp. 161–8

—, 'The Cartography of Colonialism and Decolonisation: The Case of Swaziland', in *Geography and Imperialism*, ed. M. Bell, Robin A. Butlin and Michael Heffernan (Manchester, 1995), pp. 298–324

Taylor, Christopher, 'The Plus Fours in the Wardrobe: A Personal View of Landscape History', in *Landscape: The Richest Historical Record*, ed. Della Hooke, Society for Landscape Studies Monograph (Birmingham, 2001), pp. 157–62

Thirsk, Joan, *England's Agricultural Regions and Agrarian History, 1500–1750* (London, 1987)

Thomas, J., 'The Politics of Vision and the Archaeology of Landscape', in *Landscape: Politics and Perspective*, ed. B. Bender (Oxford, 1993), pp. 19–45

Thompson, Ian B., *The Paris Basin* (Oxford, 1973)

—, *The Lower Rhône and Marseilles* (Oxford, 1975)

Trinder, Barry, *The Making of the Industrial Landscape* (London, 1982)

Trueman, A. E., *Geology and Scenery in England and Wales* (London, 1949)

Tsouvalis-Gerber, J., 'Making the Invisible Visible: Ancient Woodlands, British Forest Policy and the Social Construction of Reality', in *European Woods and Forests: Studies in Cultural History*, ed. Charles Watkins (London, 1998), pp. 215–29

Tucker, R. P., 'The Depletion of India's Forests under British Imperialism: Planters, Foresters and Peasants in Assam and Kerala', in *The Ends of The Earth: Perspectives on Modern Environmental History*, ed. Donald Worster (Cambridge, 1988), pp. 118–40

Turner, Michael, *English Parliamentary Enclosure* (Folkestone, 1980)

Turnock, David, *Patterns of Highland Development* (London, 1970)

Tuan, Yi-Fu, *Landscapes of Fear* (Minnesota, 1979)

Tyacke, S., ed., *English Map-Making, 1590–1650* (London, 1983)

Ucko, P., and Layton, R., eds, *The Archaeology of Landscape* (London, 1999)

Vernon, J., 'Border Crossing: Cornwall and the English (Imagi)Nation', in *Imagining Nations*, ed. G. Cubitt (Manchester, 1998), pp. 153–72

Viazzo, P., *Upland Communities: Environment, Population and Social Changes in the Alps since the Sixteenth Century* (Cambridge, 1989)

Wallerstein, Immanuel, *The Modern World System: Capitalist Agriculture and the Origins of the European World Economy in the Sixteenth Century* (London, 1974)

Watkins, Charles, 'Themes in the History of European Woods and Forests', in *European Woods and Forests: Studies in Cultural History*, ed. Charles Watkins (London, 1998), pp. 1–10

Watson, James Wreford, 'Geography: A Discipline in Distance', *Scottish Geographical Magazine*, LXXI (1955), pp. 1–13

Watson, James W., and O'Riordan, Tim, eds, *The American Environment:*

    Perceptions and Policies (London, 1976)

Weber, Eugene, *Peasants into Frenchmen: The Modernization of Rural France,
    1870–1914* (London, 1977)

Whatley, Christopher, 'How Tame Were the Scottish Lowlanders during
    the Eighteenth Century?', in *Conflict and Stability in Scottish Society,
    1700–1850*, ed. T. M. Devine (Edinburgh, 1990), pp. 1–30

Whittington, Graeme, 'The Regionalisation of Lewis Grassic Gibbon',
    Scottish Geographical Magazine, xc (1974), pp. 74–85

—, 'Agriculture and Society in Lowland Scotland, 1750–1870', in *An
    Historical Geography of Scotland*, ed. Graeme Whittington and Ian D.
    Whyte (London, 1983), pp. 141–64

—, and Gibson, Alexander, 'The Military Survey of Scotland 1747–1755: A
    Critique', *Institute of British Geographers Historical Geography Research
    Series*, XVIII (1986)

—, and Jarvis, J., 'Kilconquhar Loch, Fife: An Historical and Palynological
    Investigation', *Proceedings of the Society of Antiquaries of Scotland*, cxvi
    (1986), pp. 413–28

Whyte, Ian D., *Agriculture and Society in Seventeenth-Century Scotland*
    (Edinburgh, 1979)

—, 'Rural Europe since 1500: Areas of Retardation and Tradition' in *An
    Historical Geography of Europe*, ed. Robin A. Butlin and Robert A.
    Dodgshon (Oxford, 1998), pp. 243–58

—, 'William Wordsworth's Guide To The Lakes and the Geographical
    Tradition', *Area*, xxxii (2000), pp. 101–6

—, and Whyte, Kathleen A., *The Changing Scottish Landscape, 1500–1800*
    (London, 1991)

Widgren, M., 'Is Landscape History Possible? or, How Can We Study the
    Desertion of Farms', in *The Archaeology of Landscape*, ed. P. Ucko and R.
    Layton (London, 1999), pp. 96–103

Williams, Michael, *The Making of the South Australian Landscape* (London,
    1974)

—, *Americans and their Forests: A Historical Geography* (Cambridge, 1989)

—, 'Dark Ages and Dark Areas: Global Deforestation in the Deep Past',
    Journal of Historical Geography, xxvi (2000), pp. 28–46

Williams, Raymond, *The Country and the City* (London, 1973)

Williamson, Tom. 'Exploring Regional Landscapes: Woodland and
    Champion in Southern and Eastern England', *Landscape History*, x
    (1988), pp. 5–13

—, *The Norfolk Broads: A Landscape History* (Manchester, 1997)

—, *Polite Landscapes: Gardens and Society in Eighteenth-Century England*
    (Stroud, 1998)

—, 'The Archaeology of the Landscape Park', *British Archaeological Reports*,
    British Series, cclxviii (Oxford, 1999)

—, 'The Rural Landscape, 1500–1900: The Neglected Centuries', in
    Landscape: The Richest Historical Record, ed. Della Hooke, Society for
    Landscape Studies Monograph (Birmingham, 2001), pp. 109–17

Winchester, Angus J. L., *The Harvest of the Hills: Rural Life in Northern
    England and the Scottish Borders, 1400–1700* (Edinburgh, 2000)

Withers, Charles W. J., 'Place, Meaning, Monument: Memoralising The Past in Contemporary Highland Scotland', *Ecumene*, III (1996), pp. 325–444
—, 'Authorizing Landscape: 'Authority', Naming and The Ordnance Survey's Mapping of the Scottish Highlands in the Nineteenth Century', *Journal of Historical Geography*, XXVI (2000), pp. 532–54
Womack, Peter, *Improvement and Romance: Constructing the Myths of the Highlands* (London, 1989)
Wordie, J. R., 'The Chronology of English Enclosure, 1500–1914', *Economic History Review*, XXXVI (1983), pp. 483–505
Worster, Donald, 'The Vulnerable Earth', in *The Ends of the Earth: Perspectives on Modern Environmental History*, ed. Donald Worster (Cambridge, 1988), pp. 3–20
—, ed., *The Ends of the Earth: Perspectives on Modern Environmental History* (Cambridge, 1988)
Wynn, G., 'Re-Mapping Tutira: Contours in the Environmental History of New Zealand', *Journal of Historical Geography*, XXIII (1997), pp. 418–46
Yelling, James, 'Agriculture, 1500–1730', in *An Historical Geography of England and Wales*, ed. Robert A. Dodgshon and Robin A. Butlin (London, 1978), pp. 151–73
Youngson, A. J., *After the Forty-Five* (Edinburgh, 1973)

Photographic Acknowledgements

The author and publishers wish to express their thanks to the below sources of illustrative material and/or permission to reproduce it:

Photos by the author: pp. 32, 47, 53, 81, 89, 107, 112, 124, 127, 128, 174, 179, 185, 189, 211; photos G. Chapman: pp. 149, 165; photo British Library London (Map Library): p. 92; Hamburger Kunsthalle: p. 117; photos © National Gallery, London: pp. 59, 74, 125, 178; Royal Holloway Collection, University of London: p. 152; Tate Britain, London: p. 119; Elke Walford: p. 117.

Index

Page numbers in *italics* refer to illustrations

Abercrombie, Patrick 189
aerial photography 172, *213–14*
Africa 137, 140, 147, 151, 166, 195, 213
Agassiz, Louis 115
Alps, The 30, 36, 37, 49, 89, 101, 105, 115, 126, 129, 130, 166, 195, 201
Altdorfer, Albrecht 57
American Civil War 137, 158, 162
American West 135, 137, 158, 159, 162, 163, 177, 190, 191
Antarctic 153, 166, 213
Apennines 31, 44, 101, 129, 130
Appalachians 95, 156, 201
architecture 58, 144, 176
  Classical 78, 82
  Gothic 78, 82, 120–21
  neo–Classical 80, 81
Arctic 129, 146, *151*, 152, 166
Areas of Outstanding Natural Beauty 187, 193–4
Arkwright, Richard 102, 131
art 13, 19–24, 55–61 72–4, 89–91, 103–4, 118–21, 130–6, 156–8, 160–61, 177–8
  American 135, 156–8, 160–2
  Australian 135
  British 10, 16, 72–4, 90–91, 134, 177–8
  Dutch 13, 20, 24, 60–61
  French 20, 133–4
  Italian 13, 56–9, 89–90
  Picturesque 100
  Romantic 103–5, 118–21
Austen, Jane 102, 138, 176
Australia 135, 140, 146, 149, 150, 151, 165, 207

Bierstadt, Albert 158, 160
Black Death 34, 35
Blenheim Palace 82, 84
Bridgeman, Charles 81, 83
Brown, George Loring 156
Brown, Lancelot 'Capability' 19, 83, 84, 85, 86, 99, 149
Buckland, William 114
Burke, Edmund 72, 98, 135
Burnet, Thomas 104
Burns, Robert 103, 203
Byron, George Gordon, Lord 103, 110

Cairngorms 170, 194, 208
California 137, 190, 214
Camden, William 41, 55
Campagna, the 90, 100, 156
Campbell, Colen 80–81
Canada 135, 165, 181, 191
Canary Islands 61, 67, 68, 148
Caribbean 64, 66, 67, 68, 148
cartography 23–5, 50–55, 91–5, 141, 145–6, 202–3, 213–14
  estate 25, 51, 91–5
  military 25, 52–4, 145–56
  surveying 51, 91–5
Cassini, Jacques 94–5, 141, 145
Catlin, George 63, 116, 162
Catskill Mountains 116, 156, 157, 190
Clare, John 8, 76, 91, 106
Claude Gellée, 'Le Lorrain' 19, 58–9, *59*, 73, 89, 90, 98, 100, 135, 136, 144, 157
Claude glasses 100
climatic change 11, 36–8, 67, 97, 166
Cole, Thomas 116, 157, 158

Coleridge, Samuel Taylor 105, 115
Commons Preservation Society 202
Conrad, Joseph 215
Constable, John 16, 91, 103, 119–20,
    133, 157, 176, 177–8, *178*
Cook, Captain James 93, 136, 144, 152,
    153
Cooper, James Fenimore 63, 116, 157
Corot, Jean-Baptiste 134
Council for the Preservation of Rural
    England 170, 188–9, 192
country houses 45–8, 47, 79–82
Cranach, Lucas 56
Culloden, Battle of 49, 91, 108, 112,
    179, 186

Defoe, Daniel 70–72
Delaroche, Paul 136
Directorate of Colonial Survey 213,
    214
Dissolution of the Monasteries 41, 51
Dughet, Gaspard 90, 98
Durand, Asher 116, 158
Dürer, Albrecht 52, 56

Egypt 137, 140–45
Elgar, Edward 163, 175
Emerson, Ralph Waldo 116, 156, 157
England 25–6, 29, 30, 31, 34, 38, 39, 42,
    44, 46, 48, 49, 50, 51, 52, 53, 54, 55,
    68, 69, 70–71, 74, 75, 77, 80, 84, 86,
    90, 99, 103, 116, 117, 118, 122, 132,
    138, 144, 149, 151, 168, 170, 174,
    175, 176, 177, 178, 182, 192, 193,
    194, 196, 197, 198, 199, 201, 208,
    209, 210, 215
English Heritage 8, 199, 206, 208
Enlightenment, the 22–3, 69, 74, 75, 91,
    96, 104, 120, 141, 143
Environmentally Sensitive Areas 197,
    214
Europe 30, 33, 35, 36, 43, 44, 49, 50, 51,
    56, 69, 79, 87, 116, 125, 128, 129,
    145, 149, 150, 151, 152, 155, 156,
    157, 166, 168, 169, 171, 173, 181,
    182, 183, 186
European Union 11, 12, 197, 198, 200
    agricultural policy 11, 12, 197, 198

feudalism 27–8, 33–35, 69
First World War 138, 162, 164, 165,
    169, 171, 177, 178, 183, 186, 189,
    213
Flanders 34, 42, 56, 60
Flaubert, Gustave 142, 143
forestry 117–18, 140, 167, 169–70, 171,
    180
Forestry Commission 169, 170, 194,
    203
forests 18–19, 42–3, 49, 63–5, 95, 97,
    115–18, 123, 129, 140, 149, 165–7,
    172, 181
    American 63–5, 116
    clearance 38, 42–4, 63–9, 95, 97,
        129, 140, 149, 165
    England 42–3, 116–17
    Germany 42, 116–17
    regrowth 64, 167, 172
    tropical 64–5, 66–9, 166–7
France 23, 28, 29, 30, 33, 34, 38, 42, 49,
    51, 54, 66, 79, 82, 83, 89, 95, 122,
    123, 125, 130, 133, 134, 136, 140,
    141, 144, 142, 146, 147, 168, 171,
    173, 176, 180, 194, 198, 204
French Revolution, the 86, 103, 172
Friedrich, Caspar David 116, *117*, 180
Frisius, Gemma 51

Gainsborough, Thomas 16, 73, 74, 91
Gaskell, Mrs 10, 138
geology 113–15
Germany 38, 42, 51, 89, 115, 123, 136,
    153, 154, 169, 175, 177, 180,
    181–2, 186, 189
Gettysburg, Battle of 186, 215
Gibbons, Stella 175
Gilpin, Revd William 98–9, 100, 102,
    116, 135, 188
Glover, John 136
Goldsmith, Oliver 85, 91
Graham, Kenneth 175
Grand Tour, the 89, 99, 101
Gray, Thomas 70, 98, 103, 107
Great Plains, the 65, 147, 159
Great Western Railway 113, 124, 125

Hardy, Thomas 18, 138, 139, 175

Harrison, William 46
Hawthorne, Nathaniel 132, 156
Highland Clearances, the 127, 184
Howard, Ebenezer 132
Hudson Valley 66, 116, 157
Hudson, W. H. 63, 132, 156, 158
Humboldt, Alexander von 114
Hutton, James 113, 114, 115

imperialism 20, 25, 140–53
Impressionism 133–4
Industrial Revolution, the 15, 122, 174,
    175, 210
Ireland 28, 31, 32, 33, 42, 46, 47, 49, 61,
    62, 69, 78, 86, 126, 128, *128*, 145,
    171, *179*, 180, 206
    the Great Famine 78, 128
Ironbridge 122, 207, 210, 214
Irving, Washington 157
Italy 21, 24, 38, 41, 56, 58, 89, 98, 137,
    189, 207

Jacobites 49, 91, 110, 112, 138, 184–5,
    185, 212
James, Henry 132
Johnson, Samuel 44, 71, 96, 108

Kent, William 83, 99
Kingsley, Mary 151
Kipling, Rudyard 175

Lake District 10, 43, 72, 87, 98, 99, 100,
    102, 105–7, 106, *107*, 108, 117,
    119, 123, 124, 139, 156, 166, 169,
    170, 175, 176, 188, 191, 192, 201,
    203, 208, 209
Lancashire *53*, 94, 123, 124, 160, 193
landscape parks 20, 73, 79–86, *81*
Landseer, Edwin 109, 132–3, *152*,
    152–3
Lee, Laurie 175
Leeghwater, Jan 40
Le Nôtre, André 82, 83
Leonardo da Vinci 50, 52
literature 70, 72, 76, 100, 102, 103–8,
    110–12, 13–39
London 55, 71, 146, 176, 193, 200, 202
Louisiana Purchase 158

Lovecraft, H. P. 95

McCulloch, Horatio 109
MacPherson, James 107
Mediterranean 28, 29, 30, 31, 43, 146,
    172, 215
Melville, Herman 132
Military Survey of Scotland 91–4, *92*
Milne, A. A. 175
Miller, Hugh 114
Monet, Claude 134
Moran, Thomas 137, 158, 160, 161
Morton, H. V. 175, 179
Muir, John 190–91, 194
Murchison, Sir Roderick 115
Muybridge, E. J. 137

national identities 23, 130–38, 172–81,
    179
national parks 190–96
National Parks and Access to the
    Countryside Act (1949) 199
National Trust 178, 188, 208, 200,
    209–10
    NT for Scotland 194
Netherlands, The 24, 39, 40, 41, 51, 52,
    60, 61, 82, 134, 207
New England 62, 63, 64, 66, 95, 96, 154,
    155, 156, 167
New York 63, 154, 156, 157
New Zealand 136, 140, 144, 149, 150
Nightingale, Florence 142, 143
Norden, John 55
North America 16, 61, 62, 63, 65, 67,
    95–7, 135, 140, 153, 155

Ordnance Survey 93, 145, 146, 178,
    202, 203, 213
Orientalism 140, 143

Palladio, Andrea 58, 80, 81
Paris 49, 95, 134, 136, 189, 208, 214
    Basin 33, 34, 134, 145
Parliamentary enclosure 11, 15, 29,
    74–7, 84, 85, 90, 91, 94, 101, 106,
    174
Patinir, Joachim 57
photography 10, 136–8, 152

Picturesque, the 23, 97–103, 104, 105,
    106, 109, 113–14, 118, 119, 121,
    131, 135, 156, 185
Playfair, John 113, 114
Poe, Edgar Allen 132
Pont, Timothy 55
population
    decline 34–5, 38–9, 128–29
    growth 28, 37–8, 167
    migration 96, 126, 128, 172
Potter, Beatrix 175, 209
Poussin, Nicolas 58, 90, 98
Price, Uvedale 98, 99, 104, 131

railways 113, 124–5, *124*, 129–30, 147,
    201–2
Ramblers Association 202
Ransome, Arthur 175
reclamation 37–41, 75, 78, 129
Remington, Frederic 135
Renaissance, the 12, 21, 24, 50, 55, 56
Repton, Humphry 85, 118
Richardson, Samuel 138
Rocky Mountains 158, 160, 162, 191
Romantic Movement, the 103–21, 135,
    136, 156, 162, 173, 180
Rome 20, 42, 58, 81, 89
Rosa, Salvator 73, 90, 98
Rowlandson, Thomas 102
Roy, Major-General William 92, 145
Royal Geographical Society 23, 137
Ruskin, John 113, 132, 161, 188

Sandby, Paul 92–3
Saxton, Christopher 52, 53, *53*, 94
Scotland 31, 32, 33, 35, 37, 39, 44, 45,
    46, 48, 49, 55, 61, 71, 74, 77, 78,
    87, 88, 91, 93, 94, 95, 96, 100, 101,
    105, 107, 108, 109, 110, 111, 112,
    113, 122, 125, 127, 128, 130, 132,
    133, 138, 146, 169, 171, 178–9,
    184, 186, *190*, 191, 194, 198, 201
Scott, Sir Walter 18, 103, 109–12, 117,
    138, 203
    'Scott country' 111–12, *112*
Second World War 128, 164, 167, 169,
    176, 185–6, 187, 189, 192, 194,
    196, 201, 213

Sedgwick, Adam 143
Seifert, Alwin 182
settlement 28–31, 34–7, 85, 127–9,
    153–4, 165, 184
    abandonment 34–7, 39, 85, 127–9,
        128, 165, 184
    expansion of 28, 36, 37
    patterns 30–31
    planned 29, 35, 78, 126–8, *127*
Shelley, Percy Bysshe 103
Sillitoe, Alan 139
Sites of Special Scientific Interest
    (SSSIs) 170, 192, 194
soil erosion 67–9, 147, 150, 165, 196
Sorte, Cristoforo 50
Spain 34, 51, 60, 129, 145, 171, 191,
    195
Speed, John 55
Stamp, Sir Dudley 203
Stonehenge 8, 207, 208, 209
Streeton, Arthur 135
Switzer, Stephen 83
Switzerland 96, 105, 115, 154, 191, *211*,
    212

Talbot, William Henry Fox 136
Tennyson, Alfred, Lord 103, 146
Tolkein, J.R.R. 215
Thompson, Flora 175
Thomson, James 70
Thoreau, Henry 63, 104, 116, 156, 157
Tintern Abbey 99, 105, 188
tourism 98–102, 131, 200–5
    Picturesque 98–102, 109, 131–2
    resorts 200
    Romantic 109
    skiing 201
    spas 201
Town and Country Planning Act (1947)
    196, 199
township and range system 96–7
Turner, J.M.W. 104, 118, *119*, 119, 124,
    125, 131, 132, 157
Turner, Frederick Jackson 161

UNESCO 207
USA 65, 96, 125, 135, 136, 147, 153–63,
    167, 175, 180, 190–91, 196, 207

Van Eyck, Jan 56
Van Gogh, Vincent 134
Vaughan Williams, Ralph 173, 175
Venice 43, 51, 57, 58, 60, 132
Vermuyden, Cornelius 41
vernacular building 32–3, 77, 95–6, 154
Vidal de la Blache, Paul 28

Wade, General George 93
Wales 49, 52, 71, 75, 95, 99, 100, 101,
    113, 131, 168, 179, 180, 191, 193,
    207, 208
Walpole, Horace 70, 82, 120
Walpole, Hugh 139
Walpole, Robert 80, 83, 120
Waterloo, Battle of 102, 185–6
Watkins, Carlton 137
Waugh, Evelyn 175
Werner, Abraham 114
West, Thomas 10, 102
Wordsworth, William 103, 105–7, 107,
    110, 113, 114, 116, 118, 124, 188
World Heritage Sites 11, 207
Wright, Joseph 102, 131
Wye Valley 98, 99, 100, 101

Yellowstone National Park 161, 190,
    191
Young, Arthur 91, 102
Youth Hostels Association 202

Zola, Emile 122